7.50

D1359020

Sin
in
the
City

Sin in the City

Chicago

and Revivalism

1880-1920

Thekla Ellen Joiner

University of Missouri Press Columbia and London

Copyright © 2007 by
The Curators of the University of Missouri
University of Missouri Press, Columbia, Missouri 65201
Printed and bound in the United States of America
All rights reserved
5 4 3 2 1   11 10 09 08 07

Cataloging-in-Publication data available from the Library of Congress

ISBN 978-0-8262-1743-1

♾ This paper meets the requirements of the
American National Standard for Permanence of Paper
for Printed Library Materials, Z39.48, 1984.

Designer: FoleyDesign.net
Typesetter: BookComp, Inc.
Printer and binder: Thomson-Shore, Inc.
Typefaces: Garamond Three and Mrs. Eaves

To Otis, Julia, and Stephen

CONTENTS

In some ways, I should not be writing a book on sin. I am not a theologian, and I am not interested in philosophizing about the nature of good and evil. I am interested, however, in how a society defines "sin," and in how history and culture can mold its meaning. I am particularly intrigued with America's twenty-first-century "culture wars" and the way that "New Right" evangelicals tout the righteousness of "traditional family values" and label alternative or conflicting viewpoints as "sin." The passion and political activism that surrounds these issues, I suspect, is less a contemporary initiative than an outgrowth of two centuries of evangelicals working to implement their vision of morality and to change America. In particular, current commitments by evangelicals to "moral values" find clear roots in successive waves of nineteenth- and twentieth-century religious revivals that historians have anointed the "Great Awakenings." Revivalism's mandate for social transformation originated in communities of the prerevolutionary colonies, reappeared in towns of antebellum America, and, by the latter part of the nineteenth century, became a nationwide phenomenon that enveloped major urban areas in a "Third Great Awakening."[1]

Third Awakening revivals were organized during a dynamic period of American history. The thirty years between 1890 and 1920 marked the rise of urban, corporate America as well as the arduous transition from Victorian to modern culture. During these same years the country also became racialized as large immigrant groups flooded urban, industrial areas and African

---

1. Jon Butler, "Enthusiasm Described and Decried: The Great Awakening as Interpretive Fiction," 305–25; William McLoughlin, *Modern Revivalism: Charles Grandison Finney to Billy Graham;* William McLoughlin, *Revivals, Awakenings, and Reform: An Essay on Religion and Social Change in America, 1607–1977;* Robert William Fogel, *The Fourth Great Awakening and the Future of Egalitarianism,* 19–43.

Americans migrated north during World War I. The significant economic and demographic shifts of this period laid the groundwork for what we now know as modern American culture. Changes of this magnitude also impacted gender expectations, challenging many of the ideals for womanhood and manhood that had predominated throughout the Victorian era. This era also saw the construction of a color line that was formulated around ideas of ethnicity and race but supported by economic discrimination as well. The extent of this transformation was seen most clearly in the "new" American city—metropolitan areas that became microcosms of the rapid and oftentimes tumultuous change of the era.

Conservative Protestants, or evangelicals, confronted the city with a combination of optimism and dread. On the one hand, turn-of-the-century evangelicals weathered the economic, political, and social changes with little difficulty. As members of the white middle class they oftentimes were in the vanguard of American modernization. In other ways, however, evangelicals found the magnitude of change in urban America disorienting and even threatening, particularly to their sense of moral order. Evangelicals saw the tumult of the American city loosening the grip that family and community had held on an individual's belief and behavior. They saw the decline of these formative influences as "sin," and they responded with religious revivals that were highly organized assaults on evil.

This book focuses on three Chicago revivals—Dwight L. Moody's 1893 World's Fair Revival, the 1910 Chapman-Alexander Simultaneous Evangelistic Campaign, and Billy Sunday's 1918 revival—all part of the Third Awakening. The three revivals offer a longitudinal opportunity to examine this phenomenon and to observe its interaction with the city. The theology of this book is minimal because, rather than focusing on a specific theologian or denominational doctrine, I am primarily interested in studying popular religious expression and the culture in which it incubates. More specifically, the book examines the influence of gender, race, and status on evangelicalism's definition of morality, and how Third Awakening narratives and rituals expressed and reinforced this moral ideal. In response to the city, revivalists instituted a moral regime rooted in class and racial advantage that was represented by moral models of womanhood and manhood. To redeem the city, revivalists enshrined white middle-class gender norms as ideals of righteousness and worked to bring about social and political reform as evidence of religious transformation.

Despite the century that separates the Third Awakening from the hard-fought "wars" waged by evangelical conservatives and sanctioned by three Republican presidential administrations since 1980, current efforts to sustain evangelical hegemony resonate with earlier turn-of-the-century revivalist efforts. Even as America shifts from an industrial to a postindustrial economy and moves culturally from modernity to postmodernity, in both eras evangelicals espouse a lasting belief in the individual and the need for domestic arrangements to promote right behavior and protect the individual from "sin." Conservative evangelicals also follow in the steps of the Third Awakening in terms of their willingness to adapt to popular culture and to use its tools to articulate and to uphold the moral certitude of white middle-class gender ideals. Like their Third Awakening ancestors, evangelicals understand their moral regime as God's rules, and many still see the city as the center of evil. Such beliefs, which animated the leaders and followers of the Third Awakening, persist as a resilient pose in the ongoing culture wars.

Acknowledgments

I am grateful for the numerous individuals and institutions that have contributed to the research and completion of this book. At the University of Illinois at Chicago, Jon Butler initially encouraged me to think about American religion. Leo Schlebert, Daniel Scott Smith, Margaret Strobel, and Michael Perman contributed to the book in its early stages. The interest and insightful questions from R. Stephen Warner were also very useful. The archivists and researchers at a variety of institutions have also helped in significant ways. The staff of the Chicago Historical Society, the Wisconsin State Historical Society, the Billy Graham Archive, the Moody Bible Institute, and the headquarters of the Woman's Christian Temperance Union answered questions and helped me locate the historical sources on which this book is based. McCormick Theological Seminary and several Chicago Presbyterian churches (Second and Fourth) graciously allowed me to examine their records.

While writing this book I was also teaching history at two institutions—California State University–Long Beach and Los Angeles Harbor College. Both brought me into contact with individuals who have encouraged my academic work. Sharon Sievers of Cal State Long Beach, along with Bradley Young, William Loiterman, Jim Stanbery, Harvey Siegel, King Carter, Gary Miller, David Weber, Bruce Lemon, Beverly Fridley, and Jonathan Lee from Harbor College have provided help and support. I am also indebted to the president of L.A. Harbor, Dr. Linda Spink, along with vice-president Luis Rosas and dean Nancy Carson for granting me a sabbatical that allowed me to finish the book. Kerrill Kephart also contributed very timely editorial comments that kept the book on the right path.

My personal support network of friends and family are also very valuable. My friends: Judy Haenn, Jan Rife, Lois and Brian Theissen-Love, Joan and

Joel Sheesley, Mary and Brian Stein-Webber, Beth and David Brokaw, Pamela and Dave Clausen, Marion and Daniel Park, and Gerald Arata. Family members have also kindly tolerated my "historical" pursuits—Mary and John Jauchen, Cherie and David Root, Amy and David Safley, Elysia and Nathan Root, as well as my mother, Josephine Joiner, and my in-laws, Ruth and Paul Caldwell. My husband, John Caldwell, has also provided immeasurable encouragement and support. My children, Otis, Julia, and Stephen, perhaps deserve the most thanks. Their constant patience, good humor, and love make me very happy to be their Mom. The book is dedicated to them.

Sin in the City

Introduction

Protestant evangelicalism entails an individual's belief and an individual's behavior. Religious revivals cover both dimensions in terms of communicating and reinforcing evangelicalism's religious and social intent. Periodic expressions of awakening serve to revitalize Protestantism and attract more followers to the faith. American revivalism began in the eighteenth century. The First Great Awakening spread through the British colonies, toppling liturgical and denominational authority and shifting spiritual responsibility from the church to the individual. First Awakening revivals replaced Protestantism's earlier dependence upon form and sacrament with a call to make a personal decision to follow Jesus.

Revivalism's trajectory of individual decision and accountability continued through the Second Awakening, which occurred in the antebellum period. This Awakening took the responsibility for salvation further from God's hands, where it had resided under Calvinist predestination, and placed it in the hearts of individual believers who became personally responsible for "choosing" their own salvation. Second Awakening respondents did not stop being Presbyterians, Congregationalists, Methodists, or Baptists, but revivalists urged each believer, regardless of his or her church loyalty, to repent, reject evil, and choose the right path. As defined by these two Awakenings, evangelical faith was not strictly defined by any institutional or church affiliation but instead had to do with an individual's life-changing conversion that initiated a personal and ongoing relationship with Jesus Christ. The emphasis in the first two Awakenings upon individual responsibility in faith matters, however, promoted personal commitment in areas that went far beyond the religious realm. Philosophy, economics, and nine-teenth-century American culture all were significantly shaped by the indi-vidualism spurred by the Great Awakenings.[1]

"Common Sense" Morality and Political Activism

In the world of philosophy, evangelicals merged their beliefs about religion with the Scottish School of Common Sense Realism and integrated their personal faith into Enlightenment principles. Common Sense proponents, primarily theologians from nineteenth-century seminaries, took the indi-vidualized spirituality of the Awakenings and molded it into a philosophical worldview, bringing together "faith, science, the Bible, morality, and civiliza-tion." These writers argued that the empirical laws of the Enlightenment reveal spiritual reality, and that individual believers, upon reading the Bible, could know God's Truth with their own conscience. Theorists aligned the individual, experiential side of revivalism alongside the Bible and cultural norms and legitimated revival emotions with Enlightenment rationality. The bottom line of the Common Sense philosophy was that individual conscience discerned moral choices.[2] The Common Sense philosophy, at least as it was interpreted by evangelicals, affirmed in the head what revival adherents knew in their hearts: neither biblical scholars nor ministers held the edge on Truth; faith must be determined by the individual.

Common Sense writers validated personal knowledge of God and upheld an individual's ability to make both religious and behavioral choices. Realizing one's sinfulness, believing God's Truth, and accepting salvation are the central initiators of evangelical belief, but a believer's actions must outwardly manifest such faith.[3] Commitment to God entailed directing one's heart and mind, then one's actions, toward righteous living. The behavioral component of evangelical faith gave spiritual meaning to all

1. Sydney E. Ahlstrom, *A Religious History of the American People,* 280–92; Randall Balmer and Lauren F. Winner, *Protestantism in America,* 44–54.

2. Sydney E. Ahlstrom, "The Scottish Philosophy and American Theology," 257–73; George M. Marsden, *Fundamentalism and American Culture: The Shaping of Twentieth-Century Evangelicalism, 1870–1925,* 14–21; William McLoughlin, "Pietism and the American Character," 173; William McLoughlin, *The American Evangelicals 1800–1900,* 2–3; Mark A. Noll, *The Scandal of the Evangelical Mind,* 90–96; D. H. Meyer, *The Instructed Conscience: The Shaping of the American National Ethic,* 35–42.

3. Noll, *Scandal,* 61–64.

human endeavors and formed the foundation of evangelical morality. Faith cannot be left in a church pew or in the revival tabernacle; rather, conversion initiated an intentional morality that pervaded all aspects of an individual's life, including family, community, and nation.

The idea of living out one's faith also deeply influenced nineteenth-century economics and politics. When it came to making money, evangelical individualism fell in line quite well with the growth of market capitalism. Evangelicals brought their faith into the nineteenth-century workplace and translated personal righteousness into economic profit. Honesty, frugality, and diligence in the work world led to commercial and capitalist success. Evangelical capitalists also found support in the less religious but equally individualistic ideas of Adam Smith to explain economic relations, particularly the need for economic autonomy and free markets. Freedom from governmental or market restraints and free choices by individuals controlled only by contractual agreement outlined proper economic attitudes for evangelicals.[4] Sanctioned by faith, the individualistic tenets of evangelicalism laid the economic foundation of America's white middle class and its attitudes toward wealth.

Beyond philosophy and economics, however, evangelical followers were obligated to engage all aspects of society with their version of righteousness. This mandate drew numerous Protestant denominations—Presbyterians, Congregationalists, northern Baptists, and Methodists—into an ecumenical bloc that increasingly assumed a political ethos, particularly when it came to issues of temperance and observing the Sabbath. In the 1830s evangelicals joined the Whig Party, a "party of moral order and positive government." Political activism, they discovered, allowed even greater opportunity to "enforce conformity to Anglo-Protestant norms." During the antebellum period, the Whigs backed various organizations that spoke out against the growing influence of immigrants in the country. Nativist opposition was frequently couched in terms that denigrated the immigrants' Catholic loyalties, their differing or "immoral" lifestyles, and, in particular, their consumption of liquor. On the other side of the political fence, the Democratic Party was made up of the antirevival or liturgical forces. The Democrats attracted both Catholic and Episcopal followers who were more closely allied to an institutional church and supported the church hierarchy along with its creeds, rituals, and sacraments. At the liturgical end of the spectrum believers held that

4. Ibid., 75.

church doctrine, not the individual, defined issues of salvation and morality; the state should play little if any role in determining public morality.[5]

The Republican Party, which evolved out of the Whigs, held onto the evangelical tradition, particularly its demand for moral certitude. Evangelicals "prized above all, free will, the 'right to do right.'" They joined the Republicans, "not as a party, but as an antiparty crusade for righteousness." Evangelicals within the Whig and Republican parties learned that politics could be an effective tool to advance one's faith commitment and, at the same time, promote individual freedoms, modernity, and national progress. Voluntary associations, which often had both political and religious intent, provided yet another avenue for evangelical activism. Northern evangelicals in particular joined a variety of organizations that addressed education, temperance, poverty, crime, prostitution, and eventually slavery. Through Magdalene missions, temperance organizations, and antislavery societies that sprang up in the nineteenth century, evangelicals actively pursued moral righteousness in the social and political arenas. Evangelical reform associations addressed a wide variety of issues that were rooted in a religious perspective but increasingly blurred the distinction between social and religious causes and gave evangelical activism a modern and forward-looking perspective.[6] Voluntary associations and their political clout enabled evangelicals to articulate and live out their individual faith in the struggle against social evil.

Millennialism, a doctrine that focused on the end of the world, only heightened the urgency of evangelical social engagement. Protestants had traditionally believed that Christ would at some point return to earth, but millennialists argued that Christ's return was imminent and dependent upon the commitment of believers to usher in God's kingdom on earth. For evangelical believers, the millennial mandate was clear—adherents were personally responsible for changing the world so that Christ could come back and begin to rule on earth. Worldly commitments (economic activity,

5. John L. Hammond, *The Politics of Benevolence, Revival, Religion and American Voting Behavior*, 1–19; Paul Kleppner, *The Third Electoral System, 1853–1892: Parties, Voters, and Political Cultures*, 60; Richard Jensen, *The Winning of the Midwest: Social and Political Conflict, 1888–1896*, 63–64.

6. Kleppner, *Third Electoral System*, 78; Thomas R. Pegram, *Battling Demon Rum: The Struggle for a Dry America, 1800–1933*, 76; Timothy L. Smith, *Revivalism and Social Reform*; Hammond, *Politics of Benevolence*, 103; Daniel Walker Howe, "Victorian Culture in America," in *Victorian America*, 21.

social reform, or political activism) had otherworldly and compelling implications, namely, the establishment of God's earthly kingdom. Belief in millennialism strengthened evangelicalism's sociopolitical bloc by uniting its fervent work around an otherworldly agenda. What began with an individual's decision to "follow Jesus" evolved into an influential moral regime; individuals, denominations, and parachurch groups dedicated themselves to establishing Christ's earthly kingdom in the here and now.

Gendering the Moral Regime

Evangelicalism's idea of God's earthly kingdom, however, deeply reflected its own nineteenth-century attitudes toward gender and race. In terms of gender, the evangelical idea of morality was rooted in the separate-spheres ideology, a construct that distinguished between the private realm of women and the public sphere that belonged to men. In the antebellum era, distinction between the two spheres initially signaled the onslaught of market capitalism and its effect on the family. In the colonial economy women and men had worked side by side within the household, but by the nineteenth century new market forces were taking men away from the home into wage-work, while their wives stayed at home.[7] Separate spheres, however, reflected much more than a simple division of labor: it became one of the primary markers that identified membership in the middle class. According to this model, women stayed home and raised the children, while men were paid to work and support their family. Economically separate spheres meant that a husband generated enough wealth to support his wife, but socially it symbolized the middle-class family's ability to transmit and perpetuate its values within the private or domestic sphere.

Second Awakening revivals articulated a domestic ideal that helped both women and men to navigate their changing social roles. This Awakening heightened the social significance of the separate spheres along with its moral capability. The revivals also affirmed the essential place of the private sphere as the foundation for a stable society. While the revivals unequivocally affirmed an individual's right to choose salvation, the individualism

7. Carl Degler, *At Odds: Women and Family in America from the Revolution to the Present,* 66–110.

encouraged by revivalism raised some unsettling questions.[8] Realistically, evangelicals confronted a society made up of individuals who, in spite of the best persuasion, would choose to sin. In light of those who rejected all appeals to righteousness or right living, who could guarantee a virtuous nation? When the responsibility rested solely with an individual's decision to choose the right way, what individual or group could guarantee that each person would recognize the Truth and decide for the moral good? Once the revival fervor cooled, who was to ensure the continuation of religious piety and the evolution of a godly life? Second Awakening preachers and their female adherents offered hope in the face of the inevitable failings of individuals by centering morality within the home under the nurture of a godly mother. According to the separate-spheres schema, domesticity and motherhood could provide a feminized and virtuous balance to the masculinized individualism of the economic and political sectors. More important, maintaining the morality of the private sphere promised to bring order to the social and economic disruptions brought on by commercial capitalism.

Responsibility to maintain evangelicalism's moral order fell on both women and men. Woman's primary contribution came through child rearing and the process of molding a child's moral conscience. The growing individualism within American evangelicalism and the antiauthoritarian trajectory of American society in general mandated the need for inner restraint, a conscience that monitored feelings and behaviors and that facilitated self-control over one's passions apart from any external control. Woman's task of nurturing children fit the bill. Within the domestic sphere women could mold their young into productive and moral adults and in the process sustain the nation's virtuous stance. Catherine Beecher, daughter of the Congregational minister Lyman Beecher and a nineteenth-century educator, wrote about domesticity in this light. Beecher portrayed domesticity both as an indicator of middle-class status and as a stabilizing force for American society. Drawing on the Common Sense Realism philosophy, Beecher argued for the uniquely influential role of middle-class women to maintain social stability in the midst of tensions generated by status, eth-

8. Mary Ryan, *Cradle of the Middle Class: The Family in Oneida County, New York, 1790–1865;* Terry D. Bilhartz, "Sex and the Second Great Awakening: The Feminization of American Religion Reconsidered," in Philip R. Vandermeer and Robert P. Swierenga, eds., *Belief and Behavior: Essays in the New Religious History,* 117–35; Margaret Lamberts Bendroth, *Growing Up Protestant: Parents, Children, and Mainline Churches,* 21.

nic, and racial differences. Investing other prestigious groups like Protestant ministers or commercial entrepreneurs with social authority, Beecher said, would undermine the essence of the Common Sense philosophy and the country's democratic vision. Instead, moral leadership should be vested in women who act not out of self-interest but rather out of submission and self-sacrifice. A woman's willingness to sacrifice herself for her husband and children assured her moral commitment to both her family and her country. Beecher's standard of sacrificial femininity, centered in the private sphere, was widely accepted as a defining characteristic of middle-class status and respectability. Female influence, asserted through domesticity, provided a crucial balance to the dominance of capitalism and its potentially disruptive consequences.[9]

Writers such as Beecher touted the social significance of domesticity, and evangelical theologians like Archibald Alexander and Charles Hodge, both Princeton theologians, gave domesticity a more spiritual spin. Hodge argued that women were to be adorned with "inward graces, and devoted to the peculiar duties of her sex," while Alexander stated that they should claim their elevated status as Christian women and have a vested interest in preserving it. Both warned of social disorder and possible anarchy if women failed to adhere to these God-given rules. Even more influential than the Princeton theologians, however, was the widely read Horace Bushnell and his book *Christian Nurture* (1847). Bushnell raised awareness about children's spirituality and the need for parents to nurture piety in their offspring. He downplayed the role of clergy and church and put the family front and center in religious training. He also turned feminine influence into a theological tenet by arguing that maternal love best represented God's love. Whereas in the eighteenth century the discipline and devotion of fathers had personified God's love, according to Bushnell, nineteenth-century mothers now embodied this role.[10]

9. Kathryn Kish Sklar, *Catharine Beecher: A Study in American Domesticity,* 80–89; Ann Taves, "Feminization Revisited: Protestantism and Gender at the Turn of the Century," in Margaret Bendroth and Virginia Brereton, eds., *Women and Twentieth-Century Protestantism,* 303–24; Ann Taves, "Mothers and Children and the Legacy of Mid-Nineteenth Century American Christianity," 203–19.

10. Charles Hodge, "Review of Emancipation in the West Indies" by Jas. Thome and J. Horace Kimball (New York: 1838), *Biblical Repertory and Princeton Review* (October, 1838): 602–44, cited in Ronald W. Hogeland, "Charles Hodge: The Association of Gentleman and Ornamental Women," 239–55; Bendroth, *Growing Up Protestant,* 24–30; Taves, "Mothers and Children," 205–7.

Evangelicalism's widespread support for domesticity positioned women and the family as the progenitors of religion and as a bulwark of the moral order.[11] Women who lived out this virtuous ideal were obviously married and were also elevated for their sexual modesty and chastity; purity was yet another component of evangelicalism's moral order. By the nineteenth century earlier suspicions about women's potential for sexual immorality had been corralled within the institution of marriage, and any tendency or expression of female sexual desire was subsumed within marital relations. Within the domestic hierarchy, woman's sexual restraint along with her maternal qualities evidenced her right position in the home as well as in the nation.

Most white middle-class women embraced the separate spheres and the moral advantage it offered. Evangelicalism's definition of morality and its elevation of female virtue privileged woman's place at a time when she had few, if any, avenues for advancement or means of social influence. With few rights to property, the vote, or the capability to pursue a life independent of men, women were generally excluded from the American mainstream. Yet if a woman was willing to sacrifice and sublimate her own identity within the family she could show her devotion to God, uphold her reputation, and assert her social position.

Evangelical morality, however, was neither limited to the domestic sphere nor strictly the purview of women. The same Second Awakening revivals that elevated woman's moral authority also called for a male version of domesticity. Masculine righteousness was defined as being a loyal husband, a strong father, and an economic provider, one who lived his life sensibly and provided adequate support for his wife and children. Man's public assignment was based on the moral value of labor, worth that was determined by his hard work and responsibility in the workforce, along with thrift and philanthropy to his community. Like women, men were to uphold their side of the righteousness equation and to embody middle-class respectability. Living up to this assignment allowed men to demonstrate their faith while also bringing some semblance of morality to the public sphere. Protestant ministers, like Horace Bushnell and Henry Ward Beecher, who have been credited with espousing feminine influences also argued for "Calvinist muscularity," a more masculine version of Protestant

---

11. Anne Braude, "Women's History Is American Religious History," in Thomas A. Tweed, ed., *Retelling U.S. Religious History,* 99; Ryan, *Cradle of the Middle Class.*

spirituality. Later revivals, like the 1857–1858 "businessman's" revival, also played a key role in defining evangelical manhood in the nineteenth century. These revivals furthered the alliance between men's faith and the values of an emerging business culture.[12]

Evangelicalism's Moral Map

Nineteenth-century evangelicalism organized its moral regime around a moral map whose geography was distinguished by roles assigned to women and men and the order that these gender assignments brought to the family and to society as a whole. In the secular realm, woman's place in the home was "married" to man's public role as wage earner, a relationship that ensured both male and female control and determined the success of the Victorian middle-class family. In the moral realm, woman's virtue in the domestic equation offered balance to the potential excesses of individualism or its capitalist outlay. Both evangelical women and men were to be religious. But the faith's reliance upon individual virtue mandated the nurture of middle-class families, which, when confronted with the realities of market capitalism, tilted the moral scale toward the feminine side of the gender equation. Men could assert themselves in the public and economic sphere, knowing all the while that women reigned over home and family and provided the moral ballast for their more materialistic interests.

Ideals for womanhood and manhood strongly influenced evangelical expression throughout the nineteenth century. On the feminine side, evangelicalism equated a mother's love to God's love and tapped into a set of symbolic virtues that embodied woman's personal piety, her submission to God and to her husband, and her innate ability to nurture the next generation, an "evangelical domesticity" touted by ministers as the heart of spirituality. Domestic piety in turn led evangelical women numerically to dominate the major Protestant

12. Clyde Griffen, "Reconstructing Masculinity from the Evangelical Revival to the Waning of Progressivism: A Speculative Synthesis," in Mark C. Carnes and Clyde Griffen, eds., *Meanings for Manhood: Constructions of Masculinity in Victorian America,* 186–88; *Historical Sketch of the Young Men's Christian Association of Chicago,* 29; David S. Reynolds, "The Feminization Controversy: Sexual Stereotypes and the Paradoxes of Piety in Nineteenth-Century America," 96–106; Braude, "Woman's History Is American Religious History," 103–4; Kathryn Teresa Long, *The Revival of 1857–58: Interpreting an American Religious Awakening,* 81–92.

denominations, particularly the Unitarians, Congregationalists, Presbyterians, and Episcopalians. As evangelical men acquiesced to women's expanding influence in the home and church, reform activism further tilted the moral balance in a feminine direction. A burgeoning subculture of evangelical women took up their domestic assignment and formed associations that catapulted their moral influence into the public arena.[13] Standing on the central values of Protestant femininity—piety, submission, domesticity, and sexual purity— women propagated their moral authority through church work and organizations, such as the Woman's Christian Temperance Union (WCTU) and the Social Purity movement.

The WCTU emerged in the 1870s as an association committed to protecting women, children, and the home from the debilitating effects of liquor. To attack this problem, a wide variety of WCTU-sponsored programs promoted woman's moral clout to redress the array of abuses spawned by alcohol.[14] The WCTU effectively publicized woman's moral prestige and unleashed her power to domesticate and reform public space. Temperance activists frequently joined forces with the Social Purists, a movement that as early as the 1830s organized reform societies. The Social Purity movement was committed to ending prostitution and to abolishing society's double standard of turning a blind eye to male impropriety while holding women to a higher, purer standard. Purists, oftentimes in tandem with the WCTU, objected to men's uncontrolled sexual activity and vowed to end male promiscuity and to save their working-class "sisters" from prostitution. Raising the banner of domesticity, Social Purists called men to task for their immoral behavior in order to protect middle-class wives from venereal disease. Vice not only harmed prostitutes and middle-class women, the Purists argued, but it also undercut man's prescribed role as father and household head. As they publicized their causes, the WCTU and Social Purists portrayed alcohol and vice as uniquely male sins and focused critical attention on the threat that men posed to women and the domestic sphere. Both organizations pressured men to live a more responsible definition of manhood. They argued that alcohol and illicit sex destroyed the home, and that eradicating these evils would create domestic harmony and guarantee moral childrearing.

13. Sandra Sizer, *Gospel Hymns and Social Religion*, 83–110; Taves, "Feminization Revisited," 317; Lori D. Ginzberg, *Women and the Work of Benevolence: Morality, Politics, and Class in the 19th Century United States*; Griffen, "Reconstructing Masculinity," 189.

14. Taves, "Feminization Revisited," 317.

This vision of reform began with a defense of home and family but, particularly by the latter part of the nineteenth century, expanded into a critique of male immorality.[15] The public rhetoric of both the temperance and Social Purity movements publicized the ideals of evangelical domesticity and used them as the standard by which to judge manhood and the failings of modern culture. Domesticity's moral position reinforced the superiority of women over men and further distanced its middle-class proponents from working-class masculinity. The lack of discipline among the working class along with its unruliness and heavy drinking evidenced the great need for domestic control.

The "Others"

The "respectable" ideals of nineteenth-century evangelical morality also created an edifice of whiteness based upon those who were deemed moral and those "others" who did not live up to this standard. Ethnic and racial categories, like gender distinctions, are based upon historical experience that first differentiates between groups on the basis of biological difference. Biological distinctions, however, are overlaid with the economic, political, and social consequences of those distinctions. Early in America's history, whites premised early explanations for ethnic and racial differences on the biological inferiority of darker-skinned peoples. The inverse of this argument was that whiter skin color was superior. But by the latter part of the nineteenth century the biological rationale for inferiority gave way to new behavioral descriptors of difference. Although biology did not totally recede in America's explanation for discrimination, individual or group behaviors became much more prominent in determining whether or not groups "belonged" in America and could be eventually assimilated into the mainstream of society.[16] In nineteenth-century America whites set the normative standard, and when upon close monitoring of immigrants and African-Americans they found behavior that did not measure up to their norm, whites felt obligated to brand such groups as inferior, less "moral" than their social "betters." Any number

15. David J. Pivar, *Purity Crusade: Sexual Morality and Social Control, 1868–1900,* 3–12.
16. Ann Taves, "Sexuality in American Religious History," in Thomas A. Tweed, ed., *Retelling U.S. Religious History,* 41; Michael Omi and Howard Winant, *Racial Formation in the United States from the 1960s to the 1990s,* 61–69.

of religious or social behaviors—adherence to Catholicism, language varia-
tions, lack of education, family organization, housing arrangements, or use of
leisure-time activities—contributed to categorizing immigrant groups as the
"other." Sexuality also played a part in the categorizing process in that immigrant populations were portrayed by the white middle class as unclean, sexually threatening, and therefore "immoral."

Whites also raised the specter of immorality against African Americans,
particularly in terms of what whites portrayed as the rampant sexuality of
blacks. White assumptions about black illicit sexual behavior initially
evolved from the lies of white slave owners who deemed all blacks—women
and men—sexually promiscuous, and therefore in need of control. After the
Civil War brought black freedom, both the North and South continued to
coerce the black population under the guise of reining in black sexual
promiscuity. At the heart of these accusations was the "bad" black woman
who was portrayed as naturally promiscuous and open to all male advances.
When compared to white womanhood, whites saw black women as morally
"loose" and outside the parameters of respectability. The insidious nature of
this allegation held true under both slavery and freedom. Under slavery, the
idea of black female promiscuity provided sexual license to white male slave-
holders. After emancipation, the lie continued to debase black women and
justify their exploitation. As a result, whites did not rank the exploitation of
black women on the same scale as the abuse of white women. For whites,
"respectable" women were those whose sexual purity was beyond repute, and
the privilege of this respect was the prerogative of whites only.[17]

The male counterpart to the "bad" black woman was the "black rapist,"
another lie asserting that black men were primitives whose excessive sexuality threatened the purity of white women. This sexual threat, southerners
claimed, warranted control and coercion of the black population by any
means, including overt racial segregation and lynching. White illusions
about the "rapist" idea restricted the freedom of all blacks by licensing violence against the race. The South's overt justification for lynching was that it
protected white womanhood and the moral virtue of white women from the
threat of black men. The use of lynching as a form of both sexual and social
control successfully deterred much of the economic and political progress of
blacks after Reconstruction, and all was accomplished in the name of pro-

17. Paula Giddings, *When and Where I Enter: The Impact of Black Women on Race and Sex,*
85–94.

tecting the values of white society. These ideas spread beyond the South, and by the 1880s both southern and northern whites accepted not only this ideology but also lynching as a legitimate way to defend the purity of all white women and to maintain the social order of white civilization.[18]

For northern evangelicals, the moral implications of ethnic and racial discrimination were not overt. However, evangelicals' gendered understanding of morality and its emphasis on pure women and righteous men were premised upon whiteness. The social norms embedded within evangelicalism's moral regime precipitated a willingness to see cultural distinctions as morally reprehensible and strengthened the tendency of evangelicals to judge difference as "sin" and therefore as deserving of judgment and condemnation.

History and the Third Awakening

Third Awakening revivals insistently normalized the ideals of white, middle-class domesticity and backed up evangelicalism's moral regime with religious authority. By the latter part of the nineteenth century, however, the rise of corporate capitalism and the growth of cities significantly changed America's social and moral landscape. For many in the middle class, America's urban, industrial progress held great promise. At the same time, however, many of these changes threatened some of the most cherished middle-class ideals, particularly individualism and the possibility of upward mobility. The channeling of industry into even larger corporations, the disparity of wealth between status groups, and the growing influence of various ethnic groups all contributed to a sense of unsettledness within the middle class and caused many to question the social, political, and moral meaning of these changes.[19] New forms of industrial and social organization were primarily located within the "new" American city, and these relations were perceived by many as a threat to their own status and to the

18. Glenda Elizabeth Gilmore, *Gender and Jim Crow: Women and the Politics of White Supremacy in North Carolina, 1896–1920,* 55–57; Ida B. Wells-Barnett, *A Red Record,* in *Selected Works of Ida B. Wells-Barnett,* compiled by Trudier Harris, 138–252; Gail Bederman, *Manliness and Civilization: A Cultural History of Gender and Race in the United States, 1880– 1917,* 46–53.

19. T. J. Jackson Lears, *No Place for Grace: Antimodernism and the Transformation of American Culture, 1880–1920;* Alan Trachtenberg, *The Incorporation of America: Culture and Society in the Gilded Age.*

overall stability of the nation. Third Awakening revivalism both addressed and reflected the new moral geography of the city, trying to rekindle evangelical fervor and reinvigorate its moral regime through yet another Awakening era.

Third Awakening revivalists were not alone in their efforts to transform American cities. Turn-of-the-century revivals paralleled the equally intense efforts by more liberal Protestants who worked within the Progressive and Social Gospel movements to bring their own moral vision to bear on urban society. What distinguishes Third Awakening revivalism from other types of Protestant activism is not the intensity of its efforts, but rather its primary commitment to individual religious transformation as the key to social reform. As Progressives and, to a lesser degree, Social Gospelers turned their focus toward the more structural elements of social and political change, revivalists held on to the redemptive power of faith alone as urban America's salvation. Third Awakening revivalists took aim at many of the same issues that attracted Progressives and Social Gospelers, but revivalists were primarily interested in eternal matters, issues that hinged upon an individual's Christian conversion. For revivalists, a changed soul meant changed behavior that in time would change society. To pursue this goal, Third Awakening revivals allied with like-minded groups, particularly the temperance and Social Purity movements, merging their agenda for spiritual transformation with the behavioral changes demanded by these two movements. Revivalism was first and foremost about saving souls, but conversions would put a stop to drinking and sexual license and urban reform would follow. Revivalists were determined to save the city—one soul at a time.

Theorizing the Third Awakening

Much of the history written about the Third Awakening has focused on its male leaders. The names of Dwight L. Moody, R. A. Torrey, J. Wilbur Chapman, and Billy Sunday, even in more recent studies of this revival era, dominate the literature of this period. Placing men in the spotlight, however, has left a significant gap in the historical understanding of revival and its relationship to the broader society. The most obvious omission has been women and their vital role in urban evangelism. Marginalizing women within the Third Awakening is all the more glaring given the attention that has been given to women in the First and Second Awakenings. By the beginning of the twentieth century, women also dominated Protestant churches both in terms of numbers and activism. It was women who gave Protestantism much of its social and moral energy.[20] Omitting women from the Third Awakening not only hands the era over to the "great men" but also shrouds the gender dynamic that was at work. Revivalists confronted the "new" American city armed with a moral regime grounded in ideals of femininity and masculinity. This gendered moral order formed the heart of evangelicals' understanding of good and evil and provided the platform for revival outreach.

A focus on male leadership has yet another drawback. It perpetuates a "top-down" understanding that detracts from the complexities inherent within a revival event. When studied in their entirety, from the perspectives of both women and men, one sees revivals not as the feat of one man, but as a vast sequence of denominational appeal, media publicity, neighborhood outreach, pulpit oratory, and conversion praxis, all woven together into a finely tuned engine that ran according to a planned agenda for weeks and sometimes months. Pamphlet evangelism on the World's Fair midway, midnight parades to Chicago's notorious Levee, appeals to beleaguered working women, boxing with the devil—these rituals, relationships, gestures, and spatial qualities are the essence of the Third Awakening and demand our attention.

These activities, which have been frequently overlooked by historians, are important because they form participatory patterns through which revivalists did two oftentimes contradictory things. First, they defined their own identity and affirmed their status by externalizing it as part of a large-scale community activity. By promoting a moral regime based on the rightness of evangelical values, revivalists sustained their position as a white middle class. At the same time, revivals created an imaginative moral unity whose symbolic and public representation transposed racial and ethnic differences into a moral whole. In the midst of cities flooded first with immigrants and later with a growing population of African Americans, revivals implicitly addressed and sought to buffer themselves from a range of new and potential threats to their position as the normative center of American culture, and,

20. Martin E. Marty, *Pilgrims in Their Own Land,* 297–317; Marty, *The Irony of It All, 1893–1919,* vol. 1, *Modern American Religion,* 208–47; McLoughlin, *Modern Revivalism;* McLoughlin, *Revivals, Awakenings, and Reform;* Bernard Weisberger, *They Gathered at the River: The Story of the Great Revivalists and Their Impact upon Religion in America,* 167–74; Paul A. Carter, *The Spiritual Crisis of the Gilded Age,* 16; Braude, "Women's History Is American Religious History," 87–107.

through this, to resolve nagging social contradictions. Drawing on the theoretical observations of sociologist Victor Turner, these sorts of rituals, whether religious or secular, allow a specific social group to not only represent the fractures in the social order but also simultaneously resolve those disruptions that resist either expeditious political or legal remedy. The rituals of Third Awakening revivals sought to redress important social conflicts that plagued turn-of-the-century America by publicly staging and performing them and, at the same time, producing or invoking symbols that embodied the social and religious values needed for their resolution.[21]

One may categorize the contradictions evidenced within the era of the Third Awakening through a framework of bipolar opposites that emerged from the theological and social worldviews of evangelicals.[22] On an explicit level the dualities appear to be theological in nature: spiritual-material, Protestant-Catholic, fundamentalist-modernist. But implicitly rhetorical manifestations of location, status, and race also pervaded the revivals: individual-collective, rural-urban, working class–middle class, immigrant–native-born, black-white, Democrat-Republican. Revivalism's ritualistic construction and expression of these dichotomies—in a heightened public sphere—provided both the means and the opportunity to encode these cultural assumptions with spiritual or immanent meanings.

Gender and its binary opposition between female (signifying righteousness) and male (signifying sin) emerged as a central and recurrent framework in both revival talk and practice. In the early years of the Third Awakening, revivalists feminized righteousness and sin was the male prerogative. Revivals defined the very nature of urban life, spatially and rhetorically, in terms of its chaos, its anonymity, and its maleness. Salvation, on the other hand, offered revival audiences and respondents rescue and refuge from the grasp of the city. Redemption served as an antidote to the ills and threats of the city, by offering identity, order, and a return to mother, family, and home. Revivals structured Gospel and public rituals in explicitly gendered terms and used gender as a mechanism for domesticating public space and for urban redemption. In the Third Awakening, gender was a privileged allegory through which other cultural conflicts (class identity,

---

21. Sizer, *Gospel Hymns,* 70–71; Victor W. Turner, *The Ritual Process: Structure and Anti-Structure;* Catherine Bell, *Ritual Theory, Ritual Practice,* 20–21; Hammond, *Politics of Benevolence,* 28.
22. Sizer, *Gospel Hymns,* 108.

racial superiority, ethnic animosity) were symbolized. At the same time, gender represented tensions over female and male roles as well as a response to broader cultural upheavals that challenged the legitimacy of nineteenth-century Protestantism. As a central opposition within the Third Awakening, gender dualism provided a lens through which a much broader range of cultural contention was focused.

In addition to their symbolic function, the public rituals of the Third Awakening also play a consensus-building role by creating what Turner terms "liminal" (in-between, exploratory) spaces that allow participants to separate themselves from earlier social affiliations and temporarily step outside ideological conventions and pressures.[23] Such rituals allow cultures undergoing threatening forms of change (modernization, urbanization, integration) to work collectively and forge new common identities and more meaningful affiliations. Third Awakening liminal spaces—street corners, churches, circus tents, wooden tabernacles—provided the space and opportunity for revivals to negotiate contemporary anxieties, to articulate and reaffirm crucial values through symbols, and, at the same time, to point revival participants toward a transcendent authority, Jesus Christ. Within these spaces, religious rituals not only symbolized social anxieties but also worked to transform human attitudes and normalize human behaviors. In short, revivals worked to forge a moral agreement around the rightness of evangelical values and, at the same time, create a moral unity that marginalized cultural and racial differences. This kind of dramatized consensus building not only sustained the emotional needs of the revival participants but also further legitimized the social order of the white middle class. The feminine influence of early Third Awakening revivals reached out to draw observers into liminal spaces in Chicago where the domesticated ethos of the Gospel could ostensibly prevail over the more suspect masculine and public sins of the city.

Revival in the City of Disparity

Chicago offers an excellent case study for revivalism. By the latter part of the nineteenth century, Chicago was best known for its explosive economic growth. But Chicago's ability to generate money also created a city of great

23. Nick Couldry, *Media Rituals: A Critical Approach*, 32–35.

extremes. Many of the nation's most celebrated entrepreneurs lived up to their reputations as rugged individualists and built giant industries, yet the city was also home to the Socialist Party and the radical Industrial Workers of the World (IWW). In Chicago the strongest trade union movement in the country struggled in uneasy coexistence with some of the nation's most powerful corporations and their industrialist-founders. Disparities were also evident in the city's spatial layout. Chicago builders constructed imposing architectural wonders, yet refuse and its stench filled many streets. Business elites lived in houses that rivaled European castles, yet horrific tenements surrounded these same mansions. These types of insistent extremes made Chicago a model for the emerging American city.

The city's moral climate could also be characterized as extreme. Many Chicago industrialists willingly exploited the city's labor force in the railroad, manufacturing, and retail sectors. At the same time, these individuals deplored the city's lack of restraint and her reputation for sin—prostitution, crime, drunkenness, political corruption—which seemed to grow proportionate to their economic prosperity. For many Chicagoans, the city was as celebrated for its depravity as for its industrial prowess. Saloons, brothels, and gambling joints lined the city's streets in direct alliance with City Hall. But Chicago was also the headquarters of the Woman's Christian Temperance Union along with a host of other moral-reform organizations.[24] Industrial smokestacks, grain elevators, and stockyards flourished alongside Protestant churches, rescue missions, the Young Men's and Women's Christian Associations, and eventually Dwight L. Moody's Bible Institute. Many Chicagoans, who staked their economic fortunes in the city, saw Protestant activism as the way to sustain Chicago's moral base and, at the same time, uplift (and eventually subdue) its laboring classes. Through churches and parachurch organizations, these elites, along with the city's middle class, aggressively modernized their interaction with this emerging urban monolith, providing monies for many evangelical ventures and supporting periodic revivals. The three revivals in this study—the World's Fair Revival of 1893, the Chapman-Alexander Simultaneous Evangelistic Campaign of 1910, and Billy Sunday's 1918 revival—represented three more opportunities for Chicago evangelicals to engage the city in its battle against sin. Just as ambitious on the moral front as in the economic realm,

24. Donald L. Miller, *City of the Century: The Epic of Chicago and the Making of America*, 191.

evangelicals creatively staged opportunities to engage the city, hold her political leadership accountable, and save her from sin.

Sin in the City underscores two recurring themes within the Third Awakening. One focuses on the nature of evangelical morality and its adaptation to modern society. Through the study of revival practice and ritual, the book traces the gendered nature of this moral regime as it interacts with urban culture and navigates city life. Increasingly, as revivalists both defined and defended their moral stance, they would come to portray themselves as "outsiders," righteous critics who deplored urban modernity. In actuality, Third Awakening revivalists were not outsiders at all. They were in fact quite adept at employing many of the "insider" tools of modernity (organization, advertising, communication) to further their religious cause. These adaptive skills kept Protestants and their faith as major influences in urban America. But adaptation also came with a price. The Third Awakening's adaptation to urban modernity effectively changed its definition of sin from a male evil to the purview of women. As a result of this shift, the more feminine and inclusive characteristics that defined early revivals of this era were eclipsed by a moral program that was increasingly masculine, hard-nosed, and corporate in its understanding and expression of faith.

A second theme is that the moral regime sought by Third Awakening revivals was part of a broader racialized regime of whiteness that pervaded America at the turn of the century. Revivalists would rhetorically deplore hatred or racial violence, yet revivalism's perpetuation of evangelical morality, and in particular its middle-class domestic focus, reinforced a sense of difference and inferiority among those who did not fit the racial or status norms that revivalists preached. What appeared to revivalists as a means to include and persuade was in reality a way to articulate and strengthen the identity of evangelical believers. Revivalists argued for the rightness of their moral regime and assumed its moral capabilities would produce a faith-generated consensus that would prevail over the unsettling social differences that emerged at the turn of the century. This principle motivated revivalist forces to engage fervently in those political and social causes that they believed would implement their vision. The "truth" of this moral model, revivalists believed, would transpose status, ethnic, or racial differences and transform urban America. The gendered nature of this morality, however, undercut this same desired consensus and social unity. Ironically, by holding so tightly to middle-class norms and preaching them as true, evangelicals actually produced the opposite effect, effectively excluding many from its universalizing intent.

The three Chicago revivals (1893, 1910, and 1918) of this study represent hundreds of revival events organized throughout the United States at the turn of the century. Focusing on one city allows an examination of revivalism's social context over a twenty-five-year span and creates a clearer understanding of these "windows" of religious experience and expression. Despite the century that separates Third Awakening revivals from the "new right," many of the same gender, racial, and status biases continue to blind contemporary evangelical conservatives to the underlying and structural bases for "sin." Like their Third Awakening predecessors, conservative evangelicals promote "family values" and just as strongly oppose non-normative sexual activity, alternative lifestyles, and many of the behaviors associated with racial minorities. Similarly, conservative evangelicals also assume that their twenty-first-century moral regime will include all comers, subsuming or erasing racism or social inequities. Examining the Third Awakening may also shed light on "New Right" evangelicals whose political engagement furthers their moral agenda. The social issues that in many ways define the activism of the twenty-first-century evangelical Right had been defined almost a century before as the "sins" of the city.

CHAPTER 1

"True Christianity" in the Second City
CHICAGO EVANGELICALS

By 1890 Chicago had emerged as America's "second city." As the largest city in the developing West, Chicago's grain, lumber, meat-packing, and farm implement industries spurred the city to unparalleled success in both manufacturing and shipping. Canals and then railroads positioned the city as an intermediary between the East and the West, a "gateway city" that tied the western hinterland's farms and small towns to the economies of the Northeast, particularly New York. The 1871 Chicago Fire only affirmed the city's dynamic potential. Even though the fire destroyed twenty-five hundred acres with financial losses topping $250 million, the city had, in the course of two years, rebuilt itself. According to many of the city's boosters, the fire's destruction had been a blessing in disguise. By burning away the conglomeration of buildings at the city's center, the inferno had encouraged the rise of a new Chicago, a more modern, vital city, well organized and complete with skyscrapers.[1] The city's rebound from the fire also reinforced its "can do" image. Despite the horrific scenarios of the fire, the railroads continued to run, products continued to move, and the city continued to grow.

Chicago's keen ability simultaneously to process, market, and transport goods contributed to her position as a retail-wholesale giant. By initiating a new association between the city and its hinterlands, wholesalers like John V. Farwell and Company, Field, Leiter, and Company, and Potter Palmer increasingly replaced eastern suppliers and created financial networks based

---

1. Bessie Pierce, *A History of Chicago,* vol. 3, 146; Robert G. Spinney, *City of Big Shoulders: A History of Chicago,* 47–69, 104.

SOME MEN WILL NOT GO TO HEAVEN, BECAUSE THEY CANNOT RIDE.

"Heaven Is Not Reached in a Single Bound." *Ram's Horn*, April 26, 1893.

on buying and selling. This Chicago system epitomized capitalist modernization and quickly established the city as an important retailer in her own right.[2] The city's dominant position in sales was equaled by its role as manufacturer. The initial centerpiece for Chicago's manufacturing sector was the McCormick Reaper Works, but the steel and lumber industries, in addition to meatpacking and grain processing, also contributed to Chicago's explosive growth.

Evangelicals and the "Second City"

By the 1870s and 1880s, the success of both the wholesale and manufacturing sectors generated a wave of wealthy Chicago elites. This group was actually the second group of entrepreneurs to emerge from the city's burgeoning economy. The first wave of Chicago capitalists had benefited from the city's earliest speculative environment in the 1830s and 1840s. First-wave leaders, such as land developer William Ogden, had also actively engaged in city governance. The later wave of entrepreneurs, such as Potter Palmer, Marshall Field, and George Armour, achieved even greater levels of wealth and held social positions that were unrivaled in the Midwest and the nation. Unlike their predecessors, the later group of business leaders disengaged from politics and instead attended strictly to business, linking their own personal success to civic improvement. This group chose to influence the city's direction through private means, such as churches, civic clubs, and private charities.[3]

Protestant evangelicals were represented in both elite groups. Cyrus McCormick, Sr., was part of Chicago's original elite. One biographer of the McCormick family described the elder McCormick as a "John Knox Presbyterian," whose ambitions in life were to "make all the harvesting machines that were made—not one less, and to wage a one-man campaign for Old School Presbyterianism against both the schismatic forces of Higher Criticism and the new theology of liberal Presbyterianism."[4] McCormick

2. William Cronon, *Nature's Metropolis: Chicago and the Great West*, 318.

3. Donald L. Miller, *The City of the Century: The Epic of Chicago and the Making of America*, 70–76, 170, 387; Pierce, *A History of Chicago*, 207; Frederic Cople Jaher, *The Urban Establishment: Upper Strata in Boston, New York, Charleston, Chicago, and Los Angeles*, 472–98.

4. Charles O. Burgess, *Nettie Fowler McCormick: Profile of an American Philanthropist*, 18; Frank Gilbert, *Centennial History of the City of Chicago: Its Men and Institutions*, 233–35; Pierce, *A History of Chicago*, 163.

was a social conservative and a devout Presbyterian who, beginning in 1847, built his reaper works in Chicago. After making numerous technological improvements to the machine, McCormick shifted his attention to advertising and sales, turning the day-to-day management of the reaper work over to his brother, Leander. To sell his reaper McCormick adapted, or, in many instances, initiated, some of the most modern marketing strategies of the century, tactics that were all geared specifically to the needs and demands of the consumer. McCormick sold his reaper for a fixed price, $120, but in order to accommodate the consumer's large outlay of cash, McCormick allowed farmers to put $30 down to purchase the reaper, then defer payments until after the fall harvest. Commissioned salesmen, who used fliers and testimonials to promote their product, also heavily advertised McCormick's reaper. They also offered guarantees of customer satisfaction. The genius of Cyrus McCormick rested not only in his technical improvements on the reaper but also in his marketing expertise. The success of these techniques spread the reaper into the hinterlands of the Midwest and, along with John Deere's steel plow, led to the settlement and cultivation of the midwestern prairie states. Such tactics also contributed to McCormick's business success. Between 1877 and 1881, McCormick's profits quadrupled, swelling from $325,000 to $1,232,781. By 1891 when his son, Cyrus Jr., joined the American Harvester Company, McCormick's capital worth was estimated at $35 million.[5]

Other Protestant evangelicals embraced Chicago's capitalist ethos. Turlington W. Harvey was a lumber magnate and prominent evangelical. In fewer than twenty years, Harvey rose from an apprentice sash-maker to the owner of several lumberyards in the city. Harvey then vertically integrated his lumber holdings, buying Michigan forests, processing mills, and a steel car company to transport lumber to Chicago for finishing. The Chicago Fire only accelerated Harvey's success. While the city still reeled from the fire's massive destruction, Harvey (whose lumberyard had been miraculously saved from the blaze) began immediate construction on residential housing. Later, in 1888, he and his associates built the town of Harvey, Illinois, one of Chicago's first "dry" suburbs. Harvey's success in lumber positioned him for membership in an elite network of governing boards and trustees that influenced the city's finances. Harvey served as a director of Chicago's

5. Miller, *City of the Century*, 103–6; Spinney, *Big Shoulders*, 52–53; Cronon, *Nature's Metropolis*, 313–18; Kathleen McCarthy, *Noblesse Oblige: Charity and Cultural Philanthropy in Chicago, 1849–1929*, 113–14, 155–56.

National Bank and on the board of American Trust and Savings. Another evangelical, John V. Farwell, earned the title of Chicago's "merchant prince." Like Harvey, Farwell began his career on the bottom rung of the corporate ladder, working as a clerk and stock boy. By the 1890s, Farwell had expanded his initial wholesaling business into the third-largest dry-goods house in the nation.[6] These elites either instigated or oversaw what has been described as a second wave of industrial capitalism, a period of intense industrial concentration and reorganization leading to large Gilded Age corporations controlled by a few industrialist magnates.

For Chicago's evangelical elites, business success validated their religious perspective on the world; their economic achievements legitimated the individualized work ethic of their faith. Elites, like Farwell, encoded their economic accomplishments with spiritual meaning and touted their accumulation of wealth and social status as an obvious example of the rightness of their evangelical values. The material results of their own hard work, frugality, and honesty were balanced with a generosity that typified the nineteenth century's Christian ideal of manhood. As one observer noted when he described John V. Farwell, "The two potent ideas, benevolence and acquisitiveness, were married within him." This version of manhood justified evangelical economic theory and informed attitudes toward work relations.[7]

Beneath Chicago's elite was a burgeoning middle class of managers, bookkeepers, and clerks who were also invested in the city's industrial and retail success. As industrial capitalism became more corporative, its middle class became more professionalized and developed a strong social identity. As part of the "better" status groups, Chicago elites and middle class coalesced around ideals of economic individualism, capitalistic opportunity, and social order. The unity of these "better" classes, however, was somewhat illusionary, particularly in light of the second wave of industrial formation. As corporate consolidation increased in the 1880s and 1890s, more centralized forms of business organization thwarted the ambitions of the middle class and prevented many employees from achieving the same level of

6. *Biographical Dictionary and Portrait Gallery of Representative Men of Chicago and the World's Columbian Exposition*, 62–68, 113–16, 396–99; H. C. Chatfield-Taylor, *Chicago*, 95–97; *Chicago Star-Tribune*, September 7, 1972; T. W. Harvey File; McCarthy, *Noblesse Oblige*, 66–67; Miller, *City of the Century*, 484; Pierce, *History of Chicago*, 99; Gilbert, *Centennial History*, 246–47.

7. *Biographical Sketches of the Leading Men of Chicago*, 100–101; McCarthy, *Noblesse Oblige*, 53–72.

wealth or prominence that characterized elites in the headier days of Chicago's economy.

Desiring to protect its own economic stability and social status, the middle class held ferociously to its class position. At the same time, middle-class workers were frustrated by their inability to achieve the upward mobility experienced by many of their predecessors. These frustrations, however, were not directed toward elites. Rather they were directed inward toward a strong middle-class identity that focused not on potential inequalities but on its own class values, principally order and respectability. Early in the twentieth century, H. C. Chatfield-Taylor, a Chicago novelist, captured this middle-class orientation. He described Chicago as "socially a New England town, as strait-laced as Boston. . . . The majority coming from New England or northern New York, brought with them the tenets of the Pilgrim fathers, which they planted so deeply in the soil." Any discontent that existed between the elite and middle classes was subsumed by a strong middle-class sensibility that effaced their true economic differences.[8]

The middle class further defined its status by distinguishing itself from the working-class population. Disparities that existed within the "better" classes were minuscule compared to the widening gulf between the city's "betters" and its workers. By the latter part of the nineteenth century, Chicago's insatiable demand for labor drew rural, native-born workers, as well as immigrants from southern and eastern Europe, into the city. Between 1870 and 1890, the number of individuals employed in the city skyrocketed by 400 percent, providing Chicago with the largest industrial workforce west of the Appalachians. In the meatpacking industry alone, expanded rail service coupled with the advent of refrigeration to double the number of workers in those same decades. By 1893, one-fifth of the city's population was in some way connected to the meatpacking industry. The constant flow of workers into the city created a labor surplus, and many of the city's jobs were seasonal or part-time. As a result, working wages were kept low, further sharpening the distinction between those immigrant laborers who worked in manual, often low-paying jobs and the native-born workers who tended to fill the nonmanual, often professional, jobs.[9]

8. Chatfield-Taylor, *Chicago*, 95–97; Stuart Blumin, *The Emergence of the Middle Class: Social Experience in the American City, 1760–1900*, 258–96.

9. Cronon, *Nature's Metropolis*, 311; John M. Allswang, *A House for All Peoples: Ethnic Politics in Chicago, 1890–1936*, 17–20; Pierce, *History of Chicago*, 109, 220–22, 235; Spinney, *Big Shoulders*, 62; Blumin, *Emergence of the Middle Class*, 259.

By the 1870s Chicago's working and middle classes each had strong social identities. As the "better" or "respectable" classes united around the benefits of industrial capitalism, the working class unified against capitalism's exploitation of their labor. The wide gulf separating Chicago's "haves" and "have-nots" created, at best, a tumultuous labor scene. Chicago was a hotbed for trade union activism. The Knights of Labor, as well as the Socialist Party and the Industrial Workers of the World, all had deep roots in the city, and all sought to remedy the powerful disorientation of industrial work and to demand respect from their industrialist employers.

The rapid rise in Chicago's population, along with its ethnic and racial diversity, further exacerbated labor tensions. By 1880, less than a decade after the devastating 1871 fire, two hundred thousand more people had moved into the city. By 1890, 77.9 per cent of the city's people were of foreign-born parentage, particularly German, Irish, English, and Scandinavian. After 1890, the city counted more Poles, Bohemians, Croatians, Slovaks, Lithuanians, and Greeks than any other city in the country. A small number of African Americans also were drawn to the city, but by 1890 the black population was still less than 1 percent of the city's total.[10] Native or foreign-born, all migrants came to Chicago for economic opportunity; instead, they found low wages, poor housing, and an urban infrastructure weighed down by the burden of its own growth.

This population explosion created a desperate need for more land. After 1880, the city extended her boundaries by 120 square miles in order to accommodate its burgeoning population. This expansion accelerated the city's residential segregation as middle and upper classes, trying to escape the overcrowding and congestion of urban growth, moved to the suburbs. City rail service linked these growing peripheries with the urban interior. Rails provided the city with a badly needed transportation system but further divided the city along class, ethnic, and now residential boundaries; as the city's middle class moved to the suburbs, the city's laborers remained behind, caught within the industrial center.[11]

10. Melvin Holli and Peter d'A. Jones, eds., *Ethnic Chicago: A Multicultural Portrait;* Edward Kantowicz, *Polish-American Politics in Chicago 1888–1940,* 12–27; Miller, *City of the Century,* 501.

11. Harold M. Mayer and Richard C. Wade, *Chicago: Growth of a Metropolis,* 124–28, 144–50; Blumin, *Emergence of the Middle Class,* 275; John Albert Mayer, "Private Charities in Chicago from 1871 to 1915," vii–viii.

Life on the city's perimeters further strengthened Chicago's middle-class orientation. Communities of well-ordered, single-family homes sprang up around the city's edge, encouraging middle-class privacy, oftentimes as a defense against the perceived physical and moral dangers of the city. Suburbs also allowed Chicago's middle class to create personalized environments, providing refuge from the impersonal environment of the workplace, particularly for middle-class men.[12]

Defining the Perils of the Second City

The movement of Chicago's middle class to city outskirts did little to relieve its fears of rapid change and growing diversity. The city's insistent growth severely strained middle-class ideals of social order and evoked a sense of crisis. Cultural scholar Carl Smith explains, "Because of the immense changes in transportation, communications, structure of the workplace (both factory and office) and building technology, Chicago's identity was constantly transforming. . . . This combination of sudden titanic growth out of a virtually nonexistent past and continuing constant alteration combined to make Chicago seem a place hostile to traditional ideas of order and stability."[13] As a sense of change and disruption permeated Chicago's middle class, many relied upon their religious faith for support. Affiliated largely with the Presbyterian, Congregational, Methodist, and northern Baptist denominations, Chicago evangelicals understood and explained in spiritual terms the dramatic changes that enveloped the city. Ethnic diversity and class differences, the inevitable result of urban growth, held religious meaning for them, and more often than not were transposed into evil. For evangelicals, the city became a symbol of social upheaval and moral collapse, an area defined first and foremost by her sin.

In 1894, the Reverend H. B. Hartzler, a Baptist minister in Chicago, summarized the "great perils" that existed in the city and were "greatly enhanced" there. The urban "perils" cited by Hartzler included "wealth, its worship and congestion, anarchism and lawlessness, intemperance and the

12. Richard Sennett, *Families against the City: Middle-Class Homes of Industrial Chicago, 1872–1890,* 149.
13. Paul Boyer, *Urban Masses and Moral Order in America, 1820–1920,* 131; Carl Smith, *Urban Disorder and the Shape of Belief: The Great Chicago Fire, The Haymarket Bomb, and the Model Town of Pullman,* 5.

liquor power, immigration, and a superstitious Christianity."[14] Hartzler voiced a concern of many evangelicals—the desire to get ahead and to make money had surpassed all other goals. Materialism had become the defining element of urban life. Clearly, neither elite nor middle-class Protestants objected to profit, but for the acquisition of wealth to be moral, it must be moderated by good deeds or philanthropy.

In Chicago, genuine benevolence appeared to be in short supply. The city's Gilded Age extravagance defied ideals of religious stewardship, causing evangelicals to attribute urban problems directly to the subversion of Protestant economic values. The darker realities of Chicago—labor strife, political corruption, and crime—all resulted, in one way or another, from the city's unbridled pursuit of material gain without regard for spiritual or social responsibility. Business continually involved its leaders in private moneymaking, drained their civic consciousness, and contributed to the city's slide into excess. Josiah Strong, another Protestant spokesman, wrote, "It is in the city that the unprecedented increase of wealth affords unprecedented opportunities for self-gratification; and, without a corresponding increase in self-control, we shall become enervated and demoralized in the lap of luxury." When the commitment to profit was not balanced by benevolence, wealth degenerated into excess that threatened individual morality and civic growth.[15]

Protestants deplored the unprecedented accumulation of money that occurred in the city even though evangelical elites, such as McCormick and Farwell, were the epitome of Gilded Age success. Their extensive philanthropy, particularly to evangelical reform causes, deflected any criticism of business praxis or more direct accusations of greed and exploitation. For evangelicals, elite generosity balanced or moderated any unrighteous impulses. The more secular ambitions of modern manhood could be balanced by philanthropic stewardship that contributed to the city's moral and social betterment.

Evangelicals were also concerned about the growing division between the rich and the poor. In an 1894 article entitled "What Shall We Do with Our Cities?" the WCTU's Union Signal warned, "Our great and ever-growing cities, with their abject poverty and fabulous wealth are a growing menace to

14. Rev. H. B. Hartzler, Moody in Chicago or the World's Fair Gospel Campaign, 12.
15. Strong, The Challenge of the City, 49; Boyer, Urban Masses, 98; Robert T. Handy, A Christian America: Protestant Hopes and Historical Realities, 77–78; Marty, Pilgrims in Their Own Land, 310–17.

our national life." Economic disparity, however, did not generate as much sympathy for the lower classes as it contributed to seeing them as "others," questionable candidates at best for assimilation into American life. Middle-class perceptions of workers were often demeaning and patronizing; workers' problems were blamed on their sloth, intemperance, or a general lack of self-discipline. One writer for the Chicago Bible Institute noted, "We are well aware that much of the misery in which the laboring classes are does not come from outward circumstances but from intemperance, luxury, and other sins—in one word, from sin."[16] Evangelicals also disdained any effort by labor to organize and perhaps help themselves. They saw unionization as antithetical to the individualist/American work ethic, as it interfered with individualism and corporate profits. J. V. Farwell, for example, viewed labor's challenge to employers or the right to strike as "an interference with the laws of supply and demand." Because Union membership was heavily ethnic, opponents accused all unions of being infiltrated with "foreign elements" who advocated socialism or anarchism. Cyrus McCormick blamed labor problems on "professional labor agitators combined with external pernicious influences." Most evangelicals were fiercely anti-union, preferring instead to indoctrinate workers with the evangelical values—hard work, thrift, sobriety—that they believed had been their ticket to success.

Both sides accentuated these status differences. Chicago's laborers openly criticized industrialists, the capitalist system, and its rampant exploitation of the labor force. Hours, wages, and the working conditions in Chicago's industries—all provided ample fuel for chastising corporate heads, their businesses, and capitalist exploitation. Chicago's "better" classes fought back. Protestants saw working-class demands for rights and respect as a direct challenge to their economic, social, and religious values. By the mid 1880s, the chasm between labor and capital grew wider, making an urban revolution appear imminent. A. W. Williams, a Chicago minister, wrote, "Nowhere else is the struggle between capital and labor more intense and bitter. In no other city have the socialists and anarchists secured such a dangerous foothold."[17]

16. *Union Signal*, May 25, 1893; Count A. Bernstorff, "The Laboring Classes and the Church," *Record of Christian Work*, June 1895, 166.
17. Pierce, *A History of Chicago*, 298; *Biographical Dictionary and Portrait Gallery of Representative Men of Chicago and the World's Columbian Exposition*, 62–68; Smith, *Urban Disorder*, 101–46; A. W. Williams, *Life and Work of Dwight L. Moody: The Great Evangelist of the Nineteenth Century*, 275.

Chicago politics also appeared to be under siege. After the Civil War, a new generation of entrepreneurs took control of the city's civic life. They asserted their authority indirectly through private boards and committees as opposed to direct political involvement. The unwillingness of elites to hold political office created a vacuum that was filled by new leaders. Shortly after the Chicago Fire, Joseph Medill, the editor of the *Chicago Tribune*, was elected mayor of the city. Medill enmeshed himself in a struggle between Chicago's moral conservatives and the city's liquor interests. The battle line was drawn on Medill's effort to revoke saloon licenses and close saloons on Sunday. In response to this conflict, Medill essentially vacated his post and went to Europe. A Democrat, Harvey D. Colvin, replaced him in 1874. The effort to oust the Republican Medill and replace him with Colvin, a Democrat, led to a political partnership between Chicago's German American and Irish American populations.[18] The two ethnic groups along with other working-class supporters aligned within the Democratic Party to challenge Republican control, and to dominate the city's political scene. Out of ten mayoral races between 1876 and 1892, only three Republicans were elected into the mayor's office.

Chicago's Republican Party stood for many issues that were dear to the hearts of evangelicals, particularly education, temperance, and public observation of the Sabbath. The Democratic Party, on the other hand, held opposing views that, to Republicans, represented "ignorant power." John Coughlin, one of Chicago's First Ward aldermen, clarified the distinction between these two competing parties. In a preelection speech, Coughlin told his audience, "A Republican is a man who wants you t'go t'church every Sunday. A Democrat says if a man wants to have a glass of beer on Sunday, he can have it. Be a Democrat, unless you want t'be tied t'a church, a schoolhouse, or a Sunday school." For Chicago evangelicals, ward bosses like Coughlin taunted the cherished ideals of upright politics and promoted the saloon as the city's foremost political institution. Saloonkeepers in Chicago built businesses based on liquor sales, but the saloon's social environment also nurtured a political relationship between the owners and their clientele, a trust that paid off in votes. Finis Farr provides this description of First Ward politics: "Bathhouse John and his partner flourished for more than forty years, openly bartering votes, and never failing to deliver

18. Miller, *City of the Century,* 387; Spinney, *City of Big Shoulders,* 76.

their ward at election time. They accomplished this by intimidation that included mayhem and murder, by parading armies of alcoholic derelicts to vote at the polls."[19] By 1900 half of the Democratic Party's precinct captains were saloonkeepers. To Chicago Republicans the collusion of the saloon and politics signaled a political structure rooted in cronyism, not in a consciousness of right and wrong. Democratic victories meant that self-aggrandizement had replaced Republican moral civicism.

Evangelical anxiety over the seemingly downward spiral of the city focused on Protestantism's two pillars of social morality—the church and the home. The decline of these two institutions foregrounded other issues and most clearly represented the sins of the city. The exodus of the city's middle class into surrounding suburbs, coupled with the influx of immigrant populations, meant that downtown Protestant churches faced declining membership, attendance, and funding. Distance, diversity, and class differences made it difficult, if not impossible, for evangelicals to provide a middle ground between the rich and poor, between the suburban and tenement dweller, and between employers and workers.[20]

For evangelicals, secular forces appeared to be on the rise while the influence of the Protestant church grew proportionately weaker. Religious statistics only affirmed Protestant suspicions; by the latter part of the 1880s only one person in nineteen belonged to a Protestant denomination.[21] Chicago Catholics, on the other hand, outnumbered by two and a half times all the individuals listed among the seven leading Protestant denominations. Given these odds, it seemed to Chicago evangelicals that "true Christianity" appeared to be losing its spiritual claim on the city; Protestant forces could not compete with the "superstitious Christianity" of Catholicism. The authority of lofty Protestant edifices eroded as churches no longer reached individuals or families that it sought spiritually to transform and socially to reform.

19. Lloyd Wendt and Herman Kogan, *Lords of the Levee, the Story of Bathhouse John and Hinky Dink,* 19; Finis Farr, *Chicago: A Personal History of America's Most American City,* 304; Miller, *City of the Century,* 447; Pierce, *A History of Chicago,* 379–80.

20. Josiah Strong, *The Challenge of the City,* 48–51; Joseph Lee Lukonic, "Evangelicals in the City: Evangelical Protestant Social Concerns in Early Chicago, 1837–1860." Lukonic argues that evangelical influence was seriously eroded in the first twenty years of Chicago's history. While their influence may have declined, evangelicals did not abandon their attempts to bring their version of morality to the city.

21. *Daily News Almanac and Register,* 85–86; Pierce, *A History of Chicago,* 424–25.

The Christian home, yet another symbol of Protestant authority, also appeared to be under assault. Chicago evangelicals clearly distinguished between a "house" and a "home." The "home," its privatized space, its assigned gender roles, its familial harmony, and its religious orientation together carried much more religious potency than a mere residential structure or "house," but urban geography made it difficult for the private, domestic sphere to do its job. The city saw a decrease in the actual ownership of private homes, while Chicago tenements became filled with largely transient populations of working-class immigrants who found it difficult to live up to middle-class expectations of home ownership. Many Chicagoans thought that the increasing number of nonpropertied city-dwellers undermined both individual and communal accountability. For evangelicals, the nucleus of spirituality, the molder of moral conscience, was unable to uphold its influential assignment. Evangelicals were alarmed that Chicago was becoming a city of "houses" that significantly compromised the home's domestic authority and their own socioreligious influence. Protestant writer Josiah Strong, author of *The Challenge of the City,* noted, "the institution of the home with all its saving influences, may exist in the tenement, but it is less likely to do so, and it certainly cannot exist where there are several families in one room."[22]

Evangelical concerns for domesticity also reflected their larger concerns regarding the use of public and private space for all Chicagoans. For Josiah Strong, the public orientation of urban life, whether in the working-class tenements or in the rising popularity of the more elite social clubs, held similar dangers for the domestic roots of the faith. Strong warned that the home was being attacked at "each of the two social extremes . . . among the rich, hotel and club life is being substituted for home life," and the increase of interest-bearing securities was promoting "a growing idle class which is migratory."[23] Transience was not limited to the city's working class; elites were also abandoning the home to pursue Chicago's growing nightlife. Both developments were seen by evangelicals as less-than-hopeful trends.

The middle-class antidote to either the working-class tenement or the upper-class social club could be found in two places—within the haven of the private, nuclear home or in the idyllic untainted spaces of rural America.[24] Both home and field were portrayed as simple and uncomplicated spaces

22. Strong, *The Challenge of the City,* 53.
23. Ibid., 53–54.
24. Cronon, *Nature's Metropolis,* 359.

where social order and regularity were determined by seasonal cycles or by the equally predictable and well-defined roles of husband, wife, and children. In sharp contrast to the untainted space of farm life or the virtuous order of the private home, the congestion and disorder of the city threatened the well-defined parameters of middle-class life and the authority of the evangelical faith.

Responding to the Perils of Urban Life

The magnitude of the city's "great perils" prompted a broad Protestant response that was only slightly tempered by growing theological differences between liberals and conservatives. In 1907, Andrew Stevenson, a railroad executive, boasted that Chicago was *Pre-Eminently a Presbyterian City.* His book highlighted the strong numerical and social influence of Presbyterianism in the city. Chicago Presbyterians, he noted, included an inordinate number of industrialists, lawyers, and doctors whose business savvy called for a more modern Protestantism that brought business efficiency to religious activism.[25] To ensure that the tenets of the faith were correctly taught, Cyrus McCormick endowed McCormick Seminary as a center of old-school theology. Another evangelical entrepreneur, John V. Farwell, joined McCormick and formed several mission and foreign-language Sunday Schools, settlement houses, and church extensions among the major language groups of the city. In the 1870s, however, David Swing, the pastor of the prestigious Fourth Presbyterian Church, challenged the conservative hold on Presbyterian theology. Reverend Swing argued, "A creed is only the highest wisdom of a particular time and place," and raised questions regarding Reformed doctrine and biblical inerrancy. In response to this challenge, the Presbyterian Synod of Illinois charged Swing with heresy in 1874. Chicago's Methodist Conference conducted a similar trial for Hiram Thomas, pastor of the city's First Methodist Church, who denied that Jesus Christ had died for humanity's sins. Both Swing and Thomas were ousted from their denominations, and both pastors subsequently established their own churches in the city where they continued to preach a more liberal theology.[26] These trials fore-

25. Andrew Stevenson, *Chicago, Pre-Eminently A Presbyterian City.*
26. Paul H. Heidebrecht, "Chicago Presbyterians and the Businessman's Religion, 1900–1920," 42–43; Ahlstrom, *A Religious History,* 814; Spinney, *City of Big Shoulders,* 87–88.

shadowed the fundamentalist-modernist split that would divide the evangelical bloc at the beginning of the twentieth century.

Theological differences, however, could not dampen Protestant commitments to urban America. The Social Gospel movement urged believers to address environmental issues such as working conditions, wages, and housing in order to promote spiritual renewal. The practical needs of society, like child labor and city cleanup, must be addressed if spiritual transformation was to occur; sin rested within social structures, and these must be reformed. More conservative Protestants urged personal redemption from sin as the catalyst for a changed society. After providing a litany of the city's "perils," the Baptist minister Hartzler concluded, "in the face of these facts, conditions, and perils the special need and supreme importance of city evangelization need no argument."[27] Reverend Hartzler, like many conservative Protestants, believed that individual conversion would lead to social reform.

The urgency of urban evangelism was heightened by evangelicalism's shift from millennialism to the doctrine of premillennialism. Evangelicalism's earlier efforts for social reform had been driven by the millennial hope of creating God's kingdom on earth. The later doctrine of premillennialism, however, held that God's kingdom was not an earthly one, but rather that the rapture, or Christ's second coming, would take all Christians to heaven, leaving only sinners behind to face God's judgment. In the 1870s and 1880s many evangelicals embraced premillennialism because they believed it accurately explained the current depravity of society. The scale of the problems that confronted urban America left little room for optimism, so many believers placed their hope in being rescued from this earth rather than trying to reform it. As a result of premillennial teaching, many evangelicals increasingly turned their attention toward a salvational model of reform and distanced themselves from their nineteenth-century activism. Evangelicals were urged to redeem as many souls as possible before Jesus returned, and not be distracted by the seemingly hopeless goal of creating a heaven on earth. Contact and conversion, not the creation of a millennial kingdom, became the mandate.[28]

27. Balmer and Winner, *Protestantism in America,* 62; Wendy J. Deichmann Edwards and Carolyn DeSwarte Gifford, eds., *Gender and the Social Gospel,* 2–6; Rev. H. B. Hartzler, *Moody in Chicago,* 12.

28. Timothy P. Weber, *Living in the Shadow of the Second Coming: American Premillennialism;* Balmer and Winner, *Protestantism in America,* 19, 73–76.

Theological differences between liberals and conservatives had ramifications for their approaches to city work. In Chicago in the 1870s and 1880s, however, distinctions between the more conservative evangelicals and more liberal adherents of the Social Gospel were more ambiguous. Given the magnitude of urban problems, the middle-class orientation of both Protestant movements frequently surpassed the theological or motivational differences of the two camps. The personnel and implementation of Protestant reform activism aligned, not on opposing sides, but along a spectrum of motivations and techniques, some religious, some social. The urgency of urban reform often prompted evangelicals to participate in social programs, while reformers of a more liberal bent supported the moral potential of revivalism.[29] The result was a broad network of denominational and parachurch groups that promoted the rightness of middle-class values and reaffirmed these ideals as central to urban reform.

Numerous Protestant denominations began to develop a variety of approaches to urban evangelism. In 1885, Lucy Rider Meyer, a Methodist-Episcopal deaconess, established the Chicago Training School for City, Home, and Foreign Missions. This school specifically trained young women for domestic and foreign missions, providing them with education and experience in both religious and social welfare work. In 1887, eight female students from the school formed a Deaconess Home. Within the first summer, the deaconesses made 2,751 home visits, formed Sunday Schools, and visited the infirm in Chicago's tenements. Rider Meyer's school became a model for deaconess training in other denominations. Following her lead, the Mission Societies of both the Baptist and Congregational churches also engaged in training workers for city evangelism.[30] Other Protestant denominations supported their own urban missions, but also contributed to the work of parachurch organizations that supplemented the city's denominational activism. The Salvation Army, which originated in Great Britain,

29. Susan Curtis, "The Son of Man and God the Father: The Social Gospel and Victorian Masculinity," in Mark C. Carnes and Clyde Griffen, eds., *Meanings for Manhood: Constructions of Masculinity in Victorian America,* 67–78; Janet Forsythe Fishburn, *The Fatherhood of God and the Victorian Family: The Social Gospel in America,* 138–44; Rebecca Perryman Garber, "The Social Gospel and Its View of Women and the Women's Movement, 1880–1918," 68; Mayer, "Private Charities in Chicago from 1871 to 1915," 128–29; Virginia Lieson Brereton, *Training God's Army: The American Bible School, 1880–1940,* 37.

30. Rima Lunin Schultz and Adele Hast, eds., *Women Building Chicago: A Biographical Dictionary,* 587–89; Rosemary Skinner Keller, "Lay Women in the Protestant Tradition," 282–83; Pierce, *A History of Chicago,* 425; Brereton, *Training God's Army,* 61.

came to Chicago in 1885, and the Young Men's and Women's Christian Associations were organized in 1858 and 1876 respectively. The Pacific Garden Rescue Mission started in 1877. By 1900, *The Institute Tie,* a publication of the Moody Bible Institute, listed close to sixty city missions that were operating in the city, along with other tract ministries and Sabbath schools. Most of the sixty missions encompassed specific regions of the city such as the Ashland Avenue or Sheridan Park missions, or designated a specific ethnic group to be reached—Chinese, Ogden Avenue German, Italian, Bohemian, and Messiah Mission for the Jews.[31] The Woman's Christian Temperance Union, headquartered in Evanston, also gained widespread support from Protestant denominations.

Organizers of the mission outreach soon realized that urban evangelism required individuals solely committed to the endeavor. Mirroring the ongoing professionalization within the nineteenth-century economy, Protestants increasingly depended upon religious workers trained in the ways of the city and knowledgeable in the best techniques for evangelism. As middle-class Protestants distanced themselves both geographically and status-wise from the urban masses, these professional workers were needed to pick up the task. The funding and organizational expertise for city missions was oftentimes provided by elites whose business experience qualified them to create the most efficient and modern means of salvation outreach, but the actual footwork had to be carried out by middle- or working-class believers who committed themselves to the Gospel cause.[32]

Dwight L. Moody and Chicago's Unruly Men

Dwight L. Moody was a leading organizer for this professionalized version of evangelism. Like many of his Chicago supporters, Moody came to the city from New England in order to make money. Arriving in 1856, Moody began a career as a shoe salesman. His early Chicago days quickly established Moody's expertise in selling both footwear and religion. After

31. Allan Whitworth Bosch, "The Salvation Army in Chicago, 1885–1914"; Emmet Dedmon, *Great Enterprises: 100 Years of the YMCA of Metropolis Chicago,* 25. The *Handbook of the YWCA* recorded that the YWCA was formed "to promote the moral, religious, intellectual, and temporal welfare of women," 2; *Institute Tie,* October 1900, 43.

32. Ahlstrom, *A Religious History,* 737; McCarthy, *Noblesse Oblige,* 151–71.

he joined Chicago's Plymouth Congregational Church, Moody began to recruit boys from one of the city's notorious slums, Hell's Kitchen, and seat them in his rented pew. This novel and egalitarian approach to evangelism raised concerns among the church's more status-conscious members. Moody soon realized that his spiritual enthusiasm did not fit within Congregationalism, so he organized his own Sabbath School class through the Wells Street Mission School. By 1859, Moody had moved his work to the Market Hall at Van Buren and Dearborn Street. As superintendent of Moody's Sabbath School venture, John V. Farwell referred to Moody as the "Sunday-school drummer." In 1864, Moody's evangelistic recruitment led to the construction of the Illinois Street Church near Rush and another mission on Chicago Avenue and LaSalle Street. Both buildings were destroyed in the 1871 fire. After the fire, a temporary structure, the North Side Tabernacle, was constructed on the corner of Wells and Ontario, and in less than three years, another, more permanent structure, the Chicago Avenue Church, was erected. Unlike other major churches in the city, the Chicago Avenue Church did not rent pews and advertised that the church "was built by the poor people, for the poor people, and belongs to the poor people."[33] From its beginning, the Moody Church intended to engage all of Chicago's inhabitants and win their souls to Jesus.

Moody initially focused his religious appeals toward the increasing numbers of young men who besieged Chicago in the latter half of the nineteenth century. These young men, who came in search of work, significantly impacted the city in terms of numbers and affected its reputation for immorality. As early as 1850, the census reported that 50 percent of the male population in Chicago was between fifteen and thirty-nine. Lloyd Lewis and Henry Justin Smith, writers who tended to relish Chicago's carnal side, confirmed these perceptions. They noted, "Each year thousands of young men set their faces toward the adventurous city while their mothers wept for fear of Chicago's contaminating sins. Chicago was known as a 'young man's town.'" Living in boardinghouses, dormitories, or sometimes camping out in saloons, these young men lived apart from traditional forms of control and gave the city its reputation as a youthful and oftentimes raucous place. By the 1890s,

33. Kelsey Lane, ed., *Reaching toward Tomorrow: The Moody Church;* Rev. Henry Davenport Northrop, *Memorial Volume: Life and Labors of Dwight L. Moody, the Great Evangelist,* 42–44; "Historical Sketch of the Moody Church"; William R. Moody, *The Life of Dwight L. Moody,* 70; *Moody Church Paper,* January 1888.

Chicago's earlier sexual disparity became somewhat more balanced, but the perception of Chicago as a young man's town continued.[34]

By evangelical standards, these young men, without parental or community oversight, lacked the necessary guidance or discipline to become Christians or responsible adults. Numerous Protestant organizations, including the Woman's Christian Temperance Union, Sabbath Schools, and Social Purity organizations, directly associated the transient character of young men with urban sin—vice, drunkenness, and crime. A young man's ability to earn and spend money without supervision and his apparent lack of sexual control threatened Protestant ideals of manhood. Young men were also potential recruits for labor radicalism. Overall, the presence of this unchecked male force challenged evangelical prescriptions for masculinity and corrupted the moral base of the city itself.

This concern was central to the establishment of Chicago's Young Men's Christian Association. "The industrial city was becoming the home of the young men of the Protestant world," a YMCA publication observed. "These conditions with their temptations to young men living away from home in cities, called for the association."[35] Chicago's first YMCA was organized in 1866 in order to evangelize and to provide wholesome activity for the increasing number of the city's rootless young men. Like other parachurch groups in Chicago, the YMCA was funded and directed by Protestant elites, such as Cyrus H. McCormick and George Armour. John V. Farwell, Chicago's "merchant prince," donated land for the first YMCA building and served as president of its board for thirty-one years. These donors were interested in providing moral direction in the form of a surrogate parenthood for the city's young men. In 1868 George S. Phillips gave his rationale for the YMCA: "If it were possible for the trembling and prayerful mother, for the proud and hopeful father, to continue their watchful care over them, all might still be well. But the stern necessities and duties of life forbid the continuous exercise of parental love in that practical form, and the rising generation is left to its own resources and moralities."[36]

34. Dedmon, *Great Enterprises,* 16; Lloyd Lewis and Henry Justin Smith, *Chicago: The History of Its Reputation,* 176; Roger F. Dunn, "Formative Years of the Chicago YMCA—A Study in Urban History," 329–30; *Abstract of the Eleventh Census, 1890,* 34. The Census reported 568,402 men and 531,448 women in the city.

35. *Historical Sketch of the Young Men's Christian Association of Chicago,* 12–13.

36. Ibid., 15; *YMCA Records,* Box 1, Folder 16; George S. Phillips, *Chicago and Her Churches,* 130.

James L. Houghteling, president of the YMCA in 1882, also emphasized the organization's outreach to young men. The purpose of the organization, Houghteling said, was "To keep them [young men] from evil, to win them to be Christian gentlemen, industrious workmen, good citizens, loyal to their homes and church." Dwight L. Moody, who served as president of the YMCA from 1866 to 1870, also raised monies for the organization and directed many of its programs. Moody argued that "temptation could best be met by bringing young men into a personal relationship with Christ and setting them to work on behalf of others."[37]

Dwight L. Moody's innovative approach to the city's young men endeared him to many of Chicago's business leaders. Moody was particularly adept at integrating a middle-class sensibility with the linguistic and cultural style of the working class. To increase Sabbath School attendance, for example, Moody would frequently ride a pony through some of Chicago's worst neighborhoods or promise new suits to those boys who attended most regularly. J. V. Farwell, who served as superintendent of Moody's original Sabbath School, noted that Moody was often responsible for "getting the children out of bed on Sunday mornings, washing and dressing them and hurrying them to the mission by 9 o'clock." Publicity for Moody's original Sabbath School often included "before" and "after" pictures of the attendants. Students "before" the school experience were quite dirty and ragged. The pathetic picture of the boys was underscored with the title, "Does It Pay?" After Moody's influence, however, the picture was of a well-heeled, respectable group of young men entitled, "It Does Pay!" Moody supporters admired the evangelist's ability to subdue the "rowdiness" of his Sabbath crowd, often recounting the story of the "well-deserved lashing" Moody administered to one of his more disobedient pupils. Moody's manly skill at first subduing and then converting young, lower-class males contributed significantly to his evangelistic successes.[38]

Moody, whose success eventually opened wider doors to evangelistic outreach, went on to become one of the Third Awakening's most important revivalists. Two of Moody's revivals occurred in Chicago, the highly successful 1876 Revival and later the 1893 World's Fair Campaign Revival. His first Chicago revival occurred shortly after the Panic of 1876, a reces-

---

37. *Historical Sketch,* 29; William R. Moody, *The Life of Dwight L. Moody,* 97.
38. Northrop, *Life and Labors of Dwight L Moody,* 42–43; William R. Moody, *The Life of Dwight L. Moody,* 78.

sion that put large numbers of young, unemployed males on the streets and heightened middle-class fears of labor protest and possible anarchy. Chicago Protestants widely supported Moody's 1876 revival initiative and applauded the revival's initiation of some twenty-five hundred Chicagoans, mostly young men, into its Protestant churches.[39]

Moody's ability to mobilize denominations and parachurch groups became legendary among evangelicals. A significant portion of this success was the revivalist's modern, masculine image and the businesslike organization he brought to his revivals. In the latter part of the nineteenth century, several charismatic ministers dominated urban Protestantism, particularly Henry Ward Beecher of Plymouth Congregational in Brooklyn and Phillips Brooks of Trinity Episcopal in Boston. These ministers were noted for their erudite presentations and their enlightened, but increasingly liberal, approach to the Gospel. Beecher and Brooks also contributed to what has been described as the "feminization" of American Protestantism.[40] Dwight L. Moody, however, was a variation on this theme because Moody embodied a new manhood, a merger of middle-class respectability, masculinity, and morality.

Moody's contemporaries generally began their descriptions of him by noting that he was a "salesman," an occupation vital to corporate marketing, but one that was also tinged with immorality. A salesman was a "flimflam" man who cheated and then moved on. The nature of sales smacked of transience and dishonesty. Moody himself was described as "uncouth in appearance and rough in manners." Yet under the saving power of the Gospel, Moody's questionable character had been transformed, and he now embodied the values of the middle class: he was a principled and respectable man. Lyman Abbott, a ministerial peer of Moody's, observed, "As he stood on the platform he looked like a business man; he dressed like a business man; he took the meeting in hand as a business man would; he spoke in a business man's fashion; he had no holy tone."[41] Consistently attired in a black, three-piece suit, his

39. Darrell M. Robertson, "The Chicago Revival, 1876: A Case Study in the Social Function of a Nineteenth Century Revival."

40. Ahlstrom, A Religious History, 738–40; Ann Douglas, The Feminization of American Culture; Barbara Welter, "The Cult of True Womanhood, 1802–1860"; Taves, "Feminization Revisited," 304–24.

41. Lyman Abbott, "Mr. Moody's First Parish," The Illustrated Christian Weekly, February 19, 1876; Lyman Abbott, Silhouettes of My Contemporaries, 200–201.

commanding physical appearance led many observers to depict Moody as "God's businessman," and to contrast his manly dominance in the pulpit with the effeminacy of other Protestant ministers. Moody's assertion of middle-class masculinity led his followers to believe he could convert and tame Chicago's restless working class.

Unruly working-class men were not the only challenge to Protestantism; according to many evangelical leaders, middle-class men were also painfully absent from the church. In an article "Mr. Moody's Ministry to Men," Methodist Bishop Willard F. Mallalieu summarized the central reasons for men's lack of religious interest. First he described the "modern, reckless rush of business" that exhausted its male participants, causing them to use Sunday as a day for recreation, not for rest or worship. Secondly, the bishop blamed the Sunday newspaper. Distribution of the paper required delivery boys to work on the Sabbath, and the paper's secular nature tempted middle-class males to stay home on Sunday mornings. Thirdly, modern scientific theories, particularly evolution, caused men to drift toward skepticism. Lastly, Mallalieu argued, "Men of brains and good sense are not found crowding the pews of invertebrate preachers. They are not much given to seeking for preachers who deal in weak and lachrymose platitudes, or use only honeyed words." Yet Dwight L. Moody appealed to this crowd. Such men were attracted to the "pointed" preaching of Moody as well as to his ability to "command the confidence and loyal following of men." Other observers affirmed the bishop's insights. A journalist noted, "It has been proved by Mr. Moody, beyond doubt, that the consciences of men can be easily reached by honest, earnest endeavor, and manly argument, when showy but soulless phrases would hardly penetrate beyond the ear."[42]

Moody's background in sales also contributed to his appeal to men who needed a faith to complement their economic modernity. Moody built upon the tactics of earlier Second Awakening revivalists like Charles Grandison Finney and did not hesitate to advertise extensively. Asked about the benefit of advertising, Moody replied, "A man comes to the town from the country or from some other city, and he don't know anything about the meetings, and if he sees a notice of them he may attend them. I don't see why the walls should not be placarded as well." With marketing strategies

42. Willard F. Mallalieu, "Mr. Moody's Ministry to Men," in Northrop, *Life and Labors of Dwight L. Moody,* 124–34; Rev. E. J. Goodspeed, *A Full History of the Wonderful Career of Moody and Sankey in Great Britain and America,* 316.

not unlike those used by his supporter Cyrus McCormick to sell reapers, Moody extensively advertised the Gospel. Rather than view the media as a detriment to the cause of salvation, Moody enlisted newspapers to publicize his religious ventures. Chicago's daily press coverage significantly boosted the influence of his revivals. The *Chicago Tribune,* the Chicago *Inter-Ocean,* and the *Daily News* were not just publishers but also promoters of D. L. Moody's evangelistic cause, developing a symbiotic relationship with Moody that allowed each paper to promote its own conservative social agenda, boost sales, and beat competitors. "No daintiness here," one journalist wrote "A spade is a spade . . . What though Mr. Moody sometimes mispronounces a word, or gets a singular verb for a plural nominative, if he makes me feel that religion is business?"[43] The widespread support for Moody's style of evangelism reflected more than the revivalist's personal charisma or his relationships with publishers and business magnates. Moody was a man of action, a revivalist who made faith relevant to industrial, urban America by applying the most efficient and manliest tactics.

Women in the Streets

Dwight L. Moody balanced his manly, businesslike outreach with ideals of womanhood and domesticity; the godly woman and the sanctuary of the private sphere were essential counterparts to the modern male and to Mr. Moody's message. In contrast to Moody's public masculinity and as a balance to his oftentimes lower-class mannerisms and rhetoric, the revivalist instilled evangelical spirituality and middle-class respectability into his urban agenda with ideals of womanhood and domesticity.

On a practical level, this gender balance translated into Moody's strong support for women's work in urban evangelism; he encouraged evangelical women to take their redemptive authority to the streets. In addition to leaders like Lucy Rider Meyer, women in Chicago churches had already been actively engaged in meeting the spiritual and material needs of the city. Wives of Chicago's civic leaders frequently headed philanthropic outreaches,

---

43. Gamaliel Bradford, *D. L. Moody: A Worker in Souls,* 253; Cronon, *Nature's Metropolis,* 314. Cronon notes that McCormick once said, "To sell, I must advertise." Bruce J. Evensen, *God's Man for the Gilded Age: D. L. Moody and the Rise of Modern Mass Evangelism,* 123–63; Goodspeed, *Wonderful Career of Moody and Sankey,* 40.

and their organizational and administrative capabilities were well known. After the Chicago Fire, for example, the Fourth Presbyterian's Ladies Benevolent Society was one of the central administrative bodies to oversee aid to devastated families.[44] As religious work in urban areas became more professionalized, however, women's involvement in the evangelical agenda became even more essential. Denominations and parachurch groups encouraged female workers to both staff and administer city programs. As a signifier of its respectability, the middle class generally frowned upon any public presence for women in urban areas. A public woman symbolized a "loose" woman, open to possible corruption, seduction, or even prostitution. Middle-class women were to remain within the private sphere, protected by their fathers or husbands. For women in city mission work, however, the middle-class stigma of a public presence was buffered by an even stronger evangelical ideal—the moralizing potential of womanhood. Women engaged in city evangelism created another acceptable symbol for the middle class—the pure, undefiled morality of womanhood in opposition to the evil, frequently male-defined urban environment. Evangelicalism's moral designation for women legitimated their widespread participation in urban outreach. As Protestant women, generally from lower or middle-class backgrounds, responded to the challenge, many carved out full-time careers as urban missionaries. These activities, however, would run directly into more formidable and contentious challenges in the 1870s and 1880s.

Evangelical Morality Meets Class Warfare

Emma Dryer, an evangelist who allied her career with Dwight L. Moody, assumed a key role as evangelicalism navigated Chicago's increasingly unruly social environment. Dryer was influential in the formation of the Chicago Evangelization Society (later renamed the Moody Bible Institute), an institution that provided much of the personnel and revival leadership for the Third Awakening. An examination of the formative process of the institute that Dryer worked in clarifies the roles of women and men in urban work, and illuminates underlying contradictions within normative

44. Report of Ladies Benevolent Society, Fourth Presbyterian Church; Speech, Rev. James G. K. McClure, "The History of the Fourth Presbyterian Church of Chicago, Ill.," May 12, 1914, McCormick Theological Seminary; McCarthy, *Noblesse Oblige*, 3–24.

evangelical gender ideals. On the one hand, their vision for urban ministry promoted female initiative and independence. On the other, evangelical ideals of submission and acquiescence constantly constrained female missionaries. Urban work entailed men being in charge. Yet men desperately needed the expertise, footwork, and familial beachheads in urban neighborhoods that women workers could provide. These same contradictory pressures and norms characterized women's work in later Third Awakening revivals.

Prior to meeting Dwight L. Moody, Emma Dryer worked from 1864 to 1870 as the preceptress at the Illinois State Normal School. As she befriended various YWCA missionaries, Dryer familiarized herself with Chicago's network of Protestant missions. In 1870 Dryer resigned her teaching position to evangelize prostitutes, and she also began to attend Dwight L. Moody's Illinois Street Church. Following the 1871 Chicago Fire, Dryer helped with relief efforts that deepened her connection with evangelical urban workers. In 1873, the Chicago Avenue Church (formerly the Illinois Street Church) hired Dryer to head up its Bible Work of Chicago. The primary purposes of this organization were to train urban workers to lead prayer and Bible studies within neighborhoods, and to distribute Bibles for the Chicago Bible Society. Dryer herself worked primarily in the Haymarket and Union Park areas, a neighborhood characterized by a mix of industrial factories and worker's homes located on Chicago's near West Side.[45]

Like many evangelicals, Emma Dryer's missionary fervor was stimulated by her belief in premillennialism, a doctrine of implicit social disconnection that she accepted after hearing the preaching of Reverend William J. Eerdman at the Illinois Street Church. On one level, Dryer believed in premillennialism's salvation mandate, yet she did not give up the millennial ideal that Christian education was central to a convert's spiritual development. Christian education, she believed, could also bring about positive social change. Educational organizations like the Bible Work also represented one of the few empowering options open to evangelical women— education. Dryer took this opportunity to enable women very seriously, envisioning an all-female institution where women could live together while they were taught and supported in ministry. Dwight L. Moody had

45. Emma McNaughton to Dr. Wilbur Smith, October 18, 1945, and Letter, Office of Alumni Relations, Illinois State Normal University, to Bernard R. DeRemer, both in Emma Dryer File; Schultz and Hast, eds., *Women Building Chicago*, 230.

initially approached Lucy Rider Meyer, the Methodist-Episcopal deaconess, with the idea for the Bible Work. When Rider Meyer, who was already committed to the Chicago Training School, refused the revivalist's offer, Moody allied himself with Dryer.

Like Moody, Emma Dryer's work attracted the support of elites who funded many of the urban mission programs. One of Dryer's strongest advocates was Nettie Fowler McCormick, the widow of industrialist Cyrus McCormick, Sr. After her husband's death in 1884, Mrs. McCormick assumed management of the large McCormick Reaper Works as well as her late husband's estate and business affairs. She also became one of Chicago's leading philanthropists.[46] Cyrus McCormick, Sr.'s strong allegiance to Moody plus Nettie McCormick's own prominent evangelical faith motivated her continued support for Moody's programs, one of which was Emma Dryer's Chicago Bible Work. Monies provided by McCormick and other elites allowed Dryer to initiate the Bible Work in 1873.[47]

Urban outreaches like the Bible Work took on a renewed urgency for evangelicals as Chicago weathered the social and economic turmoil of the 1870s and 1880s. The 1873 depression wracked the already tenuous relationship between industrialists and their workers. Stringent wage reductions or layoffs confronted workers in all of the city's major industries, a reality that intensified union organization and calls for radical activism. In less than a year after Moody's 1876 revival in Chicago, a national railroad strike broke out. The 1877 railroad walkout that began in the East quickly spread from Maryland and West Virginia into Chicago. Albert Parsons, leader of the Socialist Working-Men's Party, urged calm and called on workers to protest nonviolently and to join a union. Instead, sporadic incidents of violence spread across the city. These incidents, though instigated by city "roughs," fueled rampant fears among the "better classes" that a

46. Emma Dryer to John Blanchard, January 1916, Emma Dryer File; William R. Moody to Caroline Waite, May 19, 1924, Caroline Waite File; Edward T. James, Janet W. James, Paul S. Boyer, eds., *Notable American Women,* 454–55; Schultz and Hast, eds., *Women Building Chicago,* 551–53.

47. "Mr. Moody and Mr. McCormick," *Interior,* January 4, 1900; Dryer to Blanchard, January 1916, 10–14, Emma Dryer File. Originally the Bible Institute was to be a woman's institution. In her letter to Blanchard, Dryer wrote that she remembered speaking to Moody, "I said. If you educate young women for Christian work, as done in Mildmay Institutions, what will you do for the young men? He (Moody) answered, 'Let the theological seminaries take 'em. We'd find ouselves in hot water quick, if we undertook to educate young men.'"

much larger and well-organized urban revolt was in the making.[48] The recently formed Illinois National Guard was called in, and retailer Marshall Field armed his employees and loaned horses and delivery wagons to the police. But the response was not solely military.

At the height of the strike, an emergency meeting was called at a large edifice located a block northeast of Market Square. The Moody and Sankey Tabernacle had been built a year earlier by J. V. Farwell to accommodate ten thousand people plus six thousand overflow. It had served as the center of Moody's revival.[49] In attendance at the tabernacle were many Chicago elites and industrialists, who discussed a variety of tactics, including the use of force by private civic groups to put down the strike and protect public order. Shortly after, the Chicago Board of Trade requested a larger standing army from the U.S. Congress, and a Law and Order League was formed to support the local militia. Chicago's overreaction to the railroad strike and its strong-handed enforcement of law and order laid the groundwork for the later, much more infamous Haymarket Riot, and evangelicals were part of the debate.

Despite an improved economic climate in the 1880s, the deep antagonism between Chicago industrialists and their workers lingered. Workers had been agitating for a shorter workday for decades, seeing this issue as a recognition of their rights and their significant contribution to industrial capitalism. By 1886 the eight-hour issue had united the labor movement in the city, but also drew employers together in their distrust of and opposition to workers. Chicago's conservative press and Protestant clergy blamed labor activism on radical organizers, whom they claimed represented "un-American" views, and fanned elite and middle-class hostility toward the eight-hour demand. By 1886, the two sides of Chicago's industrial workforce were deeply polarized and full class warfare seemed almost inevitable.

Tension over the eight-hour day finally climaxed when the McCormick Reaper Works staged a lockout in February 1886. In May, union employees who had been displaced from the Reaper Works gathered at factory exits to taunt their scab replacements. In response, the Chicago police arrived and shot at least two workers. On the evening of May 4, workers rallied at the Haymarket Square, on Randolph Street just west of DesPlaines, to protest the police killings and what the workers saw as the city's support of

---

48. Smith, *Urban Disorder,* 105–6.
49. Northrop, *Life and Labors of Dwight L. Moody,* 44.

"arrogant capitalism." The Haymarket Riot ensued, a violent melee that resulted in the death of at least four workers and seven policemen and once again raised the specter of urban anarchy in Chicago. City officials responded swiftly to Haymarket, immediately rounding up anarchists and unionists en masse, eventually prosecuting eight men for the police killings. In the wake of the legal travesty of Haymarket, conservatives solicited private donations to finance the construction of Fort Sheridan and the Great Lakes Naval Training Station, all to reassure Chicagoans that their property was protected and order had been restored.[50]

In the midst of this urban warfare, Emma Dryer's Bible Work continued, at times coordinating with Protestant churches or working alongside other parachurch groups like the WCTU. After 1879, the Bible Work was more specifically modeled on a deaconess program in Mildmay, England, that Dryer had observed firsthand on a trip to London. Like the deaconess movement, Bible Workers divided the city into districts. Each female worker was encouraged to live in or nearby her respective district and to organize prayer meetings in various homes, establish sewing schools, and make house-to-house visits to read Scripture to women and children. Although the Bible Work was primarily geared toward spiritual redemption, its social and educational outreaches were also significant parts of the ministry. The Bible Work also sponsored annual May Institutes that provided speakers and religious instruction. In November 1885, close to the eve of the Haymarket incident, Dryer enumerated her responsibilities to her patron Nettie McCormick. Included in her work was preparatory studies for four women hoping to further their Christian training in order to enter the foreign mission field. "Besides these, we are holding two night schools," Dryer wrote, "three young men have recently gone to college from these. I hold five meetings a week. Am I not busy?"[51]

Dryer's Bible Work conformed to a broad pattern of urban evangelism based on a salvation message with a strong dose of education. These two

50. Smith, *Urban Disorder*, 105–9.

51. Dryer to McCormick, August 29, 1879, Papers of Nettie Fowler McCormick (hereafter Nettie Fowler McCormick will be abbreviated McC.); Dryer to Virginia McCormick, November 11, 1885; T. W. Harvey to Board of Managers of MBI, November 16, 1888; Harvey related in this letter that the social involvements of the Bible Workers eventually came to interfere with Moody's primarily evangelistic interests. Harvey wrote, "these ladies became interested and pledged to certain localities, and had no time to attend Evangelistic services." Harvey File. Dryer to Blanchard, January 1916, 21–24, Dryer File.

elements were seemingly designed to counteract labor unrest and potential radicalism. Conversion was the key to a faith-based life, but education also taught immigrants to appreciate the basic principles of individualism and democracy. Through education, radicalism could be channeled into productive labor and citizenship. When it came to the Haymarket Riot, however, these evangelical ideals fell short. Shortly after the riot, its eight accused perpetrators were brought to trial. After an overtly theatrical and recognizably unjust trial, the jury declared the eight defendants guilty and condemned seven of them to death by hanging.

In October, the defendants were brought back to court and allowed to speak against their judgments. On October 8, 1886, Emma Dryer sat in the courtroom and listened to the impassioned speeches of August Spies, Samuel Fielden, and Albert Parsons, all of whom had been condemned for the Haymarket violence. Chicago's Haymarket region was part of the area included in Dryer's Bible Work district. It is likely that she had observed any one of the many inequities that had precipitated the Haymarket incident. If so, she recorded little if any sympathy for the convicted workers. While listening to the court, Dryer wrote to her benefactor, Nettie Fowler McCormick, noting, "I hear the name McCormick frequently," as the defendants lashed out at the McCormick family and their total disregard for the interests of labor. Dryer, however, was seemingly oblivious to these pleas for justice. Instead she articulated her belief that moral principles somehow exist above social or economic reality. "There is no justice possible out of Christ," she wrote. "Law centers in Him and as I hear these arguments from a social standpoint my heart aches to have the church of Christ see where her work lies. Over and over, these men argue and plead for justice to the poor. They are deluded. They need Christian education; and so do our courts and legislatures, and schools—who does not?"[52]

Dryer's comments identify her strong belief that only faith could overcome the chasm that existed between workers and employers. Only faith could override status difference and resolve conflict. According to Dryer, one could address anarchist pleas for justice by redeeming individual souls. Yet she did not offer these precepts from a distance. As an urban worker, she committed herself to social intervention in order to inculcate the working class with these evangelical principles. For Dryer, only Protestant morality could salve the discontent of the poor; only faith could effect class

52. Dryer to McC., October 8, 1886, McCormick Papers.

harmony and social stability. The fact that Dryer was addressing this plea to Nettie McCormick, who obviously held similar ideals, makes her observations at once more compelling and more conflicted.

True Womanhood and the City

Emma Dryer's understanding of the Bible Work was defined by an educational purpose as well as a domestic ideal. Home evangelism was a central focus for female urban missionaries. According to evangelicalism's domestic model, the home was the incubator of personal morality so it inevitably had to be the prime evangelistic target. Women's moral authority legitimized female activism and provided missionaries with a carte blanche into city households. In the case of the Bible Work, missionaries canvassed city "houses," the intended locus of the Protestant moral order, and sought to turn them into "homes." Domesticity also conveyed authority and respectability to female workers. At a time when "proper" society questioned the decency of any woman who ventured into urban space, missionaries like Dryer moved through city streets cloaked with the legitimacy of "true womanhood" as they carried out their redemptive tasks.[53]

D. L. Moody saw women's role in urban evangelism, and specifically in the Bible Work, from a conservative yet utilitarian perspective.[54] Like Dryer, Moody was influenced by premillennialism and wanted to redeem as many individuals and homes as possible. The moral authority of womanhood plus women's skills in urban work became part of the evangelist's redemptive effort. Moody advocated women leading home and neighborhood visitations as well as participating in more public forms of ministry. Dryer, however, appears to be more socially conservative than Moody. She was particularly intent on maintaining female respectability. Dryer willingly endorsed female evangelism in the city's homes, but refused to allow Bible Workers to teach men or evangelize in areas dominated by men, such as saloons or prisons. Younger women, she insisted, particularly needed protection and guidance: their work should be limited to women and children. Moody's advocacy of women's participation in a variety of evangelis-

53. Elizabeth Wilson, *The Sphinx in the City: Urban Life, the Control of Disorder, and Women*, 65.

54. Weber, *Living in the Shadow of the Second Coming*.

tic activities caused Dryer to hesitate. The more public forms of evangelism, Dryer believed, violated middle-class standards of propriety and were far too dangerous for younger women. She particularly opposed women's participation in night evangelism and considered public after-dark activities for women, which carried the stigma of prostitution, to be improper and unsafe. In response to one of Moody's night evangelistic outreaches, Dryer wrote, "I know that the Bible Work represents the legitimate work for women, but that such night work for young women is attended by dangers too many."[55] For Dryer, the Bible Work's purpose of winning souls could not override the realities of the crime-ridden city.

Dryer herself was not intimidated by public spaces. She reasoned that mature women should participate in the more public and therefore dangerous areas of ministry, and she herself did not hesitate to directly confront sin. Dryer, along with Sarah Clark, a cofounder of the Pacific Garden Rescue Mission, worked for many years in the men's department of the Chicago jail. Evangelists like Dryer and Clarke gave a public and female face to evangelicalism as it confronted the city. "Give me a woman every time," Moody said. "Women have more tact and offend less; if we had more of them as city missionaries we would have less anarchism and communism."[56]

Evangelicalism's promotion of true womanhood and Moody's acceptance of women in urban evangelism created new opportunities for female workers. At the same time, however, the constraints of this ideal often hindered the actual accomplishment of the mission. Problems were particularly evident in terms of the financial support for urban workers. According to the womanhood ideal, women were to be pious, submissive, and sacrificial, and their evangelism techniques were to embody those ideals. Despite an increased reliance on evangelical professionals to spread the Gospel, to assume that the Bible Work was a career for females or to solicit actively for funding would betray these same feminine qualities. Emma Dryer's attitude toward the finances of the Bible Work was typical of many evangelical workers. Dryer refused to take a salary, because she was "thinking that her (Dryer's) influence over other workers would be lessened and her own usefulness impaired." Many evangelical workers like Dryer had to rely on finances through self-deprecating prayer requests. "Please do not—do think when I tell you about our money affairs that I am suggesting a place for me

55. Dryer to McC., June 24, 1887, October 12, 1888, McCormick Papers.
56. *Record of Christian Work* 7, no. 5 (May 1888): 7.

in your benevolence—not so," Dryer wrote to Nettie McCormick. "Do not give to the Bible Work what you should give elsewhere, and only you—not I, know where you should give to the Lord." When Mrs. McCormick responded to Dryer's hesitant appeal and set up a regular means of support for her, a fellow Bible Worker, Mrs. Shute, wrote, "I am glad the Lord has moved you and Mr. Moody to make this appropriation for her. If it is not called a 'salary' I think she will receive it gladly and how much more independently she can act."[57] Women's urban work was clearly dictated and curtailed by their dependence upon others for funding, and as a result, Dryer's finances and those of the Bible Work itself were continually underfunded.

Women's lack of independence within evangelical work, sometimes to the point of deprivation, was justified within the broader context of female submission, another part of evangelical womanhood. Submission and suffering were considered signs of an authentic ministry. On the foreign mission field, the sacrifice and long suffering of women created missionary "heroines" whose stories were widely circulated among evangelical mission societies at home. Like their counterparts in urban work, female sacrifice in foreign missions often effaced the real independence of female missionaries and the evangelical ideological restraints they experienced.[58] By reinforcing women's sacrificial goodness in the face of heathen cultures, foreign or urban, evangelicals reaffirmed the elevated position of Protestant women whose virtue placed them above the mundane details of finance.

These financial restraints made city work for women precarious at best. Urban missionaries often worked without pay. In the case of the Bible Work, young trainees lived in substandard housing. "I find it difficult," Dryer wrote, "to get places for some of them in their districts, on account of high prices for board on the one hand, and then the miserable accommodations which their means secure on the other." Mrs. M. C. Hubbard confirmed Dryer's complaints about both housing and meeting places for the Bible Work. She described the "dark and unhealthy room where they spend so much of their time." In 1877, one of Dryer's coworkers summarized the evangelist's predicament in a letter to Nettie McCormick: "Dryer," she confirmed, "is very short of money."[59] While Moody and his supporters increas-

57. Emma Moody to McC., July 23, 1880, Dryer to McC., November 11, 1881, Shute to McC., November 11, 1881, McCormick Papers.

58. Joan Jacobs Brumberg, *Mission for Life*, 86.

59. Dryer to McC., November 11, 1881, Dryer to McC., October 26, 1881, Shute to McC., no day given, 1877, Dryer File.

ingly defined Protestant outreach as a profession, gender assignments dictated that the financial aspect of female evangelistic work was characterized by economic denial.

What support Dryer did receive resulted largely from personal commitments made to Dwight L. Moody and not to Dryer herself. By 1881, the expenses for the Bible Work had increased while facilities for the Bible Workers had worsened. Dryer desperately wanted a central location to house the young female workers. Mr. E. G. Keith, president of the Metropolitan Bank and another member of Chicago's evangelical elite, gave Dryer five hundred dollars to rent a house for the workers, which Dryer promptly accepted, praising God for this "good man." In January of 1882, Nettie McCormick donated the coal to heat the house.[60] Wealthy evangelicals like Keith, John V. Farwell, Nathaniel S. Bouton, T. W. Harvey, and the McCormicks contributed to the Bible Work, but, apart from Nettie McCormick, these payments appear to have been given out of loyalty to D. L. Moody's work and their affiliation with him through his church or the YMCA. But the tenuous nature of the Bible Work did not diminish Dryer's vision for an institution dedicated solely to the training of women for ministry. By 1886, however, Dryer became increasingly distressed with her inability to achieve this vision apart from some broader endorsement. The sacrificial tenor of her work began to wear thin, and Dryer longed for the day when she could properly educate and house her women in a women's training school.

Much of Dryer's frustration came to focus on the movement's powerhouse, Dwight L. Moody. At the start of the Bible Work in the spring of 1873, Moody and his song leader Ira Sankey left Chicago to lead several highly successful revival meetings in Britain and in cities throughout the United States. When Moody returned to Chicago in 1876 to head up a three-month revival, it was clear that greater amounts of his time and commitment were directed toward revival outreach than to urban ministry. Moody saw revivalism and urban ministry as part of the same agenda, and his ongoing ties to Chicago continued to motivate his interest in the ongoing Bible Work, but his support was erratic at best. The sporadic nature of Moody's attention to the Bible Work was only part of a growing division between the two.

Dryer began to acknowledge the differences inherent between her Bible Work and Mr. Moody's mission. One difference hinged on doctrine. Dryer believed in divine healing and Dwight L. Moody did not. Apparently at one

---

60. Dryer to McC., October 29, 1881, McCormick Papers; *Institute Tie,* June 1905.

point in her life, Dryer herself had experienced some form of either physical or spiritual healing and believed that the more physical aspect of spirituality could not be neglected. For years, Dryer held weekly prayer meetings in the YMCA Bible Room for the purpose of praying for the sick. "We taught and advised those that came—seeking the Truth for them, and for ourselves. We also secured instruction to our workers, by Lady Physicians, and put strong emphasis on healthful living, and proper care of our bodies." Moody, on the other hand, saw such activities as a distraction from the true mission of the Bible Work, which was to spread the Gospel. Dryer remembered, "Mr. Moody's devotion to direct evangelization, led him to fear any measure that might possibly detract from teaching the plain simple gospel of Christ. He was particularly watchful, lest Mothers' meetings, Industrial Schools, Kitchen Gardens, and any means adapted to Home and family life and common practical education became a substitute for the spiritual needs of sinner and saint." As salvation alone came to dominate Moody's vision, he judged Emma Dryer's more holistic perspective as no longer appropriate for his goals.[61]

A second difference between Dryer and Moody centered on the Bible Work's educational orientation and its community involvements. Education in the various urban communities by its very nature drew women workers into social interactions within their neighborhoods and away from Moody's mandate for salvation alone. As Moody's reputation as a revivalist rose, the social involvements of the Bible Work became increasingly out of sync with Moody's mission. In 1888, T. W. Harvey, one of the founding board members of the Chicago Evangelization Society (later renamed the Moody Bible Institute) explained the purpose of the institution. He noted that city evangelism was the primary objective. As a revivalist, Moody found it difficult to find laypersons whose knowledge of Scripture was sufficient to "gather in the results of the preaching of Evangelists." As a result, Mr. Moody initiated the Bible Work. Harvey continued, "While accomplishing a necessary work, in every Christian community, it [the Bible Work] did not seem to meet entirely Mr. Moody's original purpose, in that these ladies became interested and pledged to certain localities, and had not time to attend evangelistic services. His [Moody's] workers he wanted to devote their time exclusively to spiritual interests, and assisting the Evangelist."[62]

61. "Supplement," Dryer File, n.d.; Brereton, *God's Army,* 8–10.
62. Harvey to Chicago Bible Institute Board, November 16, 1888, Harvey File.

The Bible Work also associated with other women's groups, like the WCTU, that were committed to addressing broader social issues impacting the home and family. Dryer had allied with the WCTU earlier, but Mr. Moody determined again that temperance work was no longer appropriate to his goals. In an 1888 letter to Nettie McCormick, Dryer recalled a time when Moody informed her, "If you have anything to do with those temperance women, I won't come to Chicago!" In response to Moody's demand to sever ties with the WCTU, Dryer acquiesced: "I withdrew—no easy effort! For I believed God wanted him to 'come to Chicago,' and would make it right further on."[63] The widening split between Dryer and Moody also enlightens the function of gender in urban evangelism, particularly the issue of male dominance versus female submission. The nineteenth century's separate-spheres ideal dictated that woman's moral influence was to be exerted indirectly through submission to male authority. Similarly, the spiritual tenets of evangelicalism dictated that just as women were intended to submit to husbands or fathers, female evangelists were to submit to men within the ministry. The same ideology, designed to bring order to the family and to society, also dictated the professional relationship within evangelical ministries. If saving souls was the overriding goal, then women were to comply with men who were perceived as more knowledgeable or adept at the salvation business. Female evangelists, like Dryer, submitted to men for the good of the ministry; adherence to these ideals brought greater glory to the faith.

Despite Moody's encouragement of women in urban evangelism, the standard for female submission was set. Female missionaries were beholden to both this spiritual and class ideal. Young female workers, who came to the Bible Work because of their faith, were esteemed within the evangelical community because of their willingness to defer to male leaders. Because urban outreach was supported financially by middle-class Protestants, the standards of that class determined the propriety of all ministries. Females in urban ministry were allowed to go into public places as representatives of evangelicalism, but only if such activities were sanctioned by men and only if women exhibited the proper deference to male leadership. To step incorrectly out of that sphere or to challenge male authority was to violate this standard and to risk losing the respect of, and perhaps funding from, middle-class supporters. Evangelical women's continuation in ministry depended upon their acceptance of assigned gender roles and their

63. Dryer to McC., September 20, 1888, McCormick Papers.

promotion of this ideal within the work. With little or no career or financial independence, women had few options other than deference to male leaders.

Subordinate-dominant roles for women and men were apparent in the organizational styles of Dryer and Moody. Dryer, who was "thorough and systematic," believed that all female workers should be thoroughly trained before being sent out to the city as evangelists. Moody was "more impulsive and given to taking more widespread views of work and then leaving them to somehow work themselves out." Despite the fact that Dryer had organizational savvy and a working knowledge of city work, she was expected to defer to Moody's judgment. Submission came at a price, causing the Bible Work to lay victim to the uncertainty of Moody's indecisiveness. "He astonishes me," Dryer wrote, "by the evidence he exhibits that he forgets what he says and does." And in a summa that barely matched her frustration, she added, "the dear man is well named *Moody*."[64]

The central opportunity for female independence rested with all-female institutions like the one Dryer originally had envisioned for the Bible Work. In the nineteenth century, separation from males, particularly in institutional settings, allowed women to foster support among themselves and to create their own space in areas predominantly controlled by men. An example of this type of female independence is found in the career of Francis Willard, another activist deeply committed to reforming Chicago. Willard, like Dryer, was an evangelical and an educator who became the president of the Evanston College for Ladies. Early in her career, Willard also allied herself with Dwight L. Moody and traveled with him on an eastern tour leading women's prayer meetings. When Willard shared a revival platform with a more liberal Universalist, Moody's more conservative social and theological position became clear. Unlike Dryer, however, Willard was not cowed and did not acquiesce to Moody's demand for theological purity. Opting for a more latitudinarian approach, Willard pursued her social goals apart from Moody and became the influential leader of the WCTU, a women's organization that more broadly addressed the political and economic plight of women.[65]

64. Unidentified author to McC., June 24, 1887, Dryer to McC., March 22, 1887, McCormick Papers.

65. Ruth Bordin, *Francis Willard: A Biography*, 89; Nancy Hardesty, *Women Called to Witness*, 20–25; Caroline DeSwarte Gifford, "Francis Elizabeth Caroline Willard," in Schultz and Hast, eds., *Women Building Chicago*, 968–74; Barbara Leslie Epstein, *The Politics of Domesticity: Women, Evangelism, Temperance in Nineteenth Century America*, 115–46; Thomas R. Pegram, *Battling Demon Rum: The Struggle for a Dry America, 1800–1933*, 68–72.

Both Willard and Dryer's lifelong work were established within the parameters of the separate-spheres ideal that heightened the social influence of white middle-class women and validated their authority to reform public space. Bible Workers like Dryer, however, saw their societal engagement as the sole means to a spiritual end—the salvation of an individual soul. Like their more liberal counterparts, the Bible Work and other urban outreaches made use of middle-class ideals of womanhood and domesticity to expand their public participation, but in the end, because of these same ideals, the ministries of evangelical women became subsumed by male constraints. As middle-class women, Dryer and Willard lived within the social mandates of the separate spheres, but only Dryer adhered to these principles as spiritual absolutes. Willard went on to see many of these same ideals as constricting to women and limiting to their abilities and skills. As a result, Willard used the moral force of womanhood to call for gender equality and to build a movement that operated independently of male authority. Evangelicals like Dryer, on the other hand, endowed womanhood with spiritual worth and elevated its inherent female morality to a metaphysical plane. Unlike Willard, Emma Dryer continued to rely upon male sanction and approval for the continuation of the Bible Work.[66] Although Dryer, like Willard, established a career, her ultimate legitimacy depended not on other women but on men. When Dryer challenged male authority in the founding of the Chicago Bible Institute, she found herself alone. What limited success she experienced in the Bible Work depended not upon the elevation of her moral influence or upon her skills as an urban evangelist but on her willingness to fall into line with the dictates of male evangelicals and the imperatives of the domestic order.

Emma Dryer and the Chicago Evangelization Society

By 1886, the same year as the Haymarket Riot, Moody and his supporters concluded that Chicago's urban ministry would benefit significantly from an institution to train workers. Emma Dryer's hope for a well-funded educational program was about to be realized. Unbeknownst to Dryer, however, Moody had already abandoned the idea of an all-female institution and had shifted over to a coeducational model. His idea was to

66. Carolyn DeSwarte Gifford, "The Woman's Cause Is Man's—Francis Willard and the Social Gospel," in Edwards and Gifford, eds., *Gender and the Social Gospel,* 21–34.

train "gapmen," individuals (men and women) who could bridge the void between the clergy and laity, and "lay their lives alongside of the laboring classes and the poor and bring the gospel to bear upon their lives." In January 1886 Moody appealed to his Chicago business supporters for $250,000 in order to establish such a training school. The rampant fears generated by the Haymarket incident perhaps motivated Moody's supporters to give their assistance to the evangelist. Whatever the reason, by the end of the year, supporters contributed the required sum for the school's formation. But complications ensued as the program moved forward into the organizational stage. In July 1887, Nettie Fowler McCormick, one of the leading contributors to the project, intervened and objected to parts of the newly written constitution. Specifically, she objected to the provision for the ladies' work being relegated to the status of by-laws as opposed to being part of the regular constitution. "The ladies' work," McCormick argued, "is a Constitutional and important part of this society—and none is more so."[67] McCormick, who had supported Dryer's Bible Work in the past, saw the diminished constitutional status of the women's program as undermining its legitimacy in the newly formed institute, and, perhaps more importantly, as a betrayal of Emma Dryer's life goal.

Nettie McCormick's reasoned criticisms apparently insulted Dwight L. Moody, thereby prompting him immediately to resign from the project. Mrs. McCormick, in turn, desiring to see the project continue and to maintain her support of Dryer's work, then resigned her own connection with the institute. It became obvious that without Moody's favor or the McCormick money, the project could not go forward. The revivalist's spouse, Emma Moody, finally intervened and persuaded her husband to reconsider the school, and Nettie McCormick also agreed to restore her support. In February 1888 Dryer's Bible Work was legally incorporated into the Chicago Evangelization Society, and the home previously used by the Bible Workers was transferred to the society. Shortly after the merger, Dryer wrote to McCormick, "I certainly am

---

67. Brereton, *God's Army,* 52–54; Dryer to Blanchard, January 27, 1916, Dryer file; "The Woman's Department of the Bible Institute." Smith, *Urban Disorder,* 101–74, offers an in-depth analysis of the Haymarket incident. Smith's study of the language of Haymarket notes that words like "law," "order," "conspiracy," and "anarchy" were used so frequently that their meaning was blurred into an overall fear that was more specifically defined by words like "foreign," "manly," and "natural." McC. to Bouton, July 12, 1887, McCormick Papers.

68. Bible Work–Chicago Evangelization Society Incorporation document, February 14, 1888, Dryer to McC., March 12, 1888, McCormick Papers.

ready to unite the work and the Board and all concerned."[68] Charter members of the Chicago Evangelization Society included those individuals who had previously supported the Bible Work—Turlington W. Harvey, Nathaniel Bouton, E. G. Keith, John V. Farwell, and Cyrus McCormick, Jr., with Dwight L. Moody as president of the institute. As incorporated, the women's Bible Work became the Ladies' Council of the Chicago Evangelization Society with Nettie McCormick as honorary president.

In spite of the successful merger, Dryer's expertise in urban evangelism and her strong desire for the Bible Work's success soon came into conflict with the general will of the society's governing board. Within months of the incorporation, Turlington W. Harvey, spokesperson for the board, asked Dryer to verify in writing her willingness to "act under the majority of the managers of the Chicago Evangelization Society." This verification was required, Harvey noted, because "Parties that are near you and witness your daily walk and conversation report that you still refuse to work under Mr. Moody's leadership and still refuse to allow *your workers,* as you call them, to do the work laid out for them, and report to the General Manager." Dryer's independence and the ensuing disagreements with Mr. Moody increasingly alienated her from the society and caused some board members to search for reasons to move her out. In June 1888, T. W. Harvey wrote to Dryer, "you are overworked and you are in a condition of mind unsuited to the discharge of the great work you are undertaking to do." Mrs. T. W. Harvey wrote a similar criticism: "We feel that quite outside of the differences in method between Mr. Moody and Miss Dryer, Miss Dryer lacks the breadth and sympathy to mother an extensive establishment, and that her experience in life has narrowed and set her convictions to such an extent that it is quite out of the question that she work with a Board, unless she is recognized as the absolute ruler."[69]

The disagreement spread beyond Dryer and the Moody-Harvey coalition. On August 16, 1888, Nathaniel Bouton resigned from the society's board because of "the uncertain movements of Mr. Moody in connection with the work" and Bouton's belief that "no great Christian work can be accomplished until the Society is organized and entire harmony of purpose prevails . . . The course pursued towards Miss Dryer is unchristian and has

---

69. Harvey to Dryer, June 17, 1888, Dryer File; Mrs. T. W. Harvey to McC., July 19, 1888, McCormick Papers.

none of the Spirit of Christ. And agreeing in the main with Miss Dryer, I think best to withdraw."[70] Institutional "harmony of purpose," in this case, implied the need for Dryer to acquiesce to the board and to accept Moody's leadership in order to sustain the ministry.

By the summer of 1888, Harvey concluded that any agreement with Miss Dryer was unlikely and that the board should separate the Bible Work from the institute. Harvey initiated the division, transferring institute funds and property back to the Bible Work. Dryer herself refused to resign her position on the institute's Ladies' Council, but she was increasingly excluded from the workings of the board. Dryer's disciplinary comeuppance came in October 1888 when, with Dryer present, the board voted that Mrs. Capron, a missionary from India, should replace her as head of the ladies' work. "How did I feel?" Dryer wrote. "I am numb and heavy with sorrow which I try to tell our Lord about and can only ask him to lead us each and all. To see one set aside after fifteen years of work without some support." Dryer shared her desolation with her coworkers. She wrote, *"One* woman *can't* work on, so *alone . . .* to be *alone* is to be *weak* and liable to attack." At the same meeting the resignations of Mrs. Shute and Mrs. Ayrens, coworkers with Dryer, were presented. Dryer herself did not resign from the board until May 1889. The Bible Work eventually affiliated with the American Bible Society and Dryer spent the remaining years of her life dependent upon the McCormick family for funds to continue her smaller urban work. Admittedly despondent, she addressed her letters later in life from "Lonesome Blvd."[71] The Chicago Bible Institute was significantly different from that initially envisioned by Dryer and Moody. The original vision of a women's training school with its potential for specifically female training and service was washed into the department of "Ladies Work."

At one level Emma Dryer's conflict with Dwight L. Moody represents the fate of a capable woman who refused to fit into the model of submissive

70. Bouton to McC., August 16, 1888, McCormick Papers.
71. Dryer to Shute, August 1, 1888, Dryer file; Dryer to McC., October 1, 1888, McCormick Papers; Interview with Miss Emma MacNaughton, June 14, 1958, Dryer File. At Dryer's death in 1925 Harold McCormick, son of Nettie Fowler McCormick, paid all funeral expenses and "provided an automobile load of beautiful flowers and floral pieces." Letter, W. F. Gaylord to Caroline E. Waite, April 22, 1925, Waite File.
72. James Findlay, "Moody, 'Gapmen,' and the Gospel: The Early Days of Moody Bible Institute," *Church History* 31 (September 1968): 322–35.

womanhood.[72] But Dryer's career also illuminates the function of domesticity in defining the role of evangelical women. This ideal divided society into two spheres and attached a moral designation to each; the virtue of the private sphere of femininity was designed to balance the ever-present evils of the public sphere. The spiritual mandate of this doctrine was clear: women were to be society's moralizing force. In the urban-industrial turmoil of the 1870s and 1880s evangelicals saw this model as the means to address urban chaos and restore social order. Female urban missionaries, like Dryer, used the moral authority vested in women to establish careers that extended their authority into the city. Operating within their designated sphere of influence and armed with a gospel of domesticity, these workers undertook evangelistic programs aimed specifically at America's homes where female virtue would intentionally triumph over urban evil.

In asserting their virtue, women often ran into contradictory assignments that both benefited and circumscribed the women who worked within the parameters of the domestic ideology. Dryer's leadership of the Bible Work and the subsequent conflict over its institutionalization fits this contradictory pattern. Dryer's endorsement and implementation of moral womanhood empowered her career and provided her with opportunities to effect change in the public arena. Ever loyal to the model, Dryer refused a salary, refused to see the Bible Work as a career, upheld her sacrificial and deferential role, and, in general, fulfilled her evangelical assignment. In hindsight, she perhaps fulfilled her obligation too well. Dryer developed not only expertise but also a loyalty to the Bible Work. Her strong identification with the Bible Work made it impossible for her to see it as "Mr. Moody's school" or to back down even under the duress of strong pressure. Women such as Dryer were empowered, but only within the context of their moral ascription; they were granted an authority based upon their acquiescence to Protestant gender dictates. Dryer's eventual unwillingness to defer to this mandate disrupted the male evangelical order and resulted in strong repercussions for her ministry.

By the late nineteenth century, as the contention and conflict in urban America increased, the moral influence of evangelical women led to even greater female activism. Empowered by this ideal, female workers entered public space, often critiquing male behavior and promoting the power of a godly woman as a moral alternative. As evangelical women criticized male behavior and the evident failures of the city, the contradiction within this domestic ideal became more evident—female empowerment hinged upon her acquiescence to the dominant male culture. When evangelical female leaders such as Dryer stepped over their prescribed boundaries, their male counterparts were quick to halt such threats.

The Dryer-Moody exchange took place at a time when broader gender conflicts were developing for women and men. These conflicts will be evident throughout the Third Awakening. Male evangelicals struggled to define their manhood, and to control its individualistic bent. Even as the rhetoric of evangelicalism encoded urban sin as male, revivalists asserted a new businessman's religion of order and efficiency to control it, and as they reworked the ideal of masculinity, evangelicals sought the security of traditional womanhood in order to balance new male trajectories. As a result, revivalism heightened woman's authority in the spiritual realm and empowered her in urban revival. Women did not participate in the Third Awakening as totally free agents. Rather, like Emma Dryer, revival women did not challenge the gendered dictates of evangelicalism; instead they accepted and promoted these dictates because they perceived such actions to be beneficial to their faith. In response to their moral assignment, however, women's participation in the Third Awakening caused male leaders to now contend with the threatening implications of women's activism, both religious and otherwise.

Like Emma Dryer, women within Third Awakening revivals depended upon male organizers and preachers and on their control of resources to promote their cause. Revivalism in turn promoted a religion that depended upon moral womanhood and her domestic sphere for its expression and enforcement in the public arena. Revivalists created the spiritually powerful image of white, middle-class virtue to expiate the "sins" of the city and to redeem the men who succumbed to them. The three revivals that were organized in Chicago after the establishment of the Chicago Bible Institute reveal the power of moral womanhood as well as its increasingly problematic influence. Just as manhood was experiencing an overhaul, significant social changes challenged the virtue of domestic womanhood and the sanctity of the private sphere. The evangelical ethos, based on woman as society's moralizing force, became increasingly difficult to support within the society it wanted to redeem. In response to these social challenges, The Third Awakening had to make some spiritual adjustments as well.

CHAPTER 2

"Sow the Wind, Reap the Whirlwind"

THE 1893 WORLD'S FAIR CAMPAIGN

By the 1880s revivalist Dwight L. Moody was approaching the latter years of a successful evangelistic career in both Europe and the United States. In 1889, Moody was returning to the States from Europe when the drive shaft on his ship, the German Lloyd S.S. *Spree,* malfunctioned and punctured the hull. The revivalist later recounted that as the ship floundered in the dark waters of the Atlantic, he struck a bargain with the Almighty. "If God would spare my life and bring me back to America," Moody later recalled, "I would come back to Chicago and preach the gospel with all the power that He would give me."[1] Chicago was Moody's home base. His early years with the YMCA and later as the founder of the Chicago Evangelization Society had won him many supporters in the city. By 1889, Moody had become much more than a Chicago persona: he was the most celebrated evangelical revivalist in the United States and England. Now he was coming home. His mid-Atlantic encounter with God brought him back to conduct one more battle for Chicago's soul.

In that same year, Democratic Mayor DeWitt C. Creiger proposed another way to arouse the city's moral sensibilities. Mayor Creiger selected a one-hundred-member, blue-ribbon committee whose mandate was to persuade the U.S. Congress to grant the upcoming World's Columbian Exposition to Chicago. With "supervoluminous civicism," Creiger's committee peddled Chicago's unique blend of the West's raw, unrestrained

---

1. J. Ritchie Bell, "Reminiscences of D. L. Moody Saved from Death on the Atlantic," *Institute Tie,* November 1905, 73–74; Williams, *Life and Work of Dwight L. Moody,* 272.

"On Guard." *Ram's Horn*, June 21, 1893.

energy with the East's culture and sophistication. The panel argued that the city's population, which now numbered more than a million, pulsed with "complex human energy" and could accomplish "Herculean feats." What better place to celebrate the young and vibrant nation whose discovery the fair was to commemorate?[2] Chicago boosterism surpassed even the pressure of the New York lobby, and Chicago won the privilege of hosting the World's Fair.

Fair planners designed the World's Fair Exposition to be a uniquely Chicago-style celebration of America's discovery. Throughout 1892, elaborate buildings and exhibits slowly transformed what had been an undeveloped mud flat in the Jackson Park area into a sparkling White City, an extravagant display of the technological and humanitarian advances of the nineteenth century to highlight the century's intellectual and ethical advances and to create a once-in-a-lifetime event of enlightenment and world unity. Fair organizers coordinated an array of international conferences featuring the world's most eminent spokespersons in philosophy, religion, and reform causes. Hopes for the fair and its potential to accomplish good were enormous. Supporters argued that the fair would unquestionably demonstrate the superiority of Western thought and industry and, at the same time, transform lesser, "uncivilized" peoples with its sheer display of Western achievement.

Evangelicals and the Chicago World's Fair

Chicago evangelicals had misgivings about the fair; their enthusiasm was tempered by the fair's potential for excess and sin. Chicago continued to represent "a peculiar field for evangelistic work," a city whose "primary interest in commerce led only to irreligion and little moral restraint." These believers feared that the exposition would, in all probability, accelerate the less desirable trends already at work and deepen the city's social and moral disorder. One of their central concerns was that the fair would further intensify Chicago's ongoing love of money. As Chicago's manufacturing and retail sectors flourished, her raucous business climate continued to challenge the economic values of evangelicals who believed in the virtue of hard

2. Lewis and Smith, *Chicago: The History of Its Reputation,* 189–90; David F. Burg, *Chicago's White City of 1893,* 42.

work committed to the glory of God. According to the evangelical work ethic, one was to take profits honestly and spend them frugally. Such virtues were hard to find in Chicago's economy. Preaching to his Ravenswood Methodist Episcopal congregation, the Reverend J. P. Brushingham expressed evangelical concern. "All kinds and conditions of mankind come to a great city," he said, "mainly for one purpose—money getting, honestly or dishonestly." The British journalist, William T. Stead, was more direct. "Its [Chicago's] members came here to make money. The quest for the almighty dollar is their Holy Grail."[3]

The economic activity spawned by the World's Fair confirmed evangelical suspicions and challenged the enlightened projections of the fair's more liberal supporters. Even prior to Jackson Park being selected as the exposition site, nearby land values rose to what the *Chicago Tribune's* real estate editor termed "crack-brained altitudes." When the celebration finally opened, fair organizers and the railroads wrangled over the cost of transporting fair-goers. After weeks of dispute, the railroads essentially won, retaining the right to charge higher fares and to gouge potential fair attendees. These developments clearly indicated the greed of any and all that could get their hands into the fair's wallet.[4]

Contentious labor relations also surfaced. Throughout the lengthy and difficult construction process, workers threatened numerous times to walk off the job and to halt all building progress. Even the dictatorial mandates of the fair's leading architect, Daniel Burnham, were ineffective in overcoming organizational snafus and construction delays. Worker demands again raised the specter of labor conflict in Chicago and revived the deep class divisions that Haymarket had so clearly stamped on the city. Even the economic upswing from 1887 to 1892 had not effaced the dark blot of this event, and the highly publicized pardon of three Haymarket leaders only exacerbated labor tensions. In June 1893, one month after the opening of the fair, Illinois Democratic Governor John Peter Altgeld pardoned three of the accused perpetrators of the Haymarket Riot—Schwab, Fielden, and Neebe. Four of the seven accused in Haymarket had been executed shortly after their trial, yet Governor Altgeld pardoned the other three on the

3. Chicago *Inter-Ocean,* August 21, 1893; *Chicago Tribune,* March 13, 1893; William T. Stead, *If Christ Came to Chicago,* 123.
4. Homer Hoyt, *One Hundred Years of Land Values in Chicago, 1830–1930,* 156–57; Miller, *City of the Century,* 380; *Chicago Tribune,* November 1, 1893.

grounds that their "conviction was unjust and illegal." The governor's controversial pardon outraged Chicago's "better classes" and strengthened their resolve to stop further acquiescence to labor demands. At the same time, Altgeld's long-overdue pardon reminded workers of the grave injustices symbolized by the Haymarket incident. As the fair moved into late August, Chicago sank deeper into the Depression of 1893 and faced the likelihood of more class conflict. Stories of hunger and unemployed mobs covered the pages of the city's newspapers, portending even deeper economic failure and social upheaval to follow the fair's closing.[5]

A plethora of new Chicago businesses that were generated by the exposition further threatened the realization of evangelical ideals. Each month in the three years prior to the fair's opening, one new brewing company had started up production, responding to the fair's promise of big crowds and even bigger liquor profits. Seven hundred saloons opened to distribute the beer. Chicago's vice trade also capitalized on lascivious fair-goers. One brothel, Mollie Trussel's Custom House Place, on Harrison Street, reported a brisk business. Clifton Woolridge, a police detective, noted that it was "no unusual thing to see fifty to one hundred women lounging in the doors and windows . . . frequently half-clad, using vulgar and obscene language."[6] Evangelicals viewed saloons and brothels as outward symbols of the evil that pervaded the city. Indulgence in drunkenness and lust undermined evangelicalism's individualized, moral mandate. Opposition to these specific evils further cemented the evangelicals' alliance with the temperance and social purity movements. For evangelicals, alcohol and prostitution, the driving issues of these movements, were synonymous with moral decline; they were visible reminders of the sin among us. No amount of fair "uplift" could eradicate these blights.

The fair also contributed to Chicago politics as usual; the reality of continuing corruption was yet another threat to the moral code of evangelicals. Throughout the 1880s and 1890s, Democrat Carter Harrison had successfully created a party machine that had given him the mayoral victory in the

5. *Chicago Daily News,* April 10, 1893; the various pressures that confronted Daniel Burnham are expertly documented and interwoven with murder intrigue in Erik Larson, *The Devil in the White City: Murder, Magic, and Madness at the Fair That Changed America.* Miller, *City of the Century,* 384; Pierce, *A History of Chicago,* 299; *Chicago Tribune,* June 27, August 22, 27, September 2, 4, 1893; *Chicago Daily News,* September 2, 1893.

6. Perry Duis, *Public Drinking in Chicago and Boston, 1880–1920,* 38; Herbert Asbury, *Gem of the Prairie: An Informal History of the Chicago Underworld,* 116.

spring of 1893. Harrison was able to lock in his fifth term as mayor by defeating the Republican businessman candidate, Samuel W. Allerton. Harrison's victory in that election affirmed the staying power of the Irish-Catholic influence in Chicago politics, while the Republican, mostly Protestant electorate saw their candidate go down to defeat. Even though Republican mayors had engaged in their own share of fraud, many moral-minded Republican-Protestants believed that Harrison's election signaled a further escalation in political corruption. For example, Mike McDonald, or "King Mike," a central player in Chicago's gambling syndicate, contributed heavily to Harrison's reelection effort. When the mayor assumed office, McDonald continued to collect gambling percentages as guarantees against police interference. British reformer William T. Stead later noted that the "colossal fortunes" collected from the increased crowds of the World's Fair were divided among many. "But however many there were who fingered the profit en route, there was enough left to make it well worth the Mayor's while to allow the houses to run." Herbert Asbury, historian of the Chicago underworld, also observed, "Harrison had promised to give the World's Fair crowds a wide-open city and he more than kept his word. . . . It was, with the possible exception of New York in the days of Boss Tweed, the most corrupt city, and had been for a decade."[7]

The bald display of Chicago's sins rallied her moralists around the need for reform, and the World's Columbian Exposition seemed to fit the bill. In spite of their misgivings, many Chicago Protestants united around the fair's promise to uplift the city and the world. Raising the standard, they believed, meant demonstrating the superiority of Western civilization, particularly the uplifting quality of Christianity. In their attitudes about the fair's potential, however, Protestants spread themselves along a spectrum with a conservative evangelical position at one end and a much more liberal one at the other. In light of the challenges that confronted America at the

---

7. John D. Buenker, "The Dynamics of Chicago Ethnic Politics, 1900–1930," 175–99; Buenker, "Chicago Ethnics and the Politics of Accommodation," 92–100. Buenker noted that Harrison used his Irish, Swedish, and German background (even though he was from a southern, aristocratic family) to cement his affiliation with the Democratic wards. The Republican candidate Allerton proclaimed that the real choice in the 1892 election was between "the slums" and "the men who made modern Chicago." With Harrison's victory, Chicago's business-oriented moralists (one of whom was T. W. Harvey) saw their political influence decline. Miller, *City of the Century*, 482–87, 441–52; Stead, *If Christ Came to Chicago*, 223–24; Asbury, *Gem of the Prairie*, 155.

turn of the century, all Protestants wanted to reassert Christian values and to bring about social transformation, but differences surfaced in terms of how this reform was to be achieved. Protestant liberals who advocated social change through Western intellectual enlightenment believed that the World Fair's intellectual assets—its architectural grandeur and artistic display, its dedication to the education of the masses, its ability to expose fair-goers to the material and intellectual progress of the nineteenth century—would bring about social uplift. Protestant evangelicals, however, maintained that social progress began with an individual's recognition of sin followed by a conversion experience. These spiritual experiences would change lives, and those transformed by conversion would create better societies. Conservative evangelicals remained pessimistic about the likelihood of social progress apart from individual religious conversions. Only spiritually changed individuals could create an enlightened society. The fair's potential for reform was nil, they argued, without the component of individual redemption. But this redemptive focus did not rule out social involvements, and, as we will see, the World's Fair offered extensive opportunity for Chicago's evangelistic network to go into action.

Social Purity, Temperance, and "White" Morality

As part of the fair's effort to create a moral climate, supporters organized numerous congresses to bring together social activists who shared common purposes and causes. Evangelical spokespersons participated in several of the exposition's conferences, and many of these same individuals worked in the actual World's Fair Revival. As in the revival, these congresses defended Western civilization and Protestant superiority, an advantage that was symbolized by women's higher moral standard and their social esteem.

The Social Purity movement met at the World's Fair in June 1893. The congress convened at a time when the movement was engaged in a worldwide battle to end prostitution. Earlier in the nineteenth century, the cause of sexual purity had been a part of the Second Awakening's call to individual morality. Purists argued that vice was a sin and that one required a strong inner conscience to overcome the sexual temptations that led to vice. In both their diagnosis of and solution for this issue, Social Purists fit very much within the evangelical reform tradition created by the Second Awakening. By the 1890s, Social Purity had expanded this critique from the individual to society as a whole. Like other evangelical reform causes, Purists critiqued male impropriety, demanding that men adhere to the same sexual standard as women and put an end to society's double standard. The Social Purity agenda also worked to raise the entire standard of civilization by challenging the economic and political systems that supported vice, particularly in urban areas.

The primary organizer of the Social Purity conference at the World's Fair was Anthony Comstock, who served as the secretary of the Society for the Suppression of Vice in New York City. Other leaders of the international Social Purity movement—Dr. Kate Bushnell, Josephine Butler, and Lady Henry Somerset—also participated in the World's Fair conference. As a medical doctor and representative of England's Ladies' National Association, Bushnell had been responsible for exposing the British military's system of regulated vice in India. Josephine Butler was also a leading Social Purity activist from England. Lady Somerset, a close friend of Frances Willard, was leader of the worldwide temperance organization. Together, these leaders and their respective organizations were a moral police force determined to outlaw state regulation of vice and establish an "equal standard of morality for men and women."[8]

At the time of the World's Fair Congress, the Social Purity movement was divided between the "regulationists" and the "new abolitionists." The "regulationists" argued that segregating and then policing the sex trade within "red-light" districts would be the best means of controlling vice. On the opposing side, the "new abolitionists" advocated integrating Social Purity's earlier moral code with an activist agenda to eradicate vice. Abolitionists argued that ending the trade in young women (white slave trade) and freeing the prostitute required much more than regulation; they believed that only a formal recognition and institution of moral law could eliminate vice. The "new abolitionists" advocated remediation, such as rescuing "fallen women" from the trade and closing brothels, but they also endorsed a strong philosophy of moral child-rearing. The abolitionists saw the moral education of children as the best means of nipping possible temptation in the bud.[9] Speaking for the "new abolitionist" position, Purity activists at the World's Fair promoted the home as the most effective venue for teaching morals and thus society's most effective tool for ending prostitution.

8. *Chicago Tribune,* June 5, 1893.
9. Pivar, *Purity Crusade,* 157–59.

Their belief in the moral weight of domesticity also framed Social Purity's empathetic attitude toward the prostitutes themselves. Purists sympathized with the "fallen" woman because the men who violated her had abused her rightful place as a daughter, wife, or mother. A woman's ability to fulfill her domestic duties ensured her moral superiority and social respectability. To reinforce this domestic ideal, Social Purity speakers juxtaposed society's low opinion of the victimized prostitute with the spiritual eminence of mother-hood. Mirroring the dualist virgin/harlot view of women, Mrs. Anna Garland Spencer, a Social Purity speaker, referred to a "new ideal in mother-hood," whose "highest point was portrayed by the Madonna and child." Similarly, Archbishop Ireland told the conference, "The pure virgin of Nazareth, from whom was born God Incarnate, became the ideal woman of the new dispensation. . . . The woman henceforth was queen of the home, and as the power of the Christian religion grew, so grew in the minds of peo-ples the dignity of womanhood, its influence, and the respect awarded to it."[10] The Archbishop's participation in the conference signaled Catholic-Protestant unity on this issue and an eagerness to elevate motherhood as the preeminent standard for sexual purity. Theological differences between Catholics and Protestants did not deter Protestants' equating idealized womanhood with the Virgin Mary.

Just as Mary had been a virgin, Social Purists determined that Protestant women were to be pure in mind and body. Much of the spiritual and social authority of motherhood derived from its asexual character. This implied that all sexual activity was to be conducted within marriage and was to be directed toward reproduction. To promote this Purity ideal, the movement had successfully lobbied Congress to pass the Comstock Law in 1873. Named after Anthony Comstock, the influential organizer of the Purity Congress, this legislation essentially outlawed the manufacture, advertise-ment, or sale of any information or device related to contraception. Such legal restrictions severely limited a woman's access to birth control infor-mation and technologies. Through the Comstock Laws, the Social Purity movement tried to ensure that all sexual activity was linked to reproduc-tion, and that through motherhood, sex would be corralled within the domestic sphere and within society as a whole.

Social Purists argued that to separate sex from marriage and reproduc-tion would mean taking the protection of the domestic sphere away from

10. *Chicago Tribune,* June 3, 1893.

women. In its effort to outlaw prostitution, Social Purity "abolitionists" portrayed women outside the domestic sphere as victims of male advances, "fallen sisters" who were vulnerable and therefore unable to fend off masculine assaults. Without the constraints of domesticity, men became evildoers who preyed on innocent women. The Social Purists repeatedly stressed that prostitutes were not responsible for their own actions; rather, they were the victims of evil men.

By the second day of the Social Purity Congress, journalists noted the "many good words spoken for Friendless Women" and the many offers of "help for the downcast."[11] Mrs. Ballington Booth, head of the Salvation Army, clarified that uncontrolled men were the culprits in the vice issue. In an article entitled "Cries of the Innocents," Booth explained that even if it were possible to empty every house of ill repute, the next day just as many houses of assignation would reappear. Why? "Because while evil men are at large to plot and plan their deeds of ruin, while by the tens of thousands they were free to deceive, drug, force, tempt these 'cuckoos in the nest' for their own foul ends. Society had branded the woman." "Very well," Booth continued, "If you will pin the scarlet letter upon her poor breast with your ruthless hands. I demand in the name of the God of Justice that you pin it also on the coat of the man! Nay! Brand it upon his very brow, that he may forever bear the mark of Cain."[12] Booth, like many Social Purists, saw vice as a male problem, masculinity on the make, victimizing the moral essence of womanhood and disrupting her domestic sanctuary.

The fair also hosted the Woman's Christian Temperance Union. By 1893 the WCTU's president, Francis Willard, had expanded the organization's agenda far beyond the issue of liquor. Willard's "Do Everything" policy included woman's suffrage, involvement in the Prohibition Party, and labor activism that challenged the structures of industrial capitalism. The WCTU spoke the language of white evangelical women, however, and drew their sympathy toward woman's plight in an unequal society. Interestingly, even as the WCTU challenged the separate spheres, they also raised the moral standard of women and critiqued male excess.

In October 1893 the international organization of the WCTU opened its conference with the Doxology, a Psalm reading, and a prayer. Welcoming

11. Chicago *Inter-Ocean*, June 4, 1893.
12. *Chicago Tribune*, June 25, 1893.

remarks by Bertha Palmer, head of the fair's Lady Managers, were followed by those of Dr. Strong, spokesperson for the Evangelical Alliance, an organization of like-minded Protestant denominations. Dr. Strong allied the temperance cause with that of all Protestant churches, saying that the WCTU was "better at executing the mission of the churches than the churches themselves." "Close the Saloons" was the primary mission of the conference.[13]

Several days into the congress, the temperance advocates moved beyond their domestic rhetoric and took to the streets. Newspaper headlines declared, "Women Go Slumming," and detailed an extensive tour the WCTU women took of the Levee. Chicago's "red-light" Levee district was bounded at the time of the fair by Harrison Street and Twelfth on the north and south and by Clark and State on the west and east. The WCTU women saw it all. "The tour of the scarlet-curtained resorts of the 'levee' was made; its glaring immoralities and sickening degradations were viewed; the forsaken revelers in the midst of their saturnalian brawls interrupted and interviewed." The WCTU's rationale for a firsthand look at the Levee was to "more forcibly impress" and "strengthen the purpose to save other unfortunates."[14]

The publicity surrounding this visit, however, perhaps raises other possible explanations for such interventions. Public visits to the brothels allowed temperance women to describe the prostitute as "victim," whose sexual purity and whose right of domestic protection had been taken away. Expressing "sympathy" for their fallen sisters allowed WCTU women to publicly espouse unity with all women regardless of class. The drama of the visit also enabled WCTU women to promote the superiority of their own middle-class morality and, at the same time, rail at men and the masculine systems, both personal and political, that allowed prostitution to flourish. One has to conclude that the visit ("including interruptions and interviews") also must have proved a novel experience, one perhaps not without some voyeuristic lure to its WCTU observers. The WCTU also channeled their indignation with the Levee into the promotion of temperance products, one of which was Hires Root Beer. Coupled with its account of

13. Philip D. Jordan, "The Evangelical Alliance and American Presbyterians, 1867–1873," 309–26; *Chicago Tribune,* October 17, 1893. The Evangelical Alliance also organized a conference at the fair, *Chicago Evening Post,* October 10, 1893.

14. These are the boundaries of the Levee during the fair. They will shift over time. *Chicago Tribune,* October 23, 1893; Chicago *Inter-Ocean,* October 23, 1893.

temperance activism, the *Chicago Herald* proclaimed, "It's given New Life to the Old Folks, Pleasure to the Parents, Health to the Children—Hires Root Beer, the great temperance drink!"[15]

United by a common moral cause, the WCTU and Social Purity forces remained allies throughout the fair.[16] Social Purity head Anthony Comstock addressed the temperance convention and commended the WCTU's White Ribbon League, the Purity arm of the organization, for their efforts against vice. "The seed sowers of vice are all around us," Comstock said. "The society which I have the honor to represent and others of the same character are the vanguard of the church and cry out to protect the young; to protect the citadel of thought against the inroads of vice and crime." Comstock also reported on the successful work of Mr. McAfee in cleaning up Chicago. McAfee's anti-vice activism had led to the arrest of seven hundred men and the confiscation of 449,000 leaflets. In this raid, Comstock noted, eighteen thousand lewd pictures and forty tons of other literature had been destroyed. Comstock then scorned Chicago's court system for its inadequate punishment of these offenders.[17] It is difficult to verify the quantities of illicit materials described by Comstock, but his report leaves little doubt that vice, the man's problem, was out of control and the good women of Chicago were needed to halt the spread of this pernicious plague.

Temperance and Social Purity's definition of morality was also tied to whiteness, a definition that had negative implications for black women. By 1893 the tenuous support of northern whites for African Americans had all but disappeared. In the latter part of the nineteenth century, white northerners had acquiesced to the South and turned a blind eye to their increasing social, economic, and political disenfranchisement of the black man. As a result, America was a Jim Crow nation, strongly racialized and segregated. The black population in Chicago was still relatively small in the 1890s and the city itself held a more tolerant view of race. Fair policy-makers however, had given in to Jim Crow and excluded African Americans from participation in the fair. This exclusion caused African American leaders to see the fair as another glaring example of white racism. Leaders like Frederick Douglass and Ida B. Wells pressured the fair for inclusion, and finally the

15. *Chicago Record-Herald,* October 23, 1893.
16. Pivar, *Purity Crusade,* 78–130.
17. *Chicago Tribune,* October 16, 1893.

fair's Board of Lady Managers grudgingly permitted a few prominent African American women to speak at several events in the exposition.

One of the permitted speakers was Fannie Barrier Williams, the wife of a Chicago lawyer and one of the few black members of the Chicago Women's Club. As a black elite, Williams was allowed to address the Congress of Representative Women and the Parliament of Religions. Speaking before the Congress of Representative Women, she articulated the view of "respectable" African Americans who deeply resented white discrimination. Williams argued that racial exclusion was based insidiously upon the misperception that blacks were incapable of upholding the same moral standard as whites. Williams addressed the issue of female morality, implicitly speaking to the myth of the "bad" black woman and calling on white women to stop disparaging the virtue of black women by portraying them as immoral. In her speech Williams noted that she constantly received letters from the "still unprotected colored women of the South, begging me to find employment for their daughters according to their ability, and to save them from dishonor and degradation." "The colored woman," Williams continued, "deserves greater credit for what she has done and is doing than blame for what she cannot so soon overcome." In demanding greater respect for black women, Williams called for a moral model based on a person's true character and not on a presumption of immorality determined by the color of one's skin. Immorality, she argued, did not rest with black women, but with the white men who exploited them under both slavery and freedom. In one way, the indictment by Fanny Williams, particularly against white men, paralleled the same argument used by Social Purity and the WCTU—men were out of control and needed to be called to a higher moral plane. But Williams went on to challenge the "virtue" of white, middle-class domesticity and the elevation of this model of womanhood at the expense of black women. White womanhood, Williams argued, had no corner on morality, and to assume otherwise was to falsely construct a moral justification for racism.[18]

18. Gilmore, *Gender and Jim Crow,* 140–42; Jeanne Madeline Weiman, *The Fair Women: The Story of the Woman's Building—World's Columbian Exposition Chicago 1893,* 109–24; Fannie Barrier Williams, "A Northern Negro's Autobiography," *The Independent* 57, no. 2902 (July 14, 1904): 96, cited in Gerda Lerner, *Black Women in White America: A Documentary History,* 163–66; Wanda A. Hendricks, *Gender, Race, and Politics in the Midwest: Black Club Women in Illinois,* 4–7; Paula Giddings, *When and Where I Enter: The Impact of Black Women on Race and Sex in America,* 86.

Evangelical Morality and the Parliament of Religion

Moral issues were also on the discussion table at the fair's Parliament of Religions, a gathering of prestigious religious spokespersons brought together to underline the central place of religion in the fair's agenda. The parliament was designed to be "a great university ready to attack the subject (religion) without prejudice and in the pure light of reason." Even though the parliament was touted as an ecumenical "consummate triumph of liberalism," many congress participants fully expected the eminent group to verify the supremacy of Christianity and to demonstrate the superiority of Western culture. Because of its ecumenical nature, some evangelicals refused to participate in the parliament at all, and those who did join seized the opportunity to defend their version of the faith. For evangelical participants, no level of ecumenical cooperation could shake their belief in the truth of Christianity or its potential for cultural advancement. When the revivalist B. Fay Mills addressed the parliament's convocation, his faith came through loud and clear. His presentation "piled fervid argument upon argument, thickly interlarded with quotations from the Bible." Other evangelicals in the audience seized upon Mills's message as an opportunity to testify to their own faith. One individual, an "old man with long white hair and snowy beard," rose to his feet and suggested as a subject for contemplation that "we turn this Parliament into a prayer meeting." The general response of parliament members to the gentleman's request was apparently muted, but numerous "Amens" were heard throughout Mills's presentation.[19]

One of the central points of evangelical skepticism was to question the capability of other religions to provide the moral standard required of a true civilization. Evangelicals in the parliament touted Christianity—particularly what they described as the elevated status of women in Christian societies—as the grounds for America being a truly advanced civilization. The high status of Western women, evangelicals argued, sharply contrasted with woman's subordination in non-Western and non-Christian cultures. Evangelical spokespersons used this comparison to expound on female virtue and to justify the imperial attitude of American Protestantism toward the "heathen." The numerous accounts and pictures coming back to

19. *Chicago Tribune,* September 12–13, 21, 1893; Egal Feldman, "American Ecumenicism: Chicago's World's Parliament of Religions of 1893," 180–99.

the United States from the expansive overseas missionary movement provided ammunition for this argument. These missionary stories emphasized the dire treatment of women in foreign countries in direct contrast to the moral elevation of women within Protestant circles.[20]

When the issue of woman's status was raised in the Parliament of Religions, evangelical participants lost patience with the "enlightened" debate. The Reverend Joseph Cook, a Boston pastor who later participated in the World's Fair Revival, offered a comparison of faiths that "has convinced us," a *Tribune* journalist reported, "that Christianity has no rival." Cook left the parliament's platform in opposition to one speaker's defense of polygamy and declared that Christianity offered "first, the abolition of polygamy and then the elevation of women." Cook's message was then followed by a condemnation of the condition of child wives in the East and the priestesses of the Indian temples. Cook later explained, "the courtesies shown to the various strange faiths is characteristic of the American love of free discussion. It is not to be understood," he continued, "as any abandonment of the general Christian position of the management." Another evangelist, appropriately named Dr. Pentacost, attacked Hinduism's use of priestesses, most of whom, he said, were immoral women. "There are two or three Oriental bubbles which have been floating over Chicago for the last two or three weeks which need to be pricked." Pentacost said.[21] Both Cook and Pentacost, like the spokespersons for temperance and social purity, saw the morality of Western womanhood as a primary marker for the evidence of civilization.

Fanny Barrier Williams, however, was also permitted to address the exposition's Parliament of Religions. Her speech, "Religious Duty to the Negro," provided a somewhat different perspective on Christianity's moral regime. Williams began her speech by presenting Christianity's complicity in American slavery. "Religion," she said, "like every other force in America, was used as an instrument and servant of slavery." Williams then asked: "When mothers saw their babes sold by Christians on the auction block in order to raise money to send missionaries to foreign lands, when black Christians saw

---

20. Joan Jacobs Brumberg, "Zenanas and Girlless Villages: The Ethnology of American Evangelical Women, 1870–1910," 347–71. Brumberg analyzes American women's perceptions of women in other cultures, arguing that such views reflect the assumptions and anxieties about their own place in American society; Geraldine H. Forbes, "In Search of the 'Pure Heathen' Missionary Women in Nineteenth Century India," WS2–WS8.

21. *Chicago Tribune,* October 2, September 21, 26, 1893.

white Christians do everything forbidden in the Decalogue; when, indeed, they saw, as no one else could see, hypocrisy in all things triumphant everywhere, is it not remarkable if such a people have any religious sense of the purities of Christianity?" Williams confronted white accusations of black impropriety and immorality with a clear indictment of slavery's influence. "Knowing full well that the religion offered to the Negro was first stripped of moral instructions and suggestions, there are thousands of white church members even who charge, or are ready to believe, that the colored people are a race of moral reprobates."

Then Fanny Williams took on the issue of domesticity and the particularly devastating impact of slavery on the black family. "In nothing was slavery so savage and so relentless as in its attempted destruction of the family instincts of the negro race in America." Despite what Williams termed the "moral heroism" of the African Methodist Episcopal Church in the South after emancipation, she noted that "the home and social life of these people is in urgent need of the purifying power of religion." Fanny Williams's elite status contributed to her support of virtuous domesticity. For Williams, much like whites in the same socioeconomic class, the potential of the home for moral teaching guaranteed the broader social good. She said, "We do not yet sufficiently appreciate the fact that at the heart of every social evil and disorder among the colored people, especially of the rural South, is the lack of these inherent moral potencies of home and family that are the well-springs of all the good in human society."[22]

But Williams's remarks give evidence of different assumptions regarding the moral influence of that sphere. Rather than touting womanhood, which she saw as perniciously white, as the home's preeminent moral force, Williams refers to domesticity itself as a means of racial uplift. Unlike whites, who tended to elevate woman's moral standing, African Americans like Williams applied the moral assignment to both women and men and saw domestic values as relevant to each. In her study of women in the Black Baptist church, Evelyn Higginbotham notes, "racial consciousness placed Black women squarely beside Black men. . . . From the perspective of racial self-help, this movement so blurred values and behavior exclusively associ-

---

22. Mrs. Fanny B. Williams, "Religious Duty to the Negro," in J. W. Hanson, ed., *The World's Congress of Religions; the Addresses and Papers Delivered before the Parliament and an Abstract of the Congresses held in the Art Institute Chicago, Illinois, U.S.A. August 25 to October 15, 1893 under the Auspices of the World's Columbian Exposition.*

ated with either the masculine or the feminine identity that it implicitly undermined the validity of gender dichotomies."[23] Fanny Williams's speech promoted domesticity as a tool for racial progress, not as a means of maintaining woman's moral status. On this domestic issue Williams argues that Christianity, which had willingly destroyed the black family, now continues to deny African Americans respectability and an equal place in society precisely because of a seeming lack of domestic order. Fanny Williams shows that Christian domesticity could cut two ways: one, to provide a moral standard for civilization, and two, to use that moral standard as a tool for discrimination and exclusion.

Holding True to Evangelical Principles

In addition to their representation and in many instances outspokenness in various fair congresses, evangelicals held to their moral principles in other areas of the World's Fair Exposition. One issue that united evangelicals was their demand that the fair should be closed on Sunday, an issue that directly impacted the sanctity of the Sabbath. Evangelicals saw Sunday closure as a central premise of Christian practice and a visible marker of the faith; they wanted all institutions and businesses, save churches, closed on Sunday. In Chicago, Sabbath observation was an extremely contentious issue that pitted evangelical Protestants against the "barbarism and paganism in the form of Sunday lawlessness." Respect for the Sabbath was a barometer of the city's and nation's moral climate, and, by most counts, according to evangelicals, Chicago was failing the test. The fair's Sunday-opening controversy raised the ire of many evangelicals and dramatically increased their skepticism toward its moral potential. "You have some of the leading men of Chicago telling you to-day that the Sabbath is a pest," Dwight L. Moody stormed. "But I warn those men, that once the Sabbath goes, with it goes the nation."[24]

Protestant concerns about the Sabbath also hinged on the rising influence of ethnic groups who saw little reason to observe a more formulaic Protestant Sunday. Chicago Catholics and Lutherans, from primarily Irish

23. Evelyn Brooks Higginbotham, *Righteous Discontent: The Women's Movement in the Black Baptist Church 1880–1920,* 145.
24. *Chicago Herald,* May 15, July 24, 1893.

and German backgrounds, held a less doctrinaire view of the Sabbath and used the day for recreation, sometimes socializing as a family in neighborhood beer gardens, observing what became known as a "Continental Sunday." These ethnic groups also voted for like-minded politicians, such as Mayor Carter Harrison, who ignored Sabbatarian principles and in fact used the issue as a way to appeal to his ethnic voter base. The Sunday-opening issue, which was now highlighted at the World's Fair, tested this Protestant ideal along with its social and political clout.[25]

The initial decision to keep the fair open on Sunday was determined by a desperate need to generate revenue. Despite the much-touted opening of the fair on May 1, early attendance counts were poor. The dismal numbers caused many fair promoters, including its board of directors, to opt for keeping the fair open on Sundays. Open-Sunday proponents, however, did not justify their policy based on profit; supporters claimed to be counting on the fair's potential for moral uplift to bring in the money. One member of the fair board, Senator A. C. Beckworth of Wyoming, argued, "The World's Fair is not a place of amusement so much as it is a school for the enlightenment of the masses . . . enabling the most obtuse person to comprehend the vast extent and grandeur of the globe." Supporters argued that the civilizing influence of the Columbian Exposition equaled a religious experience and could be used effectively to reach the working class en masse. Agreeing with this positive potential, in the spring of 1893 the board voted to open the gates on Sunday. After making the decision, the board continued to gloat over the fair's moral potential, noting that on the exposition's first open Sunday all Chicago hotels and bars were empty. The fair's midway was dubbed a "civic cathedral" as "ten thousand people stood with uncovered heads in the presence of the Omnipotent and Omnipresent One last night and worshiped. It was plainly the people's holy day."[26]

Chicago Protestants and their parachurch organizations were outraged. They vehemently decried the absence of moral certitude among the board members who would allow the fair to remain open on Sunday. In response to the board's decision, Chicago Methodists immediately issued a manifesto denouncing the Sunday opening and threatening to withdraw the entire Methodist exhibit from the fairgrounds. All Methodists were also urged to

25. Miller, *City of the Century*, 448.

26. Larson, *Devil in the White City*, 235–42; *Chicago Tribune*, April 25, May 13, 29, 1893; *Chicago Herald*, June 3, 1893.

boycott the event. The Chicago Presbytery commended the district attorney for his ongoing prosecution in the U.S. Circuit Court to secure the closing of the exposition on Sunday, and assured him of "our deep interest in the same." The annual Christian Endeavor Convention, representing more than one and a half million American Christian young people, telegrammed Potter Palmer, the fair's president, to protest the board's decision, while the WCTU's exhibit at the fair displayed a sign that showed its disapproval for the policy—CLOSED ON THE LORD'S DAY.[27]

Keeping the fair open on Sunday meant more than invoking the righteous indignation of the Sabbatarians. It also meant sacrificing a million dollars' worth of support from the federal government that was contingent upon the exposition's adhering to the Sabbatarian principle. More liberal Sunday-openers argued that any cost was worth making the cultural and moral uplift of the fair (in addition to an increased number of attendees) available to all. Even the loss of a million dollars was far outweighed by the benefit that would be gained by Sunday events. The Reverend James Miller, an apparently dissident Methodist minister who supported Sunday-opening, used the controversy to question Protestant accomplishments. He, too, saw the fair's potential as overcoming all opposition: "This is the supreme religious problem of the hour: How shall we reach the masses? The church is not reaching them; the Sabbath school is not reaching them; the YMCA is not reaching them; the great evangelistic movements of our day are not reaching them." He continued, "The World's Fair if it were opened Sundays would reach them."[28]

By mid-July, however, Reverend Miller's hopes and those of the board had not materialized. Despite Sunday-opening approval by the U.S. Circuit Court of Appeals, strong Sabbatarian lobbying pressured many fair exhibitors to close their attractions on Sunday. As a result, fair-goers who wanted to see the fair in its entirety refused to show up. Fair attendance on Sundays dropped precipitously, making it highly unprofitable for the board to pay to keep the fair open when only a few exhibits drew Sunday attendees. The board scrambled to make the fair more attractive, even to the point of lowering the admittance price from fifty to twenty-five cents. But in the end the board was forced to admit that their policy was a disaster. Sources that

27. *Records of the Chicago Presbytery*, 1890–96, Parlor meeting, June 12, 1893; *Chicago Tribune*, July 8, June 19, 1893.
    28. *Chicago Herald*, May 22, 1893.

had earlier praised the exposition's enlightened potential began now to doubt its real influence, noting that the city's working class did not seem particularly interested in moral uplift. The *Chicago Tribune* questioned, "Did the directors agree to surrender over a million dollars, and did they stir up a hornet's nest of Sabbatarians merely in order that 48,000 people out of two million who were in the city last Sunday might go, not so much to the Exposition, but to the Midway Plaisance?" The midway was the entertainment venue of the fair, and, as the *Tribune* infers, its belly dancers and camel rides lured fair-goers away from the moral intent of the main exhibits. It soon became apparent that keeping the fair open on Sunday was a losing proposition; the board's decision was a financial flop. The board reversed its policy, and the World's Fair closed on Sunday. For the Sabbatarian forces, the board's reversal signaled divine Providence. The *Tribune* reported that a Baptist prayer meeting cheered the Sunday-closing decision. "The Lord has heard our prayers and answered them," the pastor reported.[29]

Even as some evangelicals actively promoted their ideals through the fair's conferences and its various attractions, many remained skeptical. The Sunday-opening controversy only reinforced these doubts about the moral potential of the fair. Fair supporters countered that the enlightened and uplifting qualities of the exposition were leading to a more civilized city. Chicago's evangelicals, however, noted that the fair only exacerbated the city's political corruption, economic excesses, and class tensions. They feared the fair was in all likelihood advancing immoral causes. These were sins, they believed, that could be remedied only through a revival cleansing. Chicago's redemption and hope for social restoration did not rest with the technological or humanitarian advances venerated by the fair, but with a spiritual transformation induced by religious revival. Dwight L. Moody, along with many Chicago evangelicals, believed that the fair's White City would be visited, but "so would the places of sin and sorrow. The closed church doors and the open saloons, the darkened house of God and the brilliantly lighted devil's den burdened his soul." With Moody's leadership, Chicago evangelicals organized the World's Fair Campaign as an alternative to the fair and its secularism. "Preach Christ, hold up Christ," Moody urged his followers. "Let the Parliament of Religions alone. Preach Christ."[30]

29. *Chicago Tribune*, July 4, 16, 1893.

30. William R. Moody, *The Life of Dwight L. Moody*, 410; Williams, *Life and Work of Dwight L. Moody*, 274.

Infusing the Secular with the Sacred:
The 1893 World's Fair Revival

Supporters of the World's Columbian Exposition and of the World's Fair Revival Campaign acknowledged the global possibilities of their efforts. Both viewed the exposition as a venue for expanding America's influence abroad and at home. More liberal fair supporters wanted to spread the enlightened values of Western technology and philosophy. Evangelicals saw the fair as a mini-missionary opportunity to convert international visitors and then return them to their home countries as emissaries of the Gospel. Organizers of the revival campaign emphasized the international possibilities of the revival. To reach the widest audience, revivalists throughout the event preached in various languages—French, Swedish, German, Russian, and Polish.[31] The impact of this outreach, they believed, would be felt around the world. Their Gospel message, however, was equally and emphatically directed to the many "heathen" who resided in Chicago. The majority of these domestic heathens were men who, as in the 1880s, were perceived as threats to Chicago's moral and social order.

In August 1893, the Chicago *Inter-Ocean* editorialized that the city's population was composed of "an innumerable host of homeless men who are under little or no moral restraint and give pecuniary support to the most degraded and degrading elements of the community." These men, the paper argued, constitute "a powerful factor toward evil."[32] In this context, evangelicalism's equation of masculinity and evil took on symbolic importance in the 1893 revival. Masculinity represented economic excess, political corruption, and uncontrolled sexuality, all visible at the World's Fair and heightened by the deepening depression in 1893. It was men, after all, who caused labor conflict; men who supported Democratic machines; men who visited brothels. The rightness of nineteenth-century Protestant manhood was under attack, and the revival proposed to rework masculinity into a modern yet thoroughly Christian maleness.

To corral Chicago's men, the World's Fair Campaign took on a distinctly masculine style beginning with the revival's organizer, Dwight L. Moody. Moody embodied the masculine values favored among the city's corporate leaders and symbolized the more "modern" religiosity. The press favorably

31. *Chicago Tribune*, May 4, 1893.
32. Chicago *Inter-Ocean*, August 21, 1893.

noted the overwhelming masculinity of Moody's mannerisms. One report described Moody as an "aggressive man . . . imbued with that spirit which impels men to face belching cannon and cold steel with the coolness of a dude lighting a cigarette." These virtues were seen to exert a powerful influence over other males. Contemporaries described Moody as "preeminently a strong man. His chosen friends were men. Strong natures were strongly influenced by him." Yet another Moody biographer noted the source of the revivalist's charisma: "The men flocked to Moody and he had the secret of touching them by his infinite manliness."[33]

Moody's inherent masculinity was only part of a campaign extensively oriented toward men. Evangelists conceived the event as both business venture and military assault. Chicago evangelicals took the offensive and seized the large crowds and publicity of the fair for their own redemptive goals. Periodic revivals in Chicago were commonplace, but an event that spanned the months of May through October presented a unique challenge to the resources and ingenuity of its organizers. Under ordinary circumstances, Chicago's summer humidity and heat were valid reasons, even for evangelicals, to suspend many of the city's religious activities. Many Chicago churches closed for the summer months to allow their middle-class parishioners to flee the oppressive weather. Despite the exceptionally humid summer of 1893, evangelicals, refusing to be deterred, saw the World's Fair Campaign as a unique opportunity to unify the city's Protestants ("bold, aggressive, evangelistic forces") and bring their moral influence ("the uncompromising truth of God") to bear against the masses ("selfish, preoccupied multitudes") expected to throng the fair.[34]

Organization was central to the revival's success, so organizers developed a hierarchical design that mirrored a corporate model. The recently established Chicago Bible Institute became the campaign's center-of-command. The institute housed most visiting evangelists and revival workers, which required adding two more stories to the facility to accommodate the visitors. Three outlying revival posts also were strategically located throughout the city. Northside forces were located in Moody's Chicago Avenue Church, forces to the west in the First Congregational Church, and the newly erected Sunday School Building just outside the exposition directly served the fair-

33. *Chicago Herald,* June 12, 1893; William R. Moody, *The Life of Dwight L. Moody,* 583; Bradford, *Moody: A Worker in Souls,* 238.

34. Hartzler, *Moody in Chicago,* 15.

grounds. In addition, throughout the six-month campaign, close to fifty Protestant churches organized periodic revival meetings in their church buildings, encouraging both evangelists and their regular clergy to speak. Circus-tent tabernacles were also erected to accommodate the large crowds.[35]

The World's Fair Campaign was organized like a business, and it also competed like one. Moody urgently appealed to evangelicals to "beat the World's Fair"; that is, make the Gospel so consumer-friendly that people would forgo the fair's attractions to find religion.[36] The fast pace and wide variety offered by the World's Fair Campaign purposely intended to parallel the attractions of the exposition itself. Like fair vendors, evangelists were selling product (a Gospel) for the consumption (conversion) of fair-goers, and revival attractions competed with the attendance figures and material allure of the exposition. Chicago newspapers featured a daily schedule of revival events that listed as many as four or five different speakers and locations holding meetings simultaneously. By the end of August, the revival was holding regular weekday and Sunday meetings in ten churches, seven halls, two theaters, and five tents. By September, revival successes prompted the call for "reinforcements," and five more evangelists were added. Lord Bennett and Lord Kinnaird, past associates from Moody's British revivals, joined the campaign. Speakers also included Major General O. O. Howard, the "one-armed hero of the Civil War," Major D. W. Whittle, Moody's "right hand man," and Dr. Pentacost, who was already in Chicago for the Parliament of Religions. Moody himself often preached three sermons at three different locations on Sunday and was followed, at these same meetings, by other revivalists or musicians. Two to three hundred revival workers, many of whom were Bible Institute students, organized weekly Gospel meetings held at locations throughout the city.[37]

The rivalry for attendees and publicity contributed to the commercialization of revival strategies and the use of widely advertised religious nov-

---

35. *Chicago Tribune*, May 4, 1893; Hartzler, *Moody in Chicago*, 40–42. Miller notes that Moody drew crowds of up to 150,000 per week during the campaign (Miller, *City of the Century*, 507).

36. Hartzler, *Moody in Chicago*, 63.

37. Major D. W. Whittle fought in the Civil War, earning rank of major in the 72nd Illinois Infantry Regiment. He had been seriously wounded. He also served on the staff of General O. O. Howard, who like Whittle was a "staunch aggressive soldier of Jesus Christ." *Institute Tie*, April 1901, 233. H. M. Wharton, *A Month with Moody: His Work and Workers*, 260–61; Hartzler, *Moody in Chicago*, 105.

elties. Revivalists delighted in taking what were considered highly secular sites and transforming them into sacred places. Forepaugh's Circus Tent was such a location. Pitched on the lake front, the tent, able to accommodate large crowds, appealed to revivalist ambitions for large numbers and even larger publicity. The Chicago Bible Institute regularly used smaller tents in its ongoing city evangelism programs, but the Forepaugh tent presented an unrivaled opportunity. Notices for revival meetings in the Forepaugh tent did not appear in the religious section of newspapers as was typical; instead, they were placed in the amusement section with other types of entertainment such as Buffalo Bill's Wild West Show, the Lilian Rusell Opera Comique Company, or the Chicago Racing Association. Moody's tent meetings were advertised along with the Forepaugh circus itself:

> D.L. Moody—Circus Sunday—Preaches at 10 a.m. Sunday, June 11
> In the Adam Forepaugh Show tents on Lake Front.
> Performances will begin at usual hours—2 and 8 p.m. Door opens
> at 1 and 7 p.m.[38]

Another, more sensational advertisement read:

> Ha! Ha! Ha!
> Three Big Shows!
> Moody in the Morning!
> Forepaugh in the Afternoon and Evening![39]

Adam Forepaugh, the circus owner, originally agreed to rent his tent for revival meetings but was highly skeptical that revivals had the draw required to fill it. To the glee of revivalists, Moody's first Sunday-morning meeting attracted more than fifteen thousand people. In covering the event, the *Chicago Herald* noted not only the sweltering heat but also the ironic mix of secular and sacred. "From the turf where the lady in spangles, cheese cloth and contract smile makes her daring leap to the well-rosined back of her fiery charger," the journalist observed, "hundreds of thirsty souls drank the words of comfort and assurances of divine love."[40]

---

38. *Chicago Tribune,* June 11, September 1, 1893; *Chicago Herald,* July 14, 1893; *Chicago Daily News,* September 26, 1893.
    39. William R. Moody, *The Life of Dwight L. Moody,* 415.
    40. *Chicago Herald,* June 19, 1893; Charles S. Winslow, *Historical Events of Chicago,* vol. 3, 1893.

Chicago theaters were also turned into sacred sites. At various times throughout the campaign, revivalists rented the Haymarket, Standard, Empire, and Columbia, as well as Hooley's, the Windsor, Tattersall's, and Vaudeville theaters. The campaign focused heavily on the theater district, an area of "saloons, brothels, gambling hells, murderer's dens, and all kinds of vile resorts," located near West Madison and Halsted. To evangelize the area more effectively, the Chicago Bible Institute rented a four-story building in the theater area and opened the ground floor as a mission hall. The upper stories were converted into living quarters that housed some thirty revival workers from the institute who proselytized both within the mission and throughout the surrounding area.[41]

These same workers also staffed the revival's Gospel Wagons. To reach the maximum number of city neighborhoods, these horse-drawn mobile units rumbled daily throughout the city carrying a male evangelist and female musician. Labeled the "flying artillery of the evangelistic forces," Gospel Wagons moved through neighborhoods, searching for prime locations to stop, pull out a lantern, and place a baby organ on the tailgate. From this mobile pulpit, male evangelists preached and females sang Gospel songs before neighborhood crowds. Like revival work in the circus arena or theater stage, Gospel Wagon activities transformed the secular spaces of the city into sacred sites. Urban streets were considered particularly public and therefore highly secular, but revivalists enthusiastically seized such opportunities to transform them into sites of holiness. The public character of the streets allowed revivalists to specifically target the unchurched masses who inhabited them.

Taking the Gospel to the streets allowed evangelists to approach directly those they perceived to be the source of immorality and disorder in the city. After speaking to one Gospel Wagon crowd, a Chicago pastor commented, "I realized today as never before, how Jesus must have felt as he preached to such crowds of lost, wretched souls."[42] Preaching to the "lost and wretched" reinforced perceptions of the evangelicals' social status and religious identity, an identity clarified by distinguishing themselves from the lower, less civilized masses. Work on the Gospel Wagon, as well as in other public spaces that specifically challenged middle-class values, intensified the demarcation between believers and nonbelievers. At the same time that

41. Hartzler, *Moody in Chicago,* 23–27.
42. Ibid., 154–55.

"The Gospel Wagon." The "flying artillery" of the 1893 revival. *Christian Worker's Magazine,* June 1913.

revivalists drew moral boundaries, however, they also worked to overcome them with the Gospel. Overt hostility to revival tactics and the Gospel message only heightened the resolve to win over those who resisted. Revival stories of "heathens" who tried to push over the Gospel Wagon or who blatantly resisted evangelical petitions are perhaps representative of the cultural divide that separated the devout from the secular, but for revivalists the moral rightness of faith surpasses all divisions. Narratives of those who defied revivalist efforts often concluded with their submission to Christianity. Revival narratives were overwhelmingly told from the perspective of the revivalists or their sympathetic observers, not by the revival participants themselves. Evangelicals insistently recounted the "history" of a revival in their own terms or language, thereby reinforcing the civilizing power of faith, its moral values, and evangelical hegemony.

Using Domestic Influence to Win Men to Christ

By using commercial techniques and seizing secular sites for holy purposes, Chicago revivalists worked to make the Gospel specifically relevant to the men of Chicago and to win them over to the evangelical cause. This strategy served a dual purpose: first, religious fervor would tame the masses of uncontrolled, un-Christian men who threatened the city's social stability. Second, the masculine orientation of the revival would win over middle-class men who had turned away from nineteenth-century Protestantism. Moody's preachments were intended to bring unruly men to their knees, but many of the narratives and rituals addressed middle-class male anxieties, particularly about leaving behind the feminized spirituality of the nineteenth century. To navigate the needs of bourgeois men, Moody personally represented a modern, middle-class masculinity balanced by a nineteenth-century femininity.[43] In order to redeem men, it was essential to construct a modern revivalism that mirrored corporate order and stability but at the same time upheld its spirituality through woman's moral influence. The World's Fair Revival appealed to men with rituals of businesslike efficiency; at the same time, it appealed to them with a Gospel of femininity. The campaign envisioned morality in gendered terms and defined its mission to the city in terms of appealing to males who, at least from an evangelical perspective, had failed to live up to their domestic responsibilities. The evils of the city—public immorality, political corruption, and overall social decline—demonstrated the evils of uncontrolled masculinity and the urgency of establishing a modern Christian ideal. But it was a Christian manhood that, in many ways, was demanded by and depended upon female piety. Revivalism balanced its masculine appeal with female authority and offered this moral regime as the answer to the chaos and disorder of urban life.

Evangelical womanhood's restraining power over men was a central theme of the revival. Specific traits, in particular acquiescence and submission, were seen as uniquely female. These worked to balance traits that were uniquely male. The gender balance between civilized and uncivilized, good and evil, and piety and sin were frequently depicted in descriptions of the domestic or marriage relationship itself, as in this account of Emma Moody, D. L. Moody's wife. The *Institute Tie* noted that, "Partly because of her delicate soul, largely because of her innate refinement and sweetness of disposition, she was a queen of the household. These characteristics helped much to balance up the possible lack in the sturdy and rough New Englander, in whose success and blessing she doubtless had no

43. Long, *The Revival of 1857–58,* 91.

small molding influence."[44] World Fair revivalists elevated the "queen" of middle-class domesticity, preserver of home and family, as society's ballast.

Evangelistic rituals further spiritualized these gender prescriptions. The techniques of the World's Fair Revival demonstrate the use of evangelical gender ideals to modernize and at the same time spiritualize or domesticate public space. The campaign took public, secular spaces and converted these places, if even temporarily, into sacred, private areas. Revivalists justified evangelizing in circus tents among bears and camels or in vaudeville theaters before the first act as a means of not only appealing to consumers but also domesticating the space as well. The theaters, tents, and other public places used by the revivalists stood for popular, secular, leisure-time activities. The popularity of such public places not only challenged evangelical attitudes toward work but also threatened their emphasis on middle-class life and its domestic religiosity. The public nature of Chicago's streets and places of amusements was incompatible with their more privatized, domestic model. By contrasting the innate evil of these public spaces with the virtue of evangelical domesticity, they were able to triumph over the secular and masculine forces in the public sphere.

One of these domestic rituals included the campaign's use of the portable organ. Evangelistic outreaches, whether in saloons, from Gospel Wagons, or on Chicago streets included Gospel songs sung and accompanied by a female vocalist/evangelist. Playing music and singing, in fact, was an acceptable area for women's ministry. In street evangelism, the organ attracted bystanders and its sound essentially established the spiritual boundaries for the work. More importantly, the organ was a primary symbol in the practice of evangelical domesticity. In her study of Victorian Protestantism Colleen McDannell notes, "Perhaps the most enduring legacy of Protestant iconography in Victorian households was the parlor organ." The presence of an organ in the middle-class home had become, by the 1880s, a symbol of middle-class achievement, and a woman's playing of the instrument "expressed, highlighted and cemented the mother's role as spiritual keystone of the family."[45] Evangelicalism's extensive use of the portable organ and its female accompanist represented a commercial innovation as well as revivalism's commitment to domesticating the public space.

44. *Institute Tie,* November 1903, 77–78.
45. Colleen McDannell, *The Christian Home in Victorian America, 1840–1900,* 42–45.

Evangelical domesticity also mandated that the Gospel message be taken specifically to the city's houses through a visitation program. Continuing to distinguish between a "house" and "home," evangelicals described the revival's visitation program with repeated references to the city's "houses," which implied a general lack of religion. The term "home," on the other hand, held spiritual weight as the center of familial piety. The task of evangelistic visitation, then, was to transform "houses" into "homes" and create religious space in a seemingly conflicted urban environment. One revival supporter noted, "when a family receive Christ into their hearts the household is transformed. The home becomes cleaner, the wages are spent upon it instead of upon the saloon, tastes and impulses are set toward better things." Such domestic conversion not only ensured religious values but also served as a civilizing function. "It is found that, instead of being necessary to educate these people to the point of receiving the Gospel they immediately begin to rise in intelligence," the writer noted.[46] The moral and cultural repercussions of domesticating "house" space were at the very center of revival outreach.

The World's Fair Campaign sponsored an extensive home visitation program that by now was an ongoing part of the Chicago Bible Institute curriculum. Mrs. S. B. Capron (Emma Dryer's replacement), now superintendent of the Ladies' Department of the Bible Institute, reported in August of 1890 that since the establishment of the institute in 1889, the institute ladies had made more than six thousand home visits. "Of all the forms of Christian work," she said, "house visiting is the severest test of one's personal magnetism or winning power. To fulfill the supreme aim of this branch of our work is the severest test of one's spiritual power."[47] Because the home was woman's sphere, this evangelistic tactic required female evangelists. Women from the Bible Institute regularly combed Chicago neighborhoods, knocking on doors, handing out Bible tracts, and generally trying to gain access to the houses they sought to convert into homes.

The institute's active home evangelism program, which intensified during the revival, placed major responsibility for the task on the shoulders of evangelical women. Like the Gospel Wagon and street evangelism, these women and their efforts in the domestic sphere were not always well

---

46. Wharton, *A Month with Moody*, 143–44.
47. *Record of Christian Work*, August 1890, 2.

received. The Reverend H. B. Hartzler, a Chicago minister and historian of
the 1893 revival, described "one lady visitor who, with a heart full of love
for the outcast, was met at one house with nothing but curses." Like those
who defied the Gospel Wagons, resistance to home evangelicalism allowed
revivalists to strengthen their own identities as Christian conduits of middle-
class respectability. Revivalists, in ways like Emma Dryer's response to
Haymarket, deemed their moral mission as capable of prevailing over social
or economic difference. Seemingly oblivious to the variety of structural
issues that underlay these differences, revivalists categorized those on the
other side of the economic and cultural chasm as "sinners."

Hartzler continued to describe the Christian "lady" and her long climb up
rickety tenement stairs where she received still "more vehement oaths." Such
abuse earned women workers praise for their endurance and long suffering in
the face of adversity. "Physically spent and somewhat discouraged, she boldly
tackled her assailant thus: "Now look here, I've had nothing but curses all
this afternoon, so don't you begin. Please get me a drink of water for I'm done
up!"[48] Even workers who lost their patience were encouraged to press forward
with the daunting task of saving home and family. Like both the temperance
and social purity movements, revivalism's home visitation program assumed
what evangelicals considered the innate religiosity of women and children,
and hoped that female spirituality could be directed toward husbands and
fathers. Domestic conversion and its unleashing of female and familial influence promised to be a powerful means for redeeming males.

Female involvement in the revival was not limited to visitation programs; women were encouraged to participate in both private and public
forms of ministry. Within the revival meetings themselves, women wielded
their virtue and abilities of persuasion in the conversion process in order to
bring to bear their moral influence on men. At revival meetings, women
frequently aided in the redemptive process, especially in the "inquiry
rooms," another innovation of the Third Awakening that reflected its
domestic orientation. Smaller "inquiry" rooms, located to the front or side
of a revival site, replaced the Second Awakening's more public "mourner's
bench" and provided sinners with a private place in which to "inquire" as
to the eternal state of their hearts. As in the city's homes, the "inquiry
room" was a private, more personal environment where female influence
was wielded. Referring to his wife, Emma, who was apparently quite per-

48. Hartzler, *Moody in Chicago,* 32.

suasive in the inquiry room environment, D. L. Moody noted: "When I have an especially hard case, I turn him over to my wife; she can bring a man to a decision for Christ where I cannot touch him."[49] Moody's recognition of women's importance is both ironic and contradictory given that he did not allow women to preach at his revivals, yet the inquiry room legitimated the power of female influence and encouraged their involvement in this privatized setting.

Revivals also strategically placed women in public, sinful places. While some women from the Bible Institute were assigned to home evangelism, others were located in the more public arenas of the revival—tents, theaters, streets, and at various places throughout the fairgrounds. Virginia Healey, for example, was a young Bible Institute student just beginning a lifetime career as a Third Awakening evangelist. Healey was originally Irish-Catholic, born in Chicago in 1869. As a young child she attended meetings at the Moody Church, and eventually she converted to evangelical Protestantism. After her conversion, Healey began to teach Sunday School and to work at the Pacific Garden Mission with Sarah Clark and with Jessie Ackerman, one of the WCTU's leading temperance evangelists. Healey also had a beautiful contralto voice, and with it she developed a career as a Gospel singer and teacher. At eighteen she married William Asher, a Scottish immigrant who had originally worked for the Michigan Freight Company in Chicago. Asher resigned his position and together the couple attended the Chicago Bible Institute. Eventually he also became a full-time evangelist. During the World's Fair Campaign, Healey-Asher along with eleven other women worked on the Midway Plaisance.[50] These young female missionaries served a highly practical role as they handed out Bible tracts to fair-goers on the midway. Their symbolic role, however, is equally important as they represented woman's moral authority, holding the line at one of the fair's central outposts of sin.

49. Richard Ellsworth Day, *Bush Aglow: The Life Story of Dwight Lyman Moody the Commoner of Northfield*, 100; Bradford, *Moody: A Worker in Souls*, 191.

50. *Membership Register*, Moody Church Records. The *Register* records April 1, 1883—Miss Jennie Healey, Single. *Worcester Gazette*, February 2, 1907; *World*, September 25, 1906, Box 1, Folder 1, J. Wilbur Chapman Papers; Lena S. Sanders, *The Council Torchbearer: A Tribute to Mrs. Virginia Asher*, 5; *Membership Register*, Moody Church Records, May 6, 1883, recorded as Wm. Asher—Michigan Central Freight House, City; *Chicago Ave. Church Register*, Moody Church Records; *Worcester Gazette*, February 2, 1907, Folder 1, Box 1, Chapman Papers.

The midway, Virginia Asher's revival assignment, was the most publicized and popular exhibit of the exposition. It is no wonder that during the Sunday-opening controversy, fair attendees flocked to this sector of the fairgrounds. The midway boasted the fair's central attraction, a giant Ferris Wheel with 140-foot-high towers and a 250-foot-diameter wheel, all ringed with more than three thousand electric bulbs. The Ferris Wheel was the main draw of the midway, but its other international attractions kept the fair-goers even more entertained. Early on, the *Chicago Tribune* questioned the fair's official classification of the midway as an "ethnological exhibit." Thousands of fair-goers, however, who cared little about ethnography, went to see the midway's camel and donkey rides as well as its exotic costumed dancers. By the fair's second month, midway attendance had far surpassed that of any of the other exhibits at the exposition. The popularity of the midway caused some of the fair organizers, along with numerous Christian churches, to question the moral impact of these popular attractions. In July, Chicago's Christian leadership (Catholic and Protestant) reported that "They had been besieged by members of their churches, who wandered into these theaters unawares and were disgusted at the exhibitions."[51]

In response, the churches united in their condemnation of the dances (particularly belly-dancing) that were being performed in certain villages on the Midway Plaisance. Yet, in keeping with the World Fair revival's use of tents, theaters, and Gospel Wagons, the public and highly secular space of the midway needed the moralizing influence of a good woman. On the midway, female revivalists like Virginia Healey-Asher and her evangelical sisters demonstrated woman's utilitarian function in the propagation of the Gospel and underscored the symbolic importance of female morality in combating the sins of the midway. The pious image of young female revivalists standing beneath the gigantic Ferris Wheel contrasts sharply with the exotic and more sensual displays of the midway, an image that clearly distinguished between the moral women with the Bible tracts and those of "heathen" orientation. Such public presentations only reinforced revivalism's promotion of female morality in its battle against evil.[52]

51. Miller, *City of Big Shoulders,* 496–99; *Chicago Tribune,* November 1, 1893; *Chicago Herald,* July 24, 1893.

52. Sanders, *The Council Torchbearer,* 6. This author notes that Asher "became attached to a mission near the Ferris Wheel." The American Tract Society, the central publisher of evangelical tracts, did not date their publications until later in the twentieth century. It is difficult, therefore, to determine what tracts were distributed at the World's Fair. However,

The Campaign's use of female influence for religious redemption, individual transformation, and social reform sealed their commitment and
cooperation with other moralist organizations. Revivalists joined forces
with the YWCA, the WCTU, and Social Purity, organizations that, like
revivalism, were committed to the "quiet, pervasive, personal influence" of
women to dissuade men of their sin. Mirroring the sympathy expressed by
these reform groups toward women, D. L. Moody also portrayed women as
victims of male excess. In a sermon entitled "The Prodigal Daughter,"
Moody voiced his compassion for the woman who had been "sinned
against." "She is cast out and ostracized by society. She is condemned to an
almost hopeless life of degradation and shame. . . . but the wretch who has
ruined her in body and soul holds his head high as ever and society attaches
no stain to him." The similarity of perspectives within this moral coalition
ensured that many temperance and Social Purity spokespersons would also
participate in the World's Fair Campaign. The exposition's Temperance
Congress, for example, featured John G. Woolley, a well-known temperance
speaker who was also a speaker in the World's Fair Revival. Miss Jessie
Ackerman, president of the Australian WCTU, addressed the Temperance
Congress, as did the physician Kate Bushnell, an evangelist of the WCTU's
Social Purity Department. Both of these temperance leaders had a close
association with the Chicago Bible Institute and had worked with other
revivalists in both temperance and social purity work. Mrs. E. M.
Whittemore, the founder of New York's Midnight Mission, an evangelical
mission for prostitutes and a leader in the Social Purity movement, also
addressed an afternoon meeting of the revival. Whittemore continued to
propagate her views of religion and social purity in later Chicago revivals.
Mrs. Ballington Booth, head of the Salvation Army, also addressed the
Social Purity Conference.[53]

---

the society's 1893 *Index of the General Series of Tracts,* which includes all tracts in print at
that time, listed numerous tracts on female moral influence and its importance for both
religion and society. American Tract Society, Garland, Texas. See also Stephen Elmer
Slocum, Jr., "The American Tract Society: 1825–1975. An Evangelical Effort to Influence
the Religious and Moral Life of the United States."

53. *Union Signal,* April 20, May 11, 1893. The Purity Department of the WCTU praised
the members of its White Shield Societies who took a pledge of purity. The final sentence
of this report said, "The power of this organization is not in aggressive methods, but in a
quiet, pervasive, personal influence." Dwight L. Moody, *Weighed and Wanting;* Chicago
Inter-Ocean, October 18, 1893; *Chicago Tribune,* September 23, 1893; Clara C. Chapin, ed.,
Thumb Nail Sketches of White Ribbon Women, 6–7; Minutes, State President's Address and

Unlike the social-reform orientation of the Temperance and Social Purity movements, however, Moody believed that saving individual souls was his top priority, and he, along with his revival allies, was very adept at directing these organizations' message of domestic morality toward a redemptive goal. The 1893 World's Fair Campaign continued Moody's utilitarian attitude toward women and city work.[54] The revivalist staged public performances of domesticity that dispersed women's moral authority throughout the city. For Moody, redeeming souls took precedence, even if it stepped on rules of middle-class respectability and allowed "good women" to circulate in the city streets. Moody's willingness to bypass social norms in order to place female missionaries on the streets was paralleled by his willingness to overlook racial norms. After the Civil War and Reconstruction, with very few blacks living in the city, Chicago's racial climate was considered semitolerant, at least in comparison to the South's increasingly hostile environment. The city's openness, however, was more theoretical than practical, and it was clear to both blacks and whites that a color line existed in Chicago. Illinois law, for example, prohibited discrimination in schools, municipal services, and public accommodations, but in Chicago these laws were not regularly enforced. Blacks and whites did not mix socially, and informal segregation was also evident in the city's churches. Most African Americans preferred to worship with other blacks, which motivated the major white denominations—Presbyterians, Episcopalians, Methodists, Congregationalists, and Roman Catholics—to organize churches specifically within the black community. African Americans also organized their own churches, the two largest denominations being the African Methodist Episcopal Church and the Baptist.[55]

Reports of WCTU of State of Illinois, 1893. The records of the 1893 Illinois WCTU meeting noted that arrangements were being made for the sale of tickets to Anthony Comstock's lecture to the Social Purity Conference. *Union Signal,* February 2, June 22, May 11, 1893. The May 11 article describes Ackerman as a "self-sacrificing round the world missionary" who also worked with Bible Institute students in temperance. Bushnell was a Methodist medical doctor who trained in Chicago and started the Anchorage Mission for abandoned women in the city; Janette Hassey, *No Time for Silence: Evangelical Women in Public Ministry around the Turn of the Century,* 110–14. *Chicago Tribune,* August 21, 1893; *Union Signal,* May 18, 1893.

54. Lyle W. Dorsett, *A Passion for Souls: The Life of D. L. Moody,* 86–87.

55. Hendricks, *Gender, Race, and Politics,* xii; James Grossman, *Land of Hope: Chicago, Black Southerners, and the Great Migration,* 123–28; Alan H. Spears, *Black Chicago: The Making of a Negro Ghetto, 1890–1920,* 91–94.

Dwight L. Moody, however, was willing to overlook this color line and to use evangelicalism's moral mantel in order to redeem both blacks and whites. It is likely that Moody's loyalty to the Union and his ties to the Union Army that freed the slaves during the Civil War influenced his outlook toward African Americans. Through the YMCA, Moody preached, prayed, and distributed Bibles to Union troops as well as Confederate prisoners during the war. His efforts to redeem both blacks and whites continued after the war in the 1870s when he organized several revivals in the South and preached to racially integrated audiences at open-air meetings. When whites questioned his inclusion of African Americans in a Jim Crow society, Moody made pointed remarks about whites who "might possibly be astonished some day to see these blacks marching into the kingdom of heaven while they themselves were shut out."[56]

Moody's integrationist tendencies extended into his vision of urban work. In Chicago, in spite of a growing color line between the city's churches, the Moody Church was integrated as the church continued to carry on his salvationist agenda. As a result, an African American observer noted: "The Moody Church has been the church home of many negro citizens of advanced thought among educators because of the splendid work carried on there, which is the foremost in Bible study in the city." Small numbers of African Americans also trained at the Moody Bible Institute. For example, Mary McLeod Bethune, the influential African American activist and founder of Bethune-Cookman College, attended the institute from 1894 to 1895. The inclusion of African Americans in the church and institute reflects their founder's overriding redemptive priority. Moody was willing to train and educate any person, male or female, black or white, if he or she was committed to the cause of evangelism. Chicago demographics also made it easier for Moody to reach out to blacks. In 1890, African Americans represented only 1.3 percent of the city's population.[57] The

56. Dorsett, A Passion for Souls, 92–117; James F. Findlay, Dwight L. Moody: American Evangelist 1837–1899, 280.

57. Chicago Illinois Idea, May 15, 1915; Dorsett, A Passion for Souls, 287–88. Dorsett argues that Moody strongly believed "the most effective personal workers are those who can personally identify with the people they hope to reach." Because of this, all of Moody's schools—Northfield, Mt. Hermon, and the institute in Chicago—were racially diverse. I examined the pictures of graduating classes from the Moody Bible Institute in the 1890s. These pictures show both female and male graduates, but they are all white. Mary McLeod Bethune, however, attended the school for a year, 1894–1895. Bethune's documented

small number of blacks (14,271 out of a total population of 1,099,850) did not yet challenge the city economically, politically, or spatially. This meant that race and segregation were not yet central issues for Chicago in the 1890s. Fewer African Americans in the city meant that Moody could follow his spiritual instincts and include them in his ministry.

Yet in spite of Moody's redemptive goals, I found no evidence that African Americans either preached or participated in the World's Fair Campaign. This absence may be attributed to lack of evidence or even to disinterest on the part of African Americans themselves in what they may have seen as a white event. Certainly the fair's strict limitations on black participation reflect a city and nation that willingly accepted a more stringent racial policy and imposed Jim Crow laws. By trumpeting the values and moral standards of Western Civilization over those of "inferior" cultures—including the cultures of peoples of color—the fair became a "White City" in more ways than one. The World's Fair Campaign, however, had a somewhat different agenda. With its moral message, the revival hoped to redeem those same people. Given this agenda and the fact that Chicago's color line at this point was informal, it is unlikely that the revival would have overtly excluded.

Nevertheless, revivalism's promotion of middle-class domesticity as part of its moral criteria may also have discouraged black participation. Revivalism's implicit yet insistent elevation of the moral standard of whiteness, and its repeated spiritualizing of this moral stance, entailed an inherent criticism of black respectability. Moral suspicions regarding African Americans were strengthened not by overt statement or blatant discrimination: instead, blacks simply were not part of the moral model. By undercutting blacks' spiritual acceptability, this moral standard denigrated their social standing as well. Even though there was no explicit exclusion of

---

attendance raises the probability that other African Americans attended the institute for some periods of time even though they did not graduate. Lack of economic support may partly explain why they were unable to complete a full program. "Linn's Stamp News," February 11, 1985, Bethune Biographical Folder, Moody Bible Institute. The pictures of Sunday School classes at the Moody Church show a few African American children in attendance.

Mary McLeod Bethune enrolled in the Moody Bible Institute because she felt called to be "a missionary to Negroes in Africa." At the school, she was the only African American among all white girls. When there were no openings for missionaries to Africa, Bethune began to teach in rural schools in the South. "Story of an Illustrious Negro—An Unforgettable Character, Mary Bethune," n.d., Mary McLeod Bethune file. U.S. Census Reports, 1850–1930, cited in Spears, *Black Chicago,* 12.

blacks, revivalism's moral ideology, particularly its elevation of domesticity and the inherent purity of white women, underlay those discriminatory ideas. Even though Moody and many evangelicals may have believed that blacks were spiritually equal to whites, revivalism's unrelenting portrayal of spirituality as white, middle-class, and domestic belied those more egalitarian beliefs.

Gendering Sin and Salvation

The narratives of the World's Fair Campaign elevated the moral standard of womanhood as a force for conversion and as a counterweight to evil. Innovative revival tactics created sacred, domestic space that held a sentimental and feminine message. Throughout his revival career, Dwight L. Moody openly expressed his distaste for theology. Moody saw theological issues as controversial and a distraction from a Christian's true task of evangelism. During the 1893 campaign, the revivalist quipped: "I don't know that I have any theology, and if you tell me what my theology is I would like to know it." W. C. Gannet, a Unitarian, observed, "The secret of the Evangelist's power . . . is in the fact there is so little theology and so much morality in his preaching." Given Moody's disdain for formal religion, the Gospel of the World's Fair Revival relied heavily on its ritualized patterns. Home visitations, Gospel Wagons, midway evangelism, and tent preaching all represent Victor Turner's notion of "liminal spaces," in-between spaces where individuals could be separated from their ordinary lives and brought to a realization of new values and meanings.[58] For the World's Fair Revival, creating a consensus around new values involved extensive use of domestic symbols and gendered narratives to teach the Gospel. Revival narratives reinforced the spiritual concepts of righteousness and salvation by linking them to women and the private sphere, while coupling the public, male culture with evil and sin. The World's Fair Gospel insistently referenced these gender roles and asserted their moral relevance for revival participants.

58. Chicago *Inter-Ocean,* May 8, 1893; Moody's indifference to a systematic theology is confirmed in Stanley N. Gundry's *Love Them In: The Proclamation Theology of D. L. Moody;* James Findlay refers to Moody's "moral influence theory," with an emphasis on God's love and appeal to human conscience *(Moody: American Evangelist,* 232 ff). "Things at Home Freedom with Fellowship," *Unitarian Review* 7 (May 1877): 560, in Gundry, *Love Them In,* 63; Nick Couldry, *Media Rituals: A Critical Approach,* 21–23.

By 1893, D. L. Moody had preached countless sermons in both the United States and England. Along with those of other campaign revivalists, Moody's sermons at the 1893 World's Fair Campaign—one of his last revivals—typify much of what was preached throughout this portion of the Third Awakening. Central to Moody's Gospel was God's love and an individual's response to faith, ideas symbolized by an inordinate emphasis upon men's and women's roles within the nuclear family. Within the family described by revivalists, males were moral pollutants and threats. The imagery of "sin" was most frequently embodied in the "wayward" son or father. Dr. Wharton, one of the revival speakers, began his address to a crowd at the Haymarket Theater by pointing out imaginary "sinners" in the audience. They included an "old man, wife-beater, and a young boy in the city getting away from his mother's teaching." In countless narratives like Dr. Wharton's, fathers were blamed for their son's worldly ways, and the "sins" of sons were attributed to the "lukewarmness and inconsistency of fathers who are far more solicitous for the worldly prosperity of their children than for their spiritual advantage."[59]

According to revivalists, man's "sinfulness" resulted from his inability to order the public world or to protect his family. In a sermon entitled "The Overcoming Life," delivered at the Standard Theater, Moody portrayed man's public world of economics, politics, and class relations as chaotic. The message of the sermon was that ambitious excess, corruption, and social disorder were male quandaries, problems that resulted from men selling out to the secular world. Clearly, revivalism's emphasis on male "sins" and the need for male control touched the experiences of middle-class males. On a public level, earlier nineteenth-century definitions of male success based on Christian values and right living had shifted to a new emphasis on man's corporate achievements. Evangelicalism's earlier more domesticated ideal of manhood was eclipsed by the emergence of a more ambitious corporate ideal modeled on the sensational achievements of earlier magnates like Cyrus McCormick or T. W. Harvey. But by the 1890s, the sensational careers of such industrial giants were clearly beyond the reach of most men. Corporate structure and the bureaucracy needed to sustain it now impeded the middle-class man's drive to the top. For many middle-class men, corporate commitment implied not success but a loss of control.[60]

59. Marsden, *Fundamentalism and American Culture,* 37; Findlay, *Moody: American Evangelist,* 232–37; *Chicago Herald,* June 26, 1893; *Chicago Tribune,* August 21, 1893.
60. Peter Filene, *Him/Her/Self: Sex Roles in Modern America,* 72–73; Griffen, "Reconstructing Masculinity," 194.

Men's experience was plagued by an even more unsettling issue, their loss of sexual restraint, the evidence of which appeared most clearly in the city. Activist women in the WCTU and Social Purity movement accused men of sexual impropriety and demanded that they live more responsibly in order to protect the domestic sphere. By calling for sexual restraint, these organizations mandated that men live up to their domestic assignment. Those who did not accept were then blamed for many of the issues that confronted urban, industrial America. Sexual impropriety symbolized giving into temptation, betrayal of the marriage bond, and neglect of domestic responsibility. Revivalists placed even more pressure on men to achieve victory over their sexual urges. They echoed the view of these reform organizations, that a man's behavior should reflect his Christianity and his middle-class respectability.

Throughout his career, the sermon Moody preached most frequently was entitled "Sowing and Reaping." As in "The Overcoming Life," Moody's rendition of the biblical account of the sower and the seed emphasized the evils of male excess and the necessity of male control. In a man's public life, Moody argued, "If a man is sowing for a harvest of money or ambition, he is sowing to the flesh and will reap corruption, just as surely as the liar and adulterer." The revivalist urged his listeners to pursue Christianity by recognizing their "sinfulness" and conquering it. But the phraseology of "sowing" and "reaping" clearly surpassed these public "sins" to include male sexuality. "Whenever I hear a young man talking in a flippant way about sowing his wild oats, I don't laugh," Moody said. "No man has ever sowed them without having to reap them. Sow the wind and you reap the whirlwind." Moody's imprecations urged men to seize control of their own lives, including and especially their sexual proclivities. "We have self to overcome. We must overcome it, or be overcome. Our enemies are within. We must get the victory over self, over appetites, passions, lusts."[61]

For evangelicals the two competing models of masculinity created dissonance between the values of a more feminized domestic model and those of the masculine world. In order to succeed in the public world, men must turn from a more feminized, spiritual world to pursue more material objectives. This emerging division appears within revivalism; revivalists adopted

---

61. This was such an important topic that a small book of Moody's sermon was published. Dwight L. Moody, *Sowing and Reaping*, 43, 75; Chicago *Inter-Ocean*, August 26, 1893.

Sowing and Reaping

D. L. MOODY

No. 26

"Sowing and Reaping." Dwight L. Moody's sermons warned repeatedly of the destitution and death that came from men's lack of control. D. L. Moody, New York: Revell, c. 1896.

business tactics to appeal to the modern man, yet mandated that men return to a more feminized spirituality in order to restore their more domestic identity. The spirituality of the feminine continued to be an important component to the domestic ideal; the idealized virtues of womanhood must balance the chaotic drives of men within the domestic schema. Part of this ideal included the asexual or "passionless" female who through her lack of interest in sex (purity) and her piety was able to restrain man's insatiable sex drive. The revivalist portrayal of modern society as a place of crass materialism and open sexuality put men out of control, but true manhood and domesticity could be salvaged by woman's virtuous influence. As long as women remained within domesticity's constructs of piety and purity, true womanhood provided a check on out-of-control males. This domestic formula protected society from men's unruly potential, and woman's consent to domesticity enhanced her redeeming power in both public and private spheres.[62] In order to be saved, a man indeed needed a good woman.

The need for male control fixed woman's place in the revival narratives. Femininity and, more importantly, motherhood were equated with control. The popular revival song, "Where Is My Wandering Boy To-Night?" reinforced the symbolism of the delinquent male and the power of maternal control:

> Where is my wandering boy to-night?
> The boy of my tenderest care,
> The boy that was once my joy and light
> The child of my love and care?
>
> Once he was pure as morning dew
> As he knelt at his mother's knee
> No face was so bright, no heart more true
> And none so sweet as he.
>
> O, could I see you now, my boy,
> As fair as in olden time,
> When prattle and smile made home a joy,
> And life was a merry chime.

---

62. Filene, *Him/Her/Self*, 92–93; Nancy Cott, "Passionless, An Interpretation of Victorian Sexual Ideology," in Nancy F. Cott and Elizabeth H. Pleck, eds., *A Heritage of Her Own: Toward a New Social History of American Women* (New York: Simon and Schuster, 1979), 166–69.

> Go for my wandering boy to-night
> Go, search for him where you will;
> But bring him to me with all his blight,
> And tell him I love him still.[63]

The restraint provided by mothers was not only virtuous, it was godly; the qualities of God were those of a mother. In a June 5 meeting at Tattersall's, for example, Moody preached on God's mercy as revealed through a mother's discernment. "But there are many cries that are not real," Moody said, "and as a mother knows from her child's cry whether it is a cry of peevishness or a cry of pain so God ignores a half-hearted plea and answers the heartfelt and earnest prayer." Yet female influence over sons and fathers was not proactive; revivalist narratives dictated that redemption came through the submission and sacrifice of a pious woman. Mother's never-ending prayers, her candle in the window, or her sacrificial death brought men to repentance.[64] Moody's exemplary account of the "wayward young man" who left his Christian mother concluded with his dramatic return:

> Hearing that she was dying he hastened home, but on his way from the station, passing through the family burial ground, he noticed a new-made grave beside his father's. She had died of a broken heart, and deep as was his anguish and sincere his remorse he could not call her back and give her the promise she had wanted.[65]

This schema reinforced the perception of woman as metaphysical being, aligned with evangelical piety by her unyielding compliance with the domestic ideal. Husbands and sons were returned to the faith by virtue of female passivity. While sin was characterized by departure from home, the male's "coming home" to the faithful and often dead, wife or mother, marked salvation.

The submission and sacrifice required for evangelical redemption was also found in children. Revival narratives absolved the sins of delinquent fathers through wives and through the poignant pleas or deaths of young children. When Emma Moody, the wife of D. L. Moody, died in 1903, the

63. Moody, *Sowing and Reaping*, 97.

64. *Chicago Tribune*, June 5, 1893; Sizer, *Gospel Hymns,* 118–21; Tamar Frankiel, "Ritual Sites in the Narrative of American Religion," in Tweed, ed., *Retelling U.S. Religious History,* 73.

65. Chicago *Inter-Ocean,* June 12, 1893.

Institute Tie, a publication of the Moody Bible Institute, eulogized her virtues and clarified the central prescriptions for evangelical womanhood. The article described Mrs. Moody as "amiable, judicious, sensible, prudent, self-contained, one who had her tongue and temper under remarkable control, unselfish, and self-sacrificing, yet humble and meek, simple as a little child."[66] Childish innocence and naïveté, which closely parallel the attributes of women, had a similar redemptive influence.

This definition of womanhood sanctified the family and its domestic space and idealized them in a nostalgic longing for a return to rural America. The remembrance of a now-lost rural environment again reflected middle-class anxieties over urban living.[67] In contrast to the public evils of the city, revivalism focused on a domesticity purified by the rural environment. "Home," which corresponded to a personalized, rural environment, contrasted the more anonymous and urban "house." On August 12, for example, the Reverend G. W. Briggs spoke of the "Prodigal Son" at the Epworth Hotel Tabernacle near the fairgrounds. Briggs first described the ultimate in domestic tranquility, "the brightest picture this side of heaven—a happy home! The joy of home, its repose, retreat, and rest. The home stood, its broad acres stretching away to the horizon, its rich meadows, and browsing cattle." The revivalist then recounted the prodigal's leaving home and compared him to any "decent citizen visiting the great city of Chicago." And what did Chicago offer? "Wandering revelry and waste." Similarly, on June 12, in Forepaugh's circus tent, D. L. Moody described a "young man who in his waywardness left home to escape the importunities, as he deemed them, of a Christian mother, who wanted him to seek the higher life."[68] According to the 1893 revival message, the first step on the man's road to temptation was his decision to leave the purity of rural life and its spiritualized domesticity. Most significantly, the young man abandoned his mother's love.

An End to Fair Fervor

Press coverage of the World's Fair Revival emphasized the great numbers of people who were attracted to the novelty of hearing the "old time religion"

66. *Institute Tie,* November 1903, 77–78.
67. Cronon, *Nature's Metropolis,* 359.
68. Chicago *Inter-Ocean,* June 12, August 12, 1893.

in a modern context. Although the World's Fair Campaign did not keep attendance statistics, the Chicago *Inter-Ocean* reported on September 23 that the revival had "seen its best day ever, sponsoring sixty-four different meetings held in forty-six places, with an estimated attendance of from sixty-two to sixty-four thousand people."[69] Chicago newspapers repeatedly emphasized the large crowds that attended the revival. Descriptions of long lines, masses turned away, and failed attempts at ticket taking in the face of large crowds affirmed the popularity of the revival and its successful competition with the fair itself.

Much of this publicity may be attributed to Moody's strong relationship with the editors of several of Chicago's leading newspapers. The *Inter-Ocean,* the *Herald,* and the *Tribune* all provided extensive coverage of the World's Fair Campaign and undoubtedly stirred up interest among its readership. Many attendees were also attracted by the revival's consumerlike orientation that tapped into the curiosity of the fair-goer. For those people who were the focus of Gospel Wagons or home visitation programs, the revival created spaces where such individuals could examine their lives. To what degree they were influenced by revivalism's promise of domestic harmony and social stability is unclear. For those who willingly sought out revival events, the revival's message of pure women and righteous men perhaps offered some relief from the anxieties of urban life. Despite the revival's attempt to reach the "heathen" or the masses, the largest proportion of revival participants "consisted of well dressed, sedate citizens, who joined in the prayers and swelled the chorus of the hymns." In spite of "sacred songs and sawdust, streams of pulpit oratory and perspiration, and Bible reading from circus rings," the central message of the World's Fair Revival went to its middle-class adherents who in the midst of their urban, industrial lives were looking for a means of clarifying and reaffirming their own values. Revival listeners were interested in making themselves feel more comfortable, safer, their status more secure.[70] It was reassuring to these listeners to hear a reaffirmation of traditional gender roles and to know that this revival campaign was providing the truth of the Gospel, an explanation for the chaotic disorder of urban America, and the solution for its reform. The sins of city life could be absolved by an individual's decision to return

69. Ibid., September 23, 1893.
70. *Chicago Herald,* June 19, 1893.

to a domestic and maternal God. This salvation would restore the Protestant moral order to Chicago and to the nation.

By the end of October, the World's Fair Revival, like the entire exposition, was coming to a close. The *Inter-Ocean* reported that "the same reluctance and inward protest which stands out against the closing of the World's Fair and the destruction of the beautiful White City, that has become so dear, has also arisen in many hearts against the closing of the evangelistic meetings." Despite reluctance to end their religious effort, revivalists overwhelmingly confirmed the success of the six-month religious event. Particularly in their battle against the fair's Sunday opening and their challenge to the liquor industry, revival forces had triumphed over evil. The WCTU's *Union Signal* urged its readers to take courage: "We believe the World's Fair Evangelization Campaign wrought more effectively for the Kingdom of God than all the combined forces of evil were able to accomplish against it."[71]

Despite this uplifting vision of the Columbian Exposition and the World's Fair Revival, the city shuddered from the effects of the 1893 depression. As Chicago's economy weakened, the number of home evictions rose quickly, with "many families, including small children, sleeping on the streets." Crowds of unemployed men marched to City Hall to demand work, and in Packingtown, rioting appeared imminent as "idle men" were "severely hammered" by Chicago police. Then, on October 28, two days before the close of the exposition and the end of the World's Fair Revival, Mayor Carter Harrison was assassinated in his home by a disillusioned office-seeker. Chicago's City Council immediately caucused. Republicans and Democrats each put forth a different candidate for mayor pro tem, and each party resolved to put the mayor's death to political advantage. The shock over Harrison's death caused the fair managers to abandon all fair festivities, and with little fanfare, the celebration of the century quietly closed.[72]

On November 2, 1893, the World's Fair Campaign sponsored a memorial service for Mayor Harrison at Hooley's Theater. Like other meetings of the revival, ten male evangelists took seats on the theater stage, their presence visibly representing the masculine element that characterized the

71. Chicago *Inter-Ocean,* October 28, 1893. The *Union Signal* is quoted in Hartzler, *Moody in Chicago,* 254.

72. *Chicago Tribune,* August 22, September 2, October 30, 1893.

World's Fair Revival.[73] As revivalists sought to reach out to both working- and middle-class men, their message of salvation depended upon a female counterweight, based on women's spiritual and moral influence. This feminized, domestic influence, expressed through female submission and sacrifice, distinguished white "respectable" Protestants from those they perceived as inferior to themselves, yet at the same time it was offered as the sorely needed solution to the sins of a city that was battling for redemption.

73. Ibid., November 2, 1893.

CHAPTER 3

"Convert Chicago through Its Women!"

THE 1910 CHAPMAN–ALEXANDER SIMULTANEOUS CAMPAIGN

In October 1910 the Simultaneous Evangelistic Campaign of J. Wilbur Chapman and Charles Alexander came to Chicago. The Simultaneous Revival concept was a modern addendum to Third Awakening schemas, a plan that recognized urban diversity and instituted a decidedly organized approach to spreading the Gospel. Like earlier Third Awakening revivals, the Simultaneous campaign headlined two male evangelists, J. Wilbur Chapman and his song-leader, Charles Alexander. Assisting these headliners, however, was a large staff of female and male evangelists who were assigned to different facets of the campaign. Together these revivalists distributed their moral message to a city whose "sins" had only become more visible since the World's Fair Revival.

Neither the dazzling White City nor the World's Fair Revival could ease the devastating impact of the 1893 depression. By August of that year, even before the fair's closing, twenty-four of the city's private banks had closed and unemployment was on the rise. When the fair shuttered its gates at the end of October, the city's economy entered a free-fall. By the end of 1893, business failures in Chicago totaled 566, a 50 percent increase from the previous year. Between 65,000 and 100,000 persons, representing close to 20 percent of the workforce, were out of work. Those who managed to remain on the job received a sharp reduction in wages.[1] On any given day during

---

1. Donald David Marks, "Polishing the Gem of the Prairie: The Evolution of Civic Reform Consciousness in Chicago, 1874–1900," 113; Jane Addams, *Twenty Years at Hull House,* 159; Miller, *City of the Century,* 535.

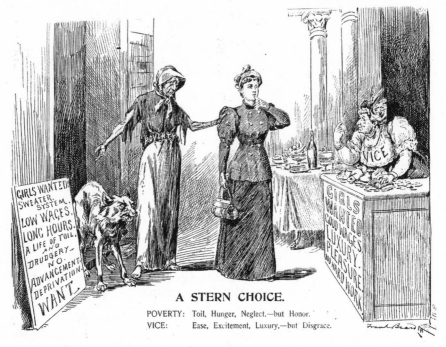

A STERN CHOICE.

POVERTY: Toil, Hunger, Neglect,—but Honor.
VICE: Ease, Excitement, Luxury,—but Disgrace.

"A Stern Choice." *Ram's Horn*, n.d.

the long winter of 1893–1894 at least 10 percent of the city's population was on the edge of starvation. Chicagoans who could not afford food or lodging now crowded police stations and the corridors of City Hall. As a result of the depression, stories of unemployment, home evictions, and hunger, not the glories of the White City, now filled the city's newspapers.

In the summer of 1894, less than one year after the World's Fair, the strain of the depression erupted into a major labor strike in the town of Pullman, located on Chicago's south side. George Pullman, owner of the Pullman Palace Car Company, had created his company town after the 1877 railway strike. The town had been purposely designed to remove the workers from the disorder of the urban environment and to alleviate the labor tensions that had caused the 1877 strike. The town of Pullman, which opened in 1880, not only housed workers but also aimed to transform them into better citizens and workers within the town's highly organized yet aesthetic setting. Mr. Pullman controlled both the wages paid to his workers and the prices (rent, groceries) that workers paid to him.[2] Living in the

2. Smith, *Urban Disorder*, 179.

town of Pullman meant having a job in the Palace Car Company; it also meant putting your life in the hands of George Pullman.

At the onset of the 1893 depression, in an effort to shore up his company, George Pullman fired thousands of employees from his Palace Car Company and reduced by 25 percent the wages of those workers retained. To add insult to injury, Pullman refused to lower rents.[3] As the depression wore on, the desperate Pullman workers joined the newly organized American Railway Workers Union and declared a strike. Other union members joined the strike and refused to handle or switch any Pullman luxury cars to their trains. The strike that stopped all train traffic in and out of Chicago quickly spread throughout the western half of the nation. The Pullman Strike, which eventually involved some 125,000 workers, sharply curtailed the nation's entire railroad system. Railroad executives, with the support of President Grover Cleveland and his attorney general, Richard Olney, determined to break the union. Citing the Sherman Anti-Trust Act, Olney ordered federal troops into Chicago. The strike was eventually broken, but not without fierce conflict and violence between government authorities and strikers.

Like the earlier Haymarket Riot, the Pullman Strike once again raised the specter of social revolution and anarchy in the city. In the wake of the depression and the strike at Pullman, Chicago elites and the middle class worked to salve the city's labor hostilities and offer some relief for human suffering. Leading industrialists/philanthropists set up soup kitchens in vacant storefronts, while Sarah Clark and her husband, coworkers with Emma Dryer, opened their Pacific Garden Mission to care for the city's unemployed. Politicians also joined the effort. Several of Chicago's aldermen distributed food and clothing to needy persons in return for votes. Michael "Hinky Dink" Kenna, one of the "Vice Lords" from Chicago's First Ward, sheltered hundreds in his saloons. Hull House founder Jane Addams observed, however, that "the lack of organization among the charitable forces of the city was painfully revealed in that terrible winter after the World's Fair." The deprivations of the depression did little to lift Chicago's moral standards. Rather, as Chicago observer Herbert Asbury noted, "Chicago stewed comfortably in the juices of its own corruption."[4]

---

3. Spinney, *City of Broad Shoulders,* 96. Mr. Pullman evicted any worker who agitated for better working conditions. He also charged a steep fee for using the Pullman library and he made the church pay rent.

4. Lewis and Smith, *Chicago: The History of Its Reputation,* 218; Addams, *Twenty Years at Hull House,* 159; Asbury, *Gem of the Prairie,* 155.

When Christ Visited Chicago—Evangelicals and the Civic Federation

The British journalist William Stead made similarly dismal observations about the city's moral state. A journalist and Christian Socialist who arrived in Chicago in early October 1893, one month before the closing of the World's Fair, Stead, like many of the Columbian Exposition's more liberal-minded supporters, initially came to celebrate the civilizing and uplifting possibilities of the White City. As a spokesperson for the "new journalism" and its advocacy of humanitarian reform, Stead had become disillusioned with what seemed to be a lack of substantive moral reform in his home country. At the same time, Stead had followed the career of Frances Willard and her effective WCTU activism in the city. Because of Willard's reputation, Stead looked to Chicago as the rising star of moral reform on this side of the Atlantic. Stead's optimism prompted him to stay on in the city after the fair's closure and to conduct a six-month investigative study of his own. Instead of finding Chicago to be the locus of Western morality, however, Stead felt compelled to initiate his own urban cleanup.

As he began to realize the true state of Chicago's transgressions, Stead set out to expose the city's cankerous evils. He accomplished this by publishing his influential book, *If Christ Came to Chicago*. With this book, Stead revealed the city's persistent social and political sores and expressed, in ways very similar to Chicago's more conservative evangelicals, his hope to revive the city's moral indignation. *If Christ Came to Chicago* reiterated the earlier observations of fellow Protestant Josiah Strong and portrayed the city's primary problem as materialism, a greed that tainted all of Chicago's economic and social relations. "The sovereign people may govern Chicago in theory," Stead wrote, but "as a matter of fact King Boodle is monarch of all he surveys." Stead used modern journalistic techniques, combined with a strong dose of righteous indignation, to publicize Chicago's major vices—prostitution, gambling, and saloons. The book provided a scientific list of the lodging houses, pawnbrokers, saloons, and brothels in the First Ward's Levee, as well as a record of the "Occupiers, Owners, and Tax-payers on Property Used for Immoral Purposes." But exposing the city's problems was only the first step; Stead then highlighted the incestuous relationship between vice and city government. The original cover of Stead's book was a lithograph of an angry Christ driving the moneychangers from the Temple. In Stead's version of the lithograph the faces of the moneychangers (cowering under a whip wielded by Christ) were those of the city's political and business officials, including Charles T. Yerkes, Chicago's transportation czar and foremost boodler.[5]

After airing the city's dark side, Stead turned his attention to the response by Chicago's religious institutions. He indicted churches for "insisting so exclusively upon the other life," that "by the substitution of Divine Worship for Human Service" they had "largely undone the work of the Incarnation." The journalist was particularly critical of those he labeled "fundamentalists" and their emphasis on biblical literalism and revival. He did note, however, that "not all of the revivalists ignored the Social Gospel, for many in the army of missionaries sent out by Dwight L. Moody and his counterparts believed that social services and spiritual ministration were inseparable."[6] Likewise, the work of evangelical parachurch organizations like the Salvation Army, the Epworth League, and the Christian Endeavor Society, according to Stead, were headed in the right direction. The journalist concluded, however, that Chicago's Protestant churches were "wealthy, comfortable, served by able and jealous ministers and sung to by choirs of ecclesiastical nightingales." Most Protestant denominations, according to Stead, had succumbed to the temptation of "being at ease in Zion." Because Protestantism had lost its reform zeal, Stead concluded that if Christ were to come to Chicago, his kingdom must come from a cleaned-up City Hall.[7] As a substitute for denominational failure, Stead instead proposed an ecumenical Civic Church, a nondenominational institution that would address social problems with Christian principles.

Within days of its publication, *If Christ Came to Chicago* sold fifteen thousand copies. The majority of the book's sales could be attributed to reviewers whose furious reaction to Stead's findings stirred many to buy the book. Some city newspapers denounced the book as a Republican plot, while the denominational press complained that Stead had falsely condemned the church for being laggards. Churches were particularly peeved that Stead's book provided a usable map of the city's brothels. Despite the book's controversial reception, no individual or church specifically refuted Stead's findings, and as Stead remained in the city, propagating his ideal of civic religion, he found many willing listeners, particularly in the wake of the 1893 depression. The call to arms initiated by Stead led to several chaotic

5. Stead, *If Christ Came to Chicago*, 172; Miller, *City of the Century*, 268–73, 537.
6. Stead, *If Christ Came to Chicago*, 13–14.
7. Stead, *If Christ Came to Chicago*, 399, 268–69.

meetings among labor, business, and religious leaders, all of whom eventually came together to form Chicago's Civic Federation.[8]

The fledgling Civic Federation's first task was to provide for Chicago's unemployed. This provision was accomplished through the Central Relief Association.[9] The president of the association was evangelical magnate Turlington W. Harvey. Mr. Harvey continued in his position as trustee of the Chicago Bible Institute and also assumed the presidency of the Central Relief Association, where he addressed the problems of the city in a "business-like fashion." The Central Relief Association was organized in a "scientific way," complete with recordkeeping and the placement of individuals in jobs for which they were qualified. In an interview with Stead, Harvey emphasized the problem of Chicago's homeless and the difficulty of finding "sleeping places for the three to four thousand men who slept in police stations, City Hall, and the Pacific Garden Mission." In keeping with his work ethic, Harvey noted that "no man was given relief without working for it," and, in fact, recipients often cleaned streets or sewed garments in exchange for their provisions.[10]

When the Civic Federation was incorporated as a nonprofit organization in 1894, Stead praised the Central Relief Association and Harvey's leadership in providing help to Chicago's unemployed. Stead described it as "the most complete realization of the Civic Church" for which he had been campaigning. T. W. Harvey's leadership in the Relief Association represented the evangelical side of a citywide coalition that pulled religious liberals and conservatives together on a specific issue, but with often differing motives. For evangelical Protestants, social commitments focused primarily upon issues specifically related to morality, ideals that were inseparable from their understanding of evangelicalism's urban mission. Evangelical participants, like Harvey, saw relief as a tool of redemption, while other members of the federation held to a more socially reformist stance.[11] In reform activism, theological differences were frequently blurred, particularly in light of the magnitude of Chicago's principal sins—vice, intemperance, and the inces-

8. Joseph O. Baylen, "A Victorian's Crusade in Chicago, 1893–1894," 418–34.

9. Asbury, *Gem of the Prairie*, 156.

10. Stead, *If Christ Came to Chicago*, 143–46; Marks, "Polishing the Gem of the Prairie," 144.

11. Baylen, "A Victorian's Crusade," 427; Norris Magnuson, *Salvation in the Slums: Evangelical Social Work, 1865–1920*; Hassey, *No Time for Silence*. These books provide extensive documentation of evangelical social involvements at the turn of the century. Both authors assume, however, that these involvements imply an evangelical liberalism. What I

tuous relationship between these issues and the city's political forces. Federation efforts, coming from both a conservative and liberal bent, successfully stopped (if only temporarily) the gambling trade in Chicago and passed the city's first Civil Service law. The work of the federation heightened the reform impulse in Chicago during the last years of the nineteenth century and continued into the next century.

In the first decade of the twentieth century, however, Chicago's rapid growth and increasing diversity continued to challenge many of the reformers' moralistic goals. By 1910 Chicago's population had reached the two million mark, affirming its position as the second-largest city in the country, and the fourth-largest city in the world. Rapid population growth further accelerated major shifts in the city's residential patterns. A substantial ethnic population now dominated the inner core of the city, and more African Americans, attracted by jobs, had joined them. By 1910 blacks represented about 2 percent of the population. Seventy-eight percent of the black Chicagoans lived in what was known to whites as the Black Belt, a thirty-block area that spread southward along State Street. As new immigrants moved into the city, Chicago's white middle class moved to its perimeter. The city's expanding transit system (funded with deals made by "King Boodle") enabled Chicago's middle-class families to flee urban congestion, take up life in the suburbs, and still commute to jobs in the city's central Loop. The improved accessibility to the city's downtown permitted tremendous growth on Chicago's outskirts.[12] Extensive growth on the city's perimeters furthered the geographical distance between the city's status groups and heightened the economic, social, and political divide as well. Many of these tensions continued to pit middle-class, now largely suburban, moral ideals against the sins of Chicago's inner core.

Sin in the First Ward

In the first decade of the twentieth century, much of Protestantism's moral indignation was focused on Chicago's First Ward. This ward

---

am arguing instead is that fundamentalists were extensively involved in social activism but it was directed more toward promoting their own "respectable" position. Asbury, *Gem of the Prairie,* 157.

12. St. Clair Drake, *Churches and Voluntary Associations in the Chicago Negro Community;* Grossman, *Land of Hope,* 123; Chicago *Inter-Ocean,* September 18, 1910; Mayer and Wade, *Chicago: Growth of a Metropolis,* 252; Wendt and Kogan, *Lords of the Levee,* 282.

included the Levee, home to the city's vice district. In the 1890s, Chicago
outgrew its "old" Levee that originally bordered the southern Loop area.
Clark Street, Wabash Avenue, and Eighteenth and Twenty-second Streets
became the boundaries for the "new" red-light district: "Here were the
brothels and peep shows and burlesque houses, the cheap saloons and
smelly cribs." As the boundaries of the Levee shifted, the city council and
the Illinois state legislature simultaneously extended the boundaries of the
First Ward, thereby ensuring that saloonkeeper-aldermen "Bathhouse
John" Coughlin and Michael "Hinky Dink" Kenna retained their political
control of the ward.[13] Both Coughlin and Kenna were Irish and were primarily interested in maintaining their own political clout and that of their
ethnic constituents. Neither was much interested in personal morality or
even civic decency for that matter. "Bathhouse John" had launched his
political career as a rubber in a Turkish bath on Clark Street. The bath's
social environs allowed Coughlin to network with politicians, saloonkeepers, and vice lords who sought out his massage services. "Bathhouse" began
to work within the Democratic Party and moved quickly into precinct
leadership. By 1892 the Democrats put him up for alderman of the First
Ward, largely as a payback for his loyalty and hard work for the Democratic
machine. In 1893 "Bathhouse John" allied with "Hinky Dink" Kenna, the
proprietor of a saloon and dice parlor, who shrewdly convinced Coughlin to
make peace with then-mayor Carter Harrison. Coughlin's renewed loyalty
to the mayor lifted much of the police pressure from "Bathhouse," enabling
Coughlin and Kenna to form a syndicate that controlled and protected
brothels, saloons, and gambling joints of the First Ward. With this economic and political foundation, "Bathhouse John" and "Hinky Dink"
presided over the First Ward for close to half a century.[14]

Expanding the vice district impacted the black as well as the white populations of Chicago. The new Levee infringed upon black residential areas
and threatened the black middle-class families that lived there. In 1907 an
African American pastor, the Reverend W. S. Bradden of the Berean Baptist
Church, deplored the extension of vice into the city's South Side. He argued
that the boundaries as they were currently being drawn would impinge
upon black churches and missions. Specifically, he cited the threat to the

13. *Centennial List of Mayors, City Clerks, City Attorneys, City Treasurers, and Aldermen
Elected by the People of Chicago, March 4, 1837–March 4, 1937*, 36–40.
14. Miller, *City of the Century*, 513–16.

Quinn Chapel, as well as the Olivet and Bethel churches. Established in 1847, Quinn Chapel A.M.E. was the first African American church in Chicago. "It will only be a matter of time," the pastor argued, "before the churches mentioned will be forced to abandon their present fields."[15]

Disregarding the moral arguments of both blacks and whites, the boundaries of the Levee marched southward. As "Hinky Dink" and "Bathhouse John" were building their careers in the First Ward, D. L. Moody was ending his career as one of the nineteenth century's most celebrated revivalists. Moody had committed much of his ministry to protecting young men from the evils represented by the Levee. In 1896, Moody preached in the First Ward, once more expressing his indignation over its sin and its incestuous relationship to Chicago politics. When questioned about the upcoming mayoral election and the influence of the vice lords Coughlin and Kenna, Moody responded, "God has forsaken this part of Chicago. Elect a saloon-keeper to the city council and he'll sell whiskey to your son. You sow whiskey and you'll reap whiskey."[16] Though Moody may have handed the First Ward over to its vices, his successors would carry on the fight.

Evangelical Activism in a Post-Moody Chicago

Dwight L. Moody died in 1896, but his legacy as a revivalist and model of Christian manhood did not fade. After his death, Moody's reputation as a great man and salesman of salvation assumed mythic proportions within evangelical circles. Moody's "larger than life" reputation caused many later evangelists such as R. A. Torrey, J. Wilbur Chapman, Gypsy Smith, and Billy Sunday to adopt many of the same revival tactics that their predecessor had used so successfully. In particular, Moody's businesslike efficiency, balanced against the virtues of womanhood and domesticity, remained an integral part of the Third Awakening. This model of evangelistic outreach

15. By the end of the century the city had more than a dozen black churches, and between 1900 and 1915 that number doubled. Most of the Baptist churches that were established were offshoots of Olivet, the oldest Baptist church in the city. Parishioners who had left the Quinn Chapel or the Bethel Church usually started the A.M.E. churches. Spears, *Black Chicago,* 91–94; Rev. W. S. Braddon, "The Segregation of Vice and Its Effect on the South Side," *Broad Ax,* 1907, as cited in Drake, *Churches and Voluntary Associations,* 116–18.

16. Wendt and Kogan, *Lords of the Levee,* 167.

was also taught to the many students who attended the Chicago Bible Institute, now renamed the Moody Bible Institute in memory of its founder. At the end of the nineteenth century, as more conservative fundamentalists shifted away from the perceived modernism of Protestant denominations, Bible schools increasingly replaced denominational authority. This shift made Moody Bible Institute a headquarters of sorts for the fundamentalist camp. The institute had created a full curriculum to instruct pastors in fundamentalist doctrine as well as to train young women and men in urban evangelism. The institute willingly trained workers of both sexes for urban work, and earlier evangelical, now fundamentalist, gender mandates continued as an integral part of the Bible School curriculum and the Gospel message.[17]

The urgency of this Gospel was heightened in light of the social changes that increasingly blurred the nineteenth century's private-public spheres and challenged its gender assignments. Revivalists continued to preach the evils of uncontrolled masculinity and its redemption through godly women and the power of domesticity. Women's moral potential expanded their opportunities in denominational and parachurch organizations, and legitimated their widespread involvement in urban evangelism. In domestic and foreign missions, temperance and brothel work, Bible and tract societies, as well as revivals, evangelical women gained experience in organizing, promoting, and financing religious work. Their wide-ranging commitments, in turn, further expanded their moral authority.

Women's influence is particularly evident in Chicago's denominational and independent city missions. In 1868, Mrs. J. V. Farwell headed the organizational meeting for the Women's Board of Mission of the Interior. The Interior Mission's first meeting, held at the Second Presbyterian Church, included a large number of women from a variety of states across the country. Over the next decades, the work of the Mission Board flourished under the leadership of capable women like Mrs. Farwell. By the end of the century, the board reported that they had funded and sent out 153 missionaries, with three more

---

17. Brereton, *God's Army*, 18, 87–103. In 1900, the Moody Bible Institute had 480 students, 299 men and 181 women. Thirty-eight countries were represented at the school and 41 denominations. That same year saw 114 graduates from Moody, 41 of whom were preachers, pastors (in frontier or rural churches), or singers. Other graduates worked in home or foreign missions, city and rescue missions, as YMCA and YWCA secretaries, and in educational or deaconess work. Margaret Lamberts Bendroth, *Fundamentalism and Gender,* 25–30.

women under appointment. The Women's Board of Mission also collected and dispersed monies from its Auxiliary Societies—Young Ladies, Mission Bands, Christian Endeavor, and Junior Christian Endeavor. It was reported that these organizations had contributed $1,318,000, with $38,000 in legacies. The resounding success of this one mission alone testifies to women's skill and influence in denominational ministry.[18]

Women were also influential in the work of city missions. An 1899 pamphlet from the Chicago Tract Society included reports from six of the leading Chicago missions, all of which distributed the society's tracts as part of their ministry. All six missions were led by women: Charlotte A. Carey and Emily S. Strong, superintendents of the Ladies Department of the Moody Bible Institute; Mrs. T. C. Rounds, superintendent of the Chicago Hebrew Mission; Miss Aphra M. Johnson, superintendent of the Italian Methodist Mission; Mrs. C. D. Morris, superintendent of the Baptist Missionary Training School, and Mrs. G. R. Clark, superintendent of the Pacific Garden Mission.[19] Each woman oversaw the relief programs and evangelistic outreach inherent in an urban ministry. Their mission leadership demonstrates that, by the turn of the century, gender prescriptions empowered women into influential positions within the evangelical urban subculture.

Female authority also expanded and became more public within the Third Awakening. Women's activism perpetuated revival success. The unmistakable power of women in urban work justified their training at the Moody Bible Institute, where they could enhance their experience and credentials as professional revival workers. Virginia Healey Asher, who had worked with the World's Fair Revival in 1893, attended the institute. Grace Saxe, a prominent authority on Bible study methods, also attended the institute from 1895 to 1897. Like Healey Asher, Saxe worked with a variety of revivalists, including M. B. Williams, R. A. Torrey, and eventually Billy Sunday. Frances Miller was also a leading figure in revival circles. Miller attended the Bible Institute from 1903 to 1905. After leading a successful Bible study for the YWCA in Chicago, Miller was ordained as a Congregational minister in 1906 and, like Grace Saxe, organized Bible studies across the country. The careers of Asher,

18. Mrs. S. J. Humphrey, *Two Decades of the Women's Board of Missions of the Interior;* Susan M. Yohn, "Let Christian Women Set the Example in Their Own Gifts": The Business of Protestant Women's Organizations," in Bendroth and Brereton, eds., *Women and Twentieth-Century Protestantism,* 213–35.

19. Chicago Tract Society, Annual Report, 1899.

Saxe, and Miller represent the willingness of the revival movement to make use of women's skills in propagating the faith.[20]

Even as women trained for careers in religious work, however, Protestant men became concerned about their power within the church and society. Women's morally superior position, in addition to their numerical advantage in most churches, caused male leaders to wonder if women perhaps had too much influence.[21] Would women's religious activism eventually betray the submissive, sacrificial qualities that legitimated their inclusion? Female visibility within urban revivals accommodated this female threat by allowing women to publicly exert their influence but, at the same time, affirm their acquiescence to the faith. Revivals also needed exemplary, godly women to counteract publicly both female secularism and society's acceptance of women who failed to fulfill their domestic mandate.

Combating Assaults on True Womanhood

During the first decade of the twentieth century Chicago ministers and business leaders organized the Laymen's Evangelistic Council, whose primary purpose was to tackle the sins of the city with revival. A council pamphlet noted, "A special evangelistic effort from time to time is essential to the awakening and continued activity and progress of the churches." The Evangelistic Council represented the interests of both business and religion. A Christian businessman presided at every council meeting, but every gathering also included a five-minute talk from a city pastor. "In this way," a council pamphlet noted, "one hundred of Chicago's business men appeared on the platform at various meetings, not only endorsing the movement, but thus declaring themselves on the Lord's side." In 1907, the Evangelistic Council enlisted R. A. Torrey, the superintendent of the Moody Bible Institute and pastor of the Moody Church, to organize a revival.[22] Torrey

20. "Billy Sunday Extra," *New York American,* 1917, William Ashley and Helen Amelia Sunday Papers; Central Records, 28th Annual Report, 1904, Young Women's Christian Association of Chicago, Box 2, Folder 1, YWCA Papers.

21. Gail Bederman, "'The Women Have Had Charge of the Church Work Long Enough': The Men and Religion Forward Movement of 1911–1912 and the Masculinization of Middle-Class Protestantism."

22. "The Laymen's Evangelistic Council of Chicago," First Campaign, October 6– December 1, 1907, pamphlet in Scrapbook 1907–1911, Moody Church Records.

was the scholar of the revival circuit, an evangelist whose zeal had been honed at Yale Seminary and who promoted the solemnity of his revival presentations by wearing a black top hat when he preached.

The Torrey revival focused primarily on threats to evangelical theology, principally the Darwinians, the liberals, and higher biblical critics. These issues, particularly biblical inerrancy, which were debated within Protestant seminaries throughout the Third Awakening period, eventually drove a wedge between the more conservative fundamentalists who argued most strongly for biblical literalism and the more liberal modernists. In the first two decades of the twentieth century, as the two sides increasingly aligned themselves into theological camps, the Divinity School at the University of Chicago emerged as a powerhouse of the modernist position, while the Moody Bible Institute, with Torrey at the helm, spoke for the fundamentalists. In 1910 with the publication of *The Fundamentals,* more conservative evangelicals symbolically threw down a gauntlet and articulated what they considered the central points of Christian Truth: biblical inerrancy, the Virgin birth, the atonement and resurrection of Christ, the veracity of Christ's miracles, and dispensational millennialism.[23] *The Fundamentals* may have clarified the theological differences within Protestantism, but in terms of urban reform, both modernist and fundamentalist hopes for moral order pushed revivalism forward. Two years after the Torrey revival, in 1909, the Evangelistic Council enlisted the British evangelist Gypsy Smith once again to revive the city's moral base.

Gypsy Smith came to Chicago on October 1, 1909, for a one-month revival. With the backing of the Layman's Evangelistic Council and three hundred Protestant churches, Smith promised to "make a lot of noise and stir things up spiritually. " He also vowed to "organize converts into an army of attack on the Chicago bulwarks of evil."[24] Smith's revival began in the middle of a heated controversy over working women and their connection to the vice trade. By 1909, the issue of prostitution and the city's tolerance of the Levee were consuming the city's attention. Publicizing prostitution and its tantalizing lure fueled the perception that the city represented an even more ominous threat to the virtue of both women and men. In his book *Chicago by Gas Light,* Samuel Paynter Wilson described his experience with

23. Roger Martin, *R. A. Torrey: Apostle of Certainty,* 182–99; Ahlstrom, *A Religious History,* 775–76; Balmer and Winner, *Protestantism in America,* 19–20.
24. *Chicago Tribune,* October 2, 1909.

Chicago: "The whole tendency was downward and nothing of elevating or ennobling influence was before me there. To me it appeared to be the death of youth and the graveyard of manhood and womanhood . . . I could see the breaking down of virtue." Another of the city's critics observed, "The spirit of the city permeates you and you display it in your every act. It is a form of intoxication that grips its victims as relentlessly as alcohol or cocaine."[25] As prostitution, segregated vice, and the Levee became more prominent in the minds of middle-class Chicagoans, the city became a more dangerous place. Urban enticements threatened a generation of the nation's young men and women. Earlier, however, "respectable" Chicagoans had obsessed about the fate of its young men; by 1910 the visibility of young working women now commanded the city's attention.

At the turn of the century, large numbers of young, unmarried women entered the industrial labor force. The number of women working not only in manufacturing jobs but also as domestics, waitresses, department store clerks, and other clerical employees skyrocketed. Nationwide, between 1860 and 1910 the percentage of women working outside the home increased from 9.7 percent to 24.8 percent. Working girls were not only economically on their own; they oftentimes lived apart from family and relatives. Because of their young age and vulnerability to industrial exploitation, working women were frequently referred to as "girls." By 1910, Chicago had approximately 31,500 wage-earning women who fit the category of "independent" working girl.[26]

The entry of women into the paid workforce, particularly in such large numbers, directly impacted the labor market and job opportunities for male workers. As industrial production required more and more unskilled labor, males with the higher-paying skilled jobs saw their trades simplified and compartmentalized into lower-paying jobs immediately filled by women. This process of "de-skilling" undercut a man's role as breadwinner and caused men to see women workers as threats to male economic authority. Employers also hired women because they could pay them less than

25. Samuel Paynter Wilson, *Chicago by Gas Light*; Leona Prall Groetzinger, *The City's Perils*.

26. Lisa Fine, "The Record Keepers of Property: The Making of a Female Clerical Labor Force in Chicago, 1870–1930"; Ruth Rosen, *The Lost Sisterhood: Prostitution in America, 1900–1918,* 43; these numbers are estimates from systematic samples taken from the federal census of Chicago cited in Joanne J. Meyerowitz, *Women Adrift: Independent Wage Earners in Chicago, 1880–1930,* 3–5.

men, a wage disparity that was at least partially justified by domesticity. Many employers falsely assumed that their female workers lived in families supported by wage-earning males. Their assumptions of traditional living arrangements justified their paying women less because they believed her male provider would protect her. Because societal norms dictated that women's "true" place was in the home, employers conveniently refused to recognize that for many women industrial work was, in fact, her primary source of income. Employers pictured wage-earning women as transient, temporary workers who would in time abandon their jobs for their socially appropriate roles of wife and mother. Working girls, even though this label also included immigrant wives and widows, were insistently portrayed as young, single women who temporarily endured poverty, harassment, and poor working conditions because, in the end, these conditions theoretically would be alleviated through marriage.

Society's support of the domestic ideal (a stay-at-home wife supported by her husband) enabled employers to exploit the transitory nature of female employment, further segregate the labor force by sex, and justify the low wages consistently paid to women. A federal survey of store and factory workers completed in 1908 found that more than half of Chicago's independent women were earning less than eight dollars a week, the recognized subsistence wage. An investigative report on Chicago vice also documented the dire straits of many young women because of their low pay. Marcella, for example, worked in the basement of a department store for six dollars a week. Her living expenses included three dollars for meals, two dollars for a room, and sixty cents for carfare. It was common knowledge that women could not exist on these meager wages, yet employers blamed the women themselves, arguing that women did not really work out of necessity and that the surplus of female workers suppressed wages. Overall, these arguments underscored women's "proper" place in the domestic sphere as well as her dependence on men for economic protection and support.[27]

Wage-earning women were exploited because of their gender and lower-class status. Inadequate wages kept many women in poverty and pushed

---

27. Meyerowitz, *Women Adrift,* 34; Vice Commission of City of Chicago, *The Social Evil in Chicago: A Study of Existing Conditions,* 186, 203; Leslie Woodcock-Tentler, *Wage-Earning Women, Industrial Work and Family Life in the U.S. 1900–1930,* 1–25; Alice Kessler-Harris, *Out to Work: A History of Wage-Earning Women in the United States,* 97–101; Ruth Rosen, ed., *The Maimie Papers;* Meyerowitz, *Women Adrift,* 39–41.

them into prostitution. Some women plied the trade full-time while others only occasionally sold their sex services depending upon their economic needs. The Vice Report's Marcella, for example, hustled three nights a week in order to pay for her laundry and new clothes. Bessie, another working girl, worked in a department store for six dollars a week. When interviewed, Bessie reported "she will go any place with fellows."[28]

The growing presence of the working girl, whether under the control of an industrialist or a madam, incensed the moral sensibilities of Chicago's middle class. In 1876 Protestant women had organized the Women's Christian Association (later the Young Women's Christian Association) to bring women under moral and religious influences. By the end of the nineteenth century, in addition to the YWCA, Chicago had at least eight homes with a similar mission to women.[29] Middle-class reformers had consistently been concerned about the commercialization of sex, but at the turn of the century the scale of this trade, represented by the expansion of the Chicago Levee, drew Chicago's reform community (both conservative and liberal) to focus their attention on the plight of Chicago's young women. In her book *A New Conscience and an Ancient Evil,* published in 1912, Hull House organizer Jane Addams identified the "long hours, the lack of comforts, the low pay, the absence of recreation" as finally overcoming a young working woman's "instincts for decency and righteousness." From Addams's perspective, the city's many working girls, innocent victims of industrial and commercial exploitation, were on the path to prostitution. Addams and other more liberal reformers saw prostitution as symptomatic of an urban-industrial system gone amuck, the intrusion of market values into life's most intimate experience.[30] Those on the more conservative side of the Social Purity movement pointed the finger at evil men. Both groups saw the working-girl/prostitute as the innocent victim of this ancient evil.

Middle-class African Americans also regarded the influx of young black women coming to Chicago with some alarm and voiced similar concerns. Like white working girls, young black women came to the city in search of jobs, but they found even greater discrimination and less protection. Chicago industries always hired white immigrant women first, which meant

28. Vice Commission of Chicago, *Social Evil in Chicago,* 186–87.
29. Meyerowitz, *Women Adrift,* 46; Fine, "The Record Keepers of Property," 213.
30. Jane Addams, *A New Conscience and an Ancient Evil,* 77; Rosen, *The Lost Sisterhood,* 42; Christopher Duffe, "Sex and the City: The White Slavery Scare and Social Governance in the Progressive Era," 411–37.

that if an African American woman needed to work, she in all likelihood would be employed in someone else's home as a domestic or a laundry worker. By 1910 nearly half of all black women in Chicago worked outside of their own homes. For a young woman new to the city, domestic work was a drudgery that isolated her from other workers and from the black community and raised the possibility of male coercion or even rape within the domestic workplace. In addition, housing for African American women was very difficult to find. Women were usually directed to live in the Black Belt, an increasingly segregated area on the South Side. Residential housing in the Black Belt shared space with dance halls and saloons, so it was considered a morally suspicious place for young women to live.[31]

Middle-class blacks saw these young women as a threat to their own status and claim to moral respectability. In 1910, the *Chicago Defender* expressed the black community's concern: "in a large city like Chicago much work must be done to save our young people." Most of the black community's outreach to young women came from within the black middle class itself. Citing differences in Protestant "family worship," as early as 1877 the Chicago YWCA had voted to deny admission to black women. Eventually a "colored branch" of the Y was formed, and middle-class leaders of the black community organized the Phyllis Wheatley Home for young women. The home provided affordable housing, taught domestic skills, and tried, with their own employment bureau, to locate respectable employment for young women. Operation and support of the Phyllis Wheatley Home was eventually taken over by the African American women's clubs. These clubs and the organizations they supported reflected the black community's concern for their vulnerable young women.[32]

The presence of more young black women continued to fuel white suspicions regarding their propriety, plaguing black-white relations. The plight of young women in Chicago's Black Belt was rendered almost invisible, however, by the city's overt and highly publicized concerns about the

---

31. Anne Meis Knupfer, *Toward a Tenderer Humanity and a Nobler Womanhood: African American Women's Clubs in Turn-of-the-Century Chicago,* 81; Grossman, *Land of Hope,* 131; Spears, *Black Chicago,* 102.

32. Grossman, *Land of Hope,* 140; *Chicago Defender,* October 29, 1910; Minutes, Chicago YWCA, July 16, 1877, YWCA Papers; Knupfer, *Toward a Tenderer Humanity,* 81; Hendricks, *Gender, Race, and Politics,* 52–55; Darlene Clark Hine, "Black Migration to the Urban Midwest: The Gender Dimension, 1915–1945," in Joe William Trotter, ed., *The Great Migration in Historical Perspective: New Dimensions of Race, Class, and Gender,* 137–38.

"white slave trade." With the upsurge in working women (both black and white) paralleled by an apparent rise in prostitution, civic leaders and reformers began to investigate this network that lured unsuspecting women into prostitution. An assumption about the purity of whites and the necessity of coercing white women to get them to enter into prostitution underlies the use of the racial descriptor "white." Unfortunately, the purity of black women still remained in question, and the lurid stories of the white slave trade reinforced the virginal purity of white womanhood and further strengthened the normative edifice of whiteness.

In 1909, the president of the Illinois WCTU reported to the state's annual convention that the white slave trade "is an organized syndicate having agents in many of the countries of Europe. These agents are scouring the country for girls that they may be bought and sold for this infamous vice, that gain may be had by these human sacrifices." Investigators deplored the coercion of working girls into the trade, along with its inhumane, businesslike organization that lustfully devoured innocent women and then demanded more victims for its "great soul market." The panic aroused by the white slave trade reflected several concerns of Chicago's middle class. First, the dramatic increase in prostitution and the subsequent expansion of the red-light district threatened property values. As the Levee crept southward, "the handsome residence district of Michigan and Prairie Ave. has suffered far more because a vice district was tolerated at 22nd and State." An Illinois Vigilance pamphlet noted: "Chicago property owners in some of the best residential districts lost many millions of dollars in property values because vice was tolerated in the proximity of their homes.[33]

Secondly, the concept of white slavery allowed the middle class to buttress its respectability against the impurity and low morals of working-class immigrants who were accused of being the central culprits in the trade. Some of the middle-class fears regarding prostitution were well founded; there was a definite increase in prostitution at the turn of the century. But the white slave trade, or organized slaving operations, was responsible for less than 10 percent of women engaged in prostitution. The alarm that surrounded this issue far surpassed the actual number of women who were affected. The concept of white slavery, however, allowed middle-class

---

33. President's Address, Report of WCTU of State of Illinois, 52; Jean Turner-Zimmerman, *Chicago's Great Soul Market: An Article on the Great White Slave Question; Protect Your Home, Property Values Injured by Immoral Neighbors.*

Americans to deflect attention away from the real social and economic factors that led women into prostitution and place the blame for the trade on a few evil men.[34]

The focus on white slavery allowed the middle class to criticize evil men, and it also allowed a venting of its nativist fears against what were described as the foreigners that organized the trade. "Shall we defend our American civilization, or lower our flag to the most despicable foreigners—French, Irish, Italians, Jews, and Mongolians?" wrote Ernest Bell, secretary of the Illinois Vigilance Association. "We do not speak against them for their nationality but for their crimes. . . . On both coasts and throughout all our cities, only an awakening of the whole Christian conscience and intelligence can save us from the importation of Parisian and Polish pollution which is already corrupting the manhood and youth of every large city in this nation."[35] Bell and other Social Purists argued that an alien, foreign force threatened the purity of American womanhood.

Dramatic revelations about the white slave trade also reinforced the middle-class picture of the prostitute as an exploited innocent. The trade was integrally linked to liquor consumption, and investigators recounted vivid stories of young women's descent into prostitution after being persuaded to take a first drink, or after being lured into hotels where they were raped and then turned over to the trade. The overriding perception of the white slave trade was that the innocence and virginity of America's young women were under assault by the highly organized interests of men.

Lurid revelations about the white slave trade gave women an opportunity to defend their moral superiority and to condemn the lewd behavior of men. Both the "regulationist" (advocates of segregating vice in one area of the city) and the "abolitionist" (proponents of closing all red-light districts) sides of the Social Purity movement attributed prostitution to the uncontrolled nature of male sexuality. Purists argued, "It is a man and not woman problem which we face today, commercialized by man, supported by man, the supply of fresh victims furnished by man."[36] The "abolitionist" goals of Social

34. Rosen, *The Lost Sisterhood,* 133.

35. Ernest A. Bell, *War on the White Slave Trade: A Book Designed to Awaken the Sleeping and to Protect the Innocent,* 260; James A. Morone, *Hellfire Nation: The Politics of Sin in American History,* 260–65.

36. Carroll Smith-Rosenberg, *Religion and the Rise of the American City, the New York City Mission Movement, 1812–1870,* 97–124; Rosen, *The Lost Sisterhood,* 47; *Vigilance* 20, no. 11 (November 1912).

Purity found strong support among fundamentalist Christians because prostitution confirmed the moral and social implications of uncontrolled masculinity, the destructive results of men who had "sowed their wild oats."
Fundamentalists saw prostitution as the triumph of masculine evil over the
moral suasion of domesticated religiosity. The city's rampant materialism had
successfully undermined the institutional foundations of social morality, the
home and the church, and now this same greed degraded and commercialized
the intended source of that morality, American women.

Mrs. Jean Turner-Zimmerman, a female physician and president of the
Chicago Rescue Mission in 1905, spent three years working in the Levee.
Her pamphlet *Chicago's Soul Market* describes the "thousands of innocent
girls from country districts who are every year entrapped into a life of hopeless slavery and degradation." The hopelessness of the lowly prostitute
prompted a patronizing, middle-class empathy that identified these women
as the "lost sisters." As Turner-Zimmerman expressed it, "as I looked the
burning fire of intense pity entered my soul for these drug and drink sod-
den, diseased, chained slaves—my sisters in Christ."[37]

Fundamentalists spearheaded a broad coalition of "abolitionist" reformers
dedicated to stopping vice and shutting down the areas where prostitution
prospered under the eyes of Chicago's aldermen and law enforcement officials.
The actual suppression of the vice trade was carried out by the police department, the Morals Court (created specifically to deal with prostitution), and
the state attorney's office, but three other organizations—the Illinois
Vigilance Association, Chicago's Law and Order League, and the Committee
of Fifteen—led the public fight to end segregated vice. In 1908, the same
year as the Gypsy Smith revival, reformers established the Illinois Vigilance
Association, an organization dedicated to the principles of "Purity,
Protection, Knowledge, Law." The association's president was the Reverend
M. P. Boynton, pastor of the Lexington Avenue Baptist Church and member
of the Ministers Advisory Council of the Laymen's Evangelistic Council of
Chicago, the organization responsible for Smith's revival. The secretary of the
Vigilance Association was Ernest A. Bell, the superintendent of Chicago's
Midnight Mission, a rescue work specifically for prostitutes.[38]

37. Turner-Zimmerman, *Chicago's Great Soul Market.*
38. Walter Reckless, *Vice in Chicago,* 234; Asbury, *Gem of the Prairie,* 295; Illinois
Vigilance Association, pamphlet, 1927; Scrapbook 1907–1911, Moody Church Records;
Bell, *War on the White Slave Trade.*

Arthur Burrage Farwell, the nephew of J. V. Farwell, Dwight L. Moody's longtime friend and supporter, headed the Law and Order League. Farwell was a Congregationalist who, as a young man, had attended his Uncle John's Sunday school class at the Plymouth Congregational Church. The young Farwell also worked at the Plymouth Mission, a social outreach of the Congregational church. In 1885 Farwell moved to Hyde Park on the South Side. As secretary of the Hyde Park Protective Association, Farwell successfully closed down its illegal saloons during the 1893 World's Fair. Although the association was unable to maintain Hyde Park's dry status, Farwell continued to campaign for the Sunday closing of saloons and for Prohibition. In 1904, Farwell became president of the Chicago Law and Order League, a watchdog organization that dedicated its reform efforts toward ending the reign of "Bathhouse" John Coughlin and "Hinky Dink" Kenna in the First Ward. While president of the league, Farwell supported Gypsy Smith's 1909 revival and his midnight march into the Levee. By 1910 Farwell was president of the Illinois Vigilance Society.

Another prominent fundamentalist, Henry P. Crowell, served on the executive board of the American Vigilance Association, a nationwide purity organization.[39] Crowell was the president of the Quaker Oats Company, member of the Fourth Presbyterian Church, trustee of the Moody Bible Institute, and president of the Laymen's Evangelistic Council of Chicago. Like elites who had earlier supported the work of Dwight L. Moody, Crowell directed his faith toward purifying the city.

Another investigative group, The Committee of Fifteen, was Chicago's leading Social Purity organization. Clifford W. Barnes, a Chicago clergyman, whose career was devoted to moral and social reform, headed the committee. Early in his career, Barnes taught at the University of Chicago and became involved in Hull House activities. It was Clifford Barnes who escorted William T. Stead on his investigatory expeditions throughout the city.[40] Barnes also pastored the Ewing Street Mission, an outreach of the Congregational church's City Mission Society. Later, Barnes took charge of missions for the New England Congregational church and served as an

---

39. John Clayton, "The Scourge of Sinners: Arthur Burrage Farwell," 68–77; American Vigilance Association, Jane Addams Papers.

40. Obituary, Clifford W. Barnes, *Chicago Daily News,* September 19, 1944; Annual Reports of the Committee of Fifteen, pamphlets, 1911 Report; American Vigilance Association, Jane Addams Papers.

assistant pastor of the Fourth Presbyterian Church, where he developed Christ Chapel, a mission on the city's North Side.

Barnes's past involvements in urban ministry led to his election as head of the Committee of Fifteen, an ecumenical group that raised funds to conduct vice investigations and report their findings to grand juries and the police. The committee was made up of Chicago's leading magnates, including Henry P. Crowell along with Julius Rosenwald of Sears, Roebuck, and Company and meatpacking giant Harold H. Swift. By 1911, the Committee of Fifteen affiliated with the American Vigilance Association, a national organization formed to conduct a "practical and systematic campaign against the traffic in girls and women." Clifford Barnes served as the chairman of its executive board. In 1908, Barnes organized the Chicago Sunday Evening Club, a nondenominational "brotherhood of Christian laymen" that met in Orchestra Hall. This weekly club provided a central meeting place and public platform for a wide array of reform activities in the city.[41]

Gypsy Smith Comes to Town

Girded with fundamentalist support, the Laymen's Evangelistic Council scheduled Gypsy Smith's campaign to begin in October. In November the issue of saloon openings was to be on the Chicago ballot. The close association between saloons and prostitution ensured that a referendum on saloons would also tap into the civic uproar over segregated vice, with many believing that a saloon shutdown would inevitably curtail the sex trade. At the beginning of the revival, the Sunday *Chicago Tribune* primed its readers for a public assault on urban sin. "Chicago now stands forth as the scene of the greatest battle in the world between the forces of good and the white slavers." From the onset, the revival, which was centered in the Seventh Regiment Armory, was represented as an Armageddon-like struggle for Chicago's soul, a battle that focused largely on prostitution. Prior to the revival, the Laymen's Evangelistic Council solicited backing from "three hundred preachers of various denominations and hundreds of business men, educators, woman's' organizations, and prominent musicians."[42]

41. Steven P. Vitrano, *An Hour of Good News: The Chicago Sunday Evening Club, A Unique Preaching Ministry,* 3.

42. *Chicago Tribune,* October 3, 13, 17, 1909; Rosen, *The Lost Sisterhood,* 117.

The council's moral cry also resounded throughout Protestant churches. On October 13, 1909, the Illinois state attorney and Chicago's chief prosecutor of white slavers, Clifford G. Roe, addressed the Buena Park Memorial Presbyterian Church. In his speech Mr. Roe, who was dubbed the "William Lloyd Garrison" of the anti-prostitution movement, provided graphic details of white slavery in Chicago and urged severe punishment for the procurers of vice. On February 5, 1909, Ernest Bell, secretary of the Vigilance Association, urged the session of Chicago's prestigious Second Presbyterian Church to allow him to speak from the pulpit on Sunday morning. Mr. Bell's address was to be followed by the collection of a special offering for the cause of Social Purity. The session adopted Bell's request, testifying to Presbyterian support of Purity activities.[43]

As the revival gathered momentum, the mayor's office and aldermen admonished Levee police to crack down on soliciting in the vice areas. Many noted, however, that Chicago mayor Fred Busse's imposition of law and order was a weak attempt to compensate for years of collaboration with Levee officials. Meager clean-up efforts did not dissuade revivalists who would settle for nothing less than the Levee's closure. At the revival's start, Gypsy Smith vowed to combat "lackadaisical" Christianity and "invade" the notorious Levee with a midnight march. The march "is going to be a great demonstration for Jesus. We are going to win the lost, the forsaken, the degraded, and the destitute. It won't be any of your sidewalk parades. It will be up the middle of the street."[44]

Churches responded favorably to Smith and his highly publicized march. Chicago Presbyterians expressed hearty sympathy with Smith's mission, and the Presbytery thanked God for the numerous conversions achieved by the revival. Chicago Prohibitionists also supported the march, convinced that the fervor directed against prostitution would also be brought to bear on the liquor trade. March publicity also generated negative opinion. Some feared that a march would be too theatrical, that the drama of the event would actually benefit the Levee. Others feared for the moral fortitude of the marchers themselves, arguing that, though well-intentioned, the parade would bring many adults into the vice

---

43. *Session Records*, vol. 4, no. 2 (April 1902–February 5, 1911), Second Presbyterian Church; *Chicago Tribune*, October 15, 1909; *Record of Chicago Presbytery, 1904–1910*, October 18, 1910, 434.
44. *Chicago Tribune*, October 16, 1909.

district where first-time marchers might receive "injurious impressions despite their religious fervor."[45]

Deaf to any resistance, Gypsy Smith prayed for "divine aid against the cohorts of evil," and, after concluding his nightly service, began the march. The participants, all dressed in black, were estimated to be somewhere between three and twelve thousand strong. "The marchers," one observer wrote, "like the crusaders of old, sought to reclaim the region for Christianity." As they reached the Levee, they lit torches as three brass bands struck up "Where He Leads Me I Will Follow" and advanced at a dirge-like pace into the district. Despite a large disparity regarding accounts of the actual number of marchers, all reports agreed that spectators on the sidelines bordered on twenty thousand. At the Everleigh House, the Levee's most famous brothel, the marchers paused to sing "Where Is My Wandering Boy Tonight?" then proceeded to the Alhambra Theater for yet another religious meeting. Filing into the theater, the marchers transformed the secular space into a holy spectacle. The stage of the Alhambra was converted from the "finale of a burlesque show to the opening of a religious revival meeting," and reporters noted that many show-goers remained in their seats.[46]

Some Chicagoans responded to the midnight march with cynicism. Opponents of the march liked to quote one Levee madam who observed, "We were certainly glad to get all this business, but I was sorry to see so many nice young men down here for the first time." Others, however, noted that not since the exploits of William T. Stead had the Levee received so much moral condemnation. Despite the failure of the saloon referendum in the November election, many were emboldened by the perception of Gypsy Smith's courageous confrontation on the Levee. In January 1910, the WCTU staged a similar march. This time they took their cause straight to city hall. At the seat of city government, the predominantly female marchers demanded that Mayor Busse enforce the municipal code, forbid the operation of brothels, and impose a fine of two hundred dollars on anyone convicted of being a "keeper, inmate, or patron of an immoral resort."

Busse was a Republican who was beholden to his WCTU constituents. Like all Chicago mayors, however, Busse knew that Democratic aldermen, many of whom were saloonkeepers, limited his political command. Politician

45. Asbury, *Gem of the Prairie*, 281–82; Reckless, *Vice in Chicago*, 3.
46. *Chicago Tribune*, October 19, 1909.

that he was, the mayor diplomatically advised the WCTU marchers that he would investigate the problem. His diplomacy, however, could not stanch the moral outcry against vice and its unholy alliance with municipal government. On January 31, 1910, the Chicago Federation of Churches, six hundred congregations strong, petitioned the mayor for an investigative committee to study vice in the city. By March, Busse had selected a thirty-member Vice Commission, whose appointment passed the City Council unanimously in June. Even "Hinky Dink" Kenna and "Bathhouse John" Coughlin, hoping for an eventual "regulationist" opinion from the commission, voted for the commission's formation.[47]

Professionals for Christ

With the Vice Commission now in full investigative mode, the public fury over vice continued into 1910. In October, the Laymen's Evangelistic Council organized for yet another moral assault, the Simultaneous Campaign of J. Wilbur Chapman and Charles Alexander. The Simultaneous concept entailed the organization of multiple revival meetings that met "simultaneously" throughout the city. This method of evangelism required a high level of organization and coordination with churches and the community. Chapman's campaign evidences the increased professionalization and specialization that took place within the Third Awakening. The size and organization of the campaign required numerous evangelists who focused their energies on specific populations. Bible Institute training or apprenticeships with other revivalists usually qualified these professionals for the revival circuit and their unique focus on saloon and jail ministries, outreaches to factories, or brothel evangelism. Although each of these ministries was part of the ongoing urban work in Chicago, a revival highlighted each activity and directed professional expertise toward the redemption of specific portions of the city's population.

As revivalism became a profession, many evangelicals began to reflect on its most current methodologies. The Moody Bible Institute began to publish "The Evangelist's Calendar" in its monthly publication, the *Institute Tie.* The calendar listed scheduled meetings for a wide network of evangelists organizing revivals throughout the nation. Revivalists themselves began to

47. *Union Signal,* February 3, 1910, 8; Asbury, *Gem of the Prairie,* 283–86.

theorize and advise about revival techniques and the tools for success. Revivalist R. A. Torrey, for example, published such works as "How to Bring Men to Christ" and "How to Conduct a Successful Revival." Specific equipment was also advertised and sold as a means of increasing revival effectiveness. The *Institute Tie* promoted folding organs that could be purchased with "Liberal Discounts to Evangelists and Missionaries" and advised its readers that "A Waterproof Tent is a Great Boon to Every Preacher."[48]

The leader of the campaign, J. Wilbur Chapman, was a clergyman. Unlike Dwight L. Moody, whose education was probably limited to the fifth grade, Chapman was a seminary-trained and ordained minister in the Presbyterian Church. In 1878, however, under the guidance of Moody, Chapman converted from what he considered a nominal brand of Christianity to a fervent evangelical faith. While pastoring four Presbyterian churches in New York and Pennsylvania between 1882 and 1902, Chapman became increasingly committed to revivalism. In 1893, Chapman preached at the World's Fair Revival and worked in the Interdenominational Association of Evangelists, an organization that unified and standardized Protestant evangelism. Chapman was also influential in establishing the Winona Lake Bible Conference, a meeting and conference ground for evangelists. He also worked for a time as vice-president of the Moody Bible Institute and was appointed the corresponding secretary of the Presbyterian General Assembly's Committee on Evangelism in 1901. In 1903 Chapman resigned his pastoral responsibilities in order to promote the simultaneous evangelistic concept. John H. Converse, a Philadelphia businessman who, in 1905, established a two-hundred-thousand-dollar trust fund to finance Chapman's work in urban revivalism, supported him.[49] With Converse's support, Chapman and his evangelistic team traveled nationally and internationally. In 1907, Charles Alexander, a revivalist song leader who attended the Moody Bible Institute and worked with Torrey, joined the Chapman group. By October 1910 the Chapman evangelistic entourage, many of whom had Chicago roots, was finishing an international tour, and in response to the request of the Laymen's Evangelistic Council prepared to come to Chicago.

48. R. A. Torrey, "How To Bring Men To Christ," and "How to Conduct a Successful Revival," pamphlets, Torrey File; *Institute Tie,* September 1908.

49. Edward Wagenknecht, *Ambassadors for Christ: Seven American Preachers,* 155; Biographical File, J. Wilbur Chapman Papers; McLoughlin, *Modern Revivalism,* 365, 378; Converse Trust Document, Chapman Papers.

The Laymen's Evangelistic Council was ready to welcome the revival team, hoping that revival fervor could revitalize the city's churches and clean up the city. In his endorsement of the campaign, the Reverend W. O. Shepard, superintendent of the northern Rock River Methodist Conference, lamented, "In the city the footfalls of the myriads never cease day or night as they tramp by—not into—our doors. Saloons and amusement places are full. Churches are often nearly empty. It is indeed deplorable. It is awful." The churches' cry for revival underscored its own sense of urgency— "Chicago is facing a great crisis in its religious and social life and upon the members of the church devolves the duty of uniting in a solid phalanx to fight the devil to his lair." The Chicago Presbytery justified its support by "recognizing the moral and spiritual needs of our city," as well as the "earnest demand for righteousness in social and political life." Every member, every church, and every minister should be prepared "for most helpful service in this campaign." The weekly calendar of Chicago's Fourth Presbyterian Church on October 2, 1910, called for the congregation to "unite for prayers that these services beginning October 16th throughout our city may prove a great blessing."[50]

Other Presbyterian as well as Methodist-Episcopal, Baptist, and Congregational churches financed the revival through cooperating subscriptions. Overall, four hundred local Protestant pastors and some thirty thousand members of Chicago churches participated in the revival. Business elites also lent support. The revival's leader, J. Wilbur Chapman, asked businessmen throughout the city to start and end the workday with short prayer services and to encourage employees to attend revival meetings. The revivalist lauded the city for its business cooperation—"more men conspicuous in business and civic life are enlisted in this service than we have ever known before."[51]

Widespread support for the Simultaneous Campaign hinged on several factors. First, as the white slave trade hysteria swept the city, Protestants saw the revival as yet another opportunity to bring city churches into the battle against vice. In a public address, Dr. A. W. Harris, president of

50. *Chicago Record-Herald,* October 24, 1910; Chicago *Inter-Ocean,* October 17, 1910; *Records of Chicago Presbytery, 1910–1916,* June 20, 1910, 32; September 12, 19, 1910, 42; *Chicago Record-Herald,* October 13, 25, 1910; Weekly Calendar, Fourth Presbyterian Church, Chicago, October 2, 1910; Jerald Brauer, *Protestantism in America,* 208.
51. *Chicago Evening Post,* October 13, 1910; Chicago *Inter-Ocean,* October 16, 1910.

Northwestern University and a member of the Chicago Vice Commission, pointed at denominational failure when it came to appealing to a young person's desire for entertainment. In his speech, Dr. Harris quoted a saloon owner's observation that the saloon was the "only decent place of amusement." "She cannot find amusement by going into a church for the churches are all shut up. She may pass a dozen closed churches in coming to my saloon. She cannot get into one of them and if she did get in, they would want her to play tiddledewinks, and go home by half past nine."[52] By 1910, Chicago's urban landscape was characterized by countless entertainment opportunities. Nightclubs and amusement parks, along with movie theaters and dance halls, represented the hallmarks of a new society of commercialized leisure. This was the social environment for the Simultaneous Campaign. Revivalists still held the idea that like D. L. Moody they could compete with these more secular and alluring aspects of modern culture.

A timely urban revival could also have political ramifications—the Simultaneous Campaign was scheduled just prior to the mayoral election on November 8, 1910. Like most of the city's political bouts, this mayoral contest hinged on the issue of political corruption. In 1907, Fred Busse was elected as Chicago's first mayor to hold a four-year term. At the time of his election, Busse had been perceived by many of his Republican, business-oriented supporters as a moderate, a man who could reverse the more "radical" trends in municipal government that had been instigated by Mayor Edward Dunne.[53] By 1910, however, Busse had miserably disappointed his Republican supporters.

The Democrats, in the meantime, accused the Busse administration of "Extravagance, Corruption, and Graft," and predicted a landslide victory for their party. The timing of the revival suggests that the Republicans wanted and needed God on their side for this political contest. The Reverend M. P. Boynton summarized the hopes of Chicago Protestants, many of whom were also Republicans. "Revival," Boynton said, "not only strengthens the church but cleanses politics, ennobles business enterprises and arouses citizens to better civic conditions, and tends to wipe out the vast vice districts." The contentious political climate guaranteed that the

52. D. W. Harris, "Work of the Chicago Vice Commission," in *The City Club Bulletin* 4, nos. 1–25 (January 1911–December 1911).

53. Maureen A. Flanagan, "Fred A. Busse: A Silent Mayor in Turbulent Times," in Paul M. Green and Melvin G. Holli, eds., *The Chicago Political Tradition*, 55.

Simultaneous Campaign's battle for Chicago would be waged on a political as well as a moral level. "Chicago is at the beginning of the most thoroughly organized and most comprehensive evangelistic movement ever undertaken in this city of ambitious achievements," the *Chicago Tribune* announced as the revival began.[54]

Unlike the earlier Gypsy Smith revival that centered its outreach in the Seventh Regiment Armory, the distinctive element of a Simultaneous Campaign was its dispersal of meetings throughout the city and suburbs. The central revival began with two weeks of nightly meetings in the White City Casino, then shifted to an amphitheater in Evanston on the North Side, and after two more weeks, to a temporary structure in Austin on the West Side.[55] Like the 1893 revival, the Chapman-Alexander Campaign took secular spaces like the White City Casino and made them sacred. White City Casino, the revival's first locale, was an amusement park. Located at Sixty-third and Cottage Grove, it had opened in 1904 to a billing of the "city of a million electric lights." Amusement parks were entertainment hubs with carnivals, bowling alleys, roller rinks, and, in most cases, a roller coaster. Parks provided entertainment for the masses, places where the social rules that usually governed class, ethnic, and gender relations were temporarily suspended. Precisely because these public places were more open and were in the vanguard of how Chicagoans used their leisure time, revivalists sought them out to claim a moral turf. Locating a religious revival in these seemingly secular locations could ensure, at least temporarily, a restoration of social norms and order.

In addition to the meetings in three central locations, thirty-five to forty nightly meetings met "simultaneously" in a variety of places throughout the city. The campaign also included "morning prayer meetings, special meetings in the business and factory districts, services for men, women, and children by special workers, and visits to the red-light district, the county and city jails, almshouse, and the saloons." The campaign was devised to physically engulf the city and to create a "far flung battle-line opening fire in every direction."[56]

---

54. Chicago *Inter-Ocean,* September 20, October 24, 1910; *Chicago Tribune,* October 18, 1910.
55. Lauren Rabinovitz, *For the Love of Pleasure: Women, Movies, and Culture in Turn-of-the-Century Chicago,* 140; James R. Grossman, Ann Durkin Keating, and Janice L. Reiff, eds., *The Encyclopedia of Chicago,* 471.
56. Chicago *Inter-Ocean,* October 16, 1910; *Chicago Tribune,* October 18, 1910.

This revival was seen as uniquely "modern" in its personnel, organization, and implementation. One Chicago editor noted Chapman's and Alexander's recent return from a worldwide evangelistic tour. "They are used to thinking world thoughts. They live in an atmosphere purified from the fogs of petty denominational division and strife," he wrote. The city's conservative news-papers praised J. Wilbur Chapman for his businesslike skill in conducting a revival. The *Evening Post* editorialized: "He has the spirit of the Wesleyan revival and the method of the Trust. He is a commingling of John Wesley and John Rockefeller."[57] Chapman's associates, experienced revivalists who trav-eled with him and coordinated a wide variety of activities within the simul-taneous format, also enhanced the organizational quality of the revival.

The most visible members of the campaign staff were married couples who worked together in urban revivalism. D. L. Moody's wife, Emma, had maintained a low profile in her husband's work, but both Mabel Chapman and Helen Alexander were highly visible. Mabel Moulton Chapman had recently married the campaign's leader, J. Wilbur Chapman. As a newly-wed, Mabel worked as an organizer and spoke at women's meetings and to church groups throughout the revival. Helen Cadbury Alexander was the daughter of Richard Cadbury, one of England's leading cocoa manufactur-ers and a devout Quaker. She was an organizer-evangelist in her own right. Prior to her marriage, Helen Cadbury had founded the Pocket Testament League, an organization that distributed Bibles internationally and encour-aged young women in particular to carry a Bible at all times, and to read one chapter daily in order to be prepared effectively for evangelism.[58] Helen Cadbury had met Charles Alexander while he was leading a revival in Birmingham, England, and they too had just recently married. The faith-ful viewed the young woman's willingness to marry Alexander and to sac-rifice her elite status in England for the sake of her revivalist husband as exemplary of wifely submission and faith.

Mr. and Mrs. William Asher also played an active role in the Simul-taneous Campaign. By 1910, Virginia and William Asher were well-known saloon evangelists. After training at the Moody Bible Institute, William Asher became the assistant pastor of the Jefferson Park Presbyterian Church

57. *Chicago Evening Post,* October 26, 1910.

58. *New York Tribune,* June 26, 1907, Biographical File, Chapman Papers; George T. B. Davis, *Torrey and Alexander: The Story of a World-Wide Revival,* 117–18; *Ledger-Dispatch* (Norfolk, Va.), May 6, 1908; *Springfield Homestead,* February 27, 1909, Chapman Papers.

while Virginia continued her own evangelistic work with women. After several years in Chicago, the Ashers moved to Duluth, Minnesota, where William Asher directed the Duluth Bethel, a local rescue mission for lumberjacks and sailors. This ministry involved working in local saloons as well as organizing periodic revival meetings. While her husband evangelized in saloons, Virginia Asher ministered in Duluth's brothels and eventually established a home for pregnant prostitutes and their newborns. The Ashers' reputation for rescue work with poorer classes led to their affiliation with J. Wilbur Chapman, who featured Virginia and William Asher as an integral part of his Simultaneous Crusade staff.[59]

Winning Men (and Women) to Christ

The 1910 revival was marked by a strong female presence and influence. "Convert Chicago through Its Women!" one headline read.[60] The high visibility of revivalist women reinforced the Third Awakening's utilitarian stance toward saving souls, and its willingness to use women to do so. By the early twentieth century, women had educational and practical expertise in evangelism and were recognized as highly effective in the redemptive cause. Female influence could also mitigate the masculine businesslike aspects of revivalism. At the same time, the campaign's extensive use of married couples underscored revivalism's emphasis on the virtue of domesticity. Elevating women and their marital status counteracted two threats—male immorality and female independence. Couples such as Mr. and Mrs. J. Wilbur Chapman, Mr. and Mrs. Charles Alexander, and Virginia and William Asher were not only revival leaders but also representatives of marriage, an institution that appeared to be on the decline.

In the nineteenth century the separate-sphere ideology had wedded male productivity to female morality, a relationship that was symbolized by middle-class marriage. By the turn of the century, however, a nationwide increase in divorce threatened this equilibrium. In 1890 there were three divorces per one thousand existing marriages, but within a decade the number had risen to 4.5. To many, severing the marital knot threatened the very

59. Central Records; *Bethel Record*, December 1907; *Worchester Gazette*, February 11, 1907, box 1, folder 1, Chapman Papers.

60. *Chicago Daily News*, October 25, 1910.

foundation of society and evoked a sense of "crisis." This urgency was by no means limited to fundamentalists; rather, a diverse coalition of conservatives and progressives emerged that deplored the emergence of a "dangerous individualism" which undermined the unity of the family and the nation. Most divorce opponents used the somewhat unisex term of "dangerous individualism," but their primary concern was woman's role in the break-ups and particularly her initiation of divorce. Opponents noted with alarm that about twice as many women as men actually filed for divorce, a trend that revealed either a growing demand for more egalitarian and companionate marriages on the part of women, or, even more disturbing, their desire to be independent from men altogether.[61]

Revivalism's promotion of marriage paralleled a strong emphasis on motherhood. The prominence of marriage and maternalism reflects yet another corrective to what was seen as an ominous fissure in domesticity— the declining birth rate among white, native-born women. Like divorce, the decline in fertility, or the "race suicide" issue, prompted alarm across a wide spectrum of the middle class which insisted that preserving both the class and its values depended upon a woman's willingness to bear children.

Another important part of the "race suicide" issue pertained to sexuality and the necessity to preserve the link between coitus and reproduction. Social Purists believed the possibility of pregnancy in effect guaranteed sexual restraint for women and men. Domesticity and the pure, passionless woman controlled the male sex drive by appropriately channeling any sexual desire into reproduction. Fears of "race suicide" also provided opportunity for the middle class to criticize both their social inferiors and their social "betters." Critics of ethnic lower-class lifestyles voiced a near hysteria at the onslaught of ethnic groups that poured into cities at the turn of the century. The realization by middle-class Americans that ethnic, often Catholic, families were producing more children than were white Protestants raised the worst of nativist fears. Looking to the upper end of the social scale, critics viewed the fertility decline among elite women as evidence of their decadence and obvious failure to lead society in a moral

61. Elaine Tyler May, *Great Expectations: Marriage and Divorce in Post-Victorian America,* 49; Marilyn Yalom, *A History of the Wife,* 286; William L. O'Neill, *Divorce in the Progressive Era,* 1–32, 87; "Marriage and Divorce—A Committee's Report," *Christian Worker's Magazine,* April 1913, 505–6.

direction. It was rumored among them that the highest goal for elites was sexual pleasure, not reproduction.[62]

Childbearing within marriage, at least in principle, ensured purity and created a female restraint that would, in turn, control male sexual desire. Women's reluctance to marry or mother challenged this domestic equation and indicated their unwillingness to accept their "proper" roles as mother and domestic nurturer.[63] On a social level, divorce and the fertility decline signaled challenges to middle-class status and, perhaps more ominously, the emergence of female independence. Revivalism worked to counteract both the divorce and "race suicide" issues with revival couples who symbolized a companionate marriage model. Labeling a female revivalist as an "evangelist's wife" deflected attention away from her actual independence and at the same time calmed fears regarding women's growing influence in revivalism. Revivalists evoked the spiritual nature of motherhood and also criticized women who failed to carry out their maternal responsibilities. For revivalists the appearance of independent women was cause for social concern, but it also challenged the spiritual and acquiescent definition of womanhood.

The display of revivalist "wives" also defused an underlying philosophical tension raised by women's religious activism—the threat of emotionalism over reason. In the nineteenth century, evangelicalism's intellectual foundation rested upon a unified perception of the world, a faith rationally understood through the Scriptures and one's common sense. By the beginning of the twentieth century, however, the rational side of evangelical belief was challenged by scientific empiricism and the historical relativity underlying biblical criticism. These intellectual paradigms challenged evangelicalism's belief in Creation and biblical literalism, but more importantly, these ideas also questioned any empirical basis for faith. Religious modernists criticized fundamentalism and argued that evangelical belief had become anti-intellectual, subjective, and emotional; hence it had great appeal to women. A faith based on emotionalism had little basis in either empirical knowledge

62. John Higham, *Strangers in the Land: Patterns of American Nativism 1860–1925,* 147–48; "Birth Control, Unnatural and Immoral," *Christian Worker's Magazine,* March 1917, 539.

63. Barbara Epstein, "Family, Sexual Morality, and Popular Movements in Turn-of-the-Century-America," in Ann Snitow, Christine Stansell, and Sharon Thompson, eds., *Powers of Desire, The Politics of Sexuality,* 117–130; Linda Gordon, *Woman's Body, Woman's Right: A Social History of Birth Control in America,* 137–42; "The Vanishing Mother," *Northwestern Christian Advocate,* July 29, 1914, 940.

or observation.[64] Fundamentalists worried that the presence of women in religion, revivals included, might confirm these criticisms. In order to strengthen the objectivity and rationality of faith, fundamentalists wanted to control this emotionalism, which was most frequently equated with women. Keeping women subordinate to their husbands even within a companionate model lent credibility to revival ministry.

However, subduing emotionalism was problematic. Removing the experiential element from a revival severely limited its impact and reduced the number of conversions. At the same time, the male leaders feared that females and their emotions could overwhelm a revival and thereby repel men. As a solution, the Simultaneous Campaign advertised itself as a "rational" phenomenon, untainted by the sensational or the frivolous. "There is a feeling of sanity about this religious campaign that marks it as individual," wrote the *Tribune*.[65] Revival participants who disrupted meetings with excessive amounts of religious fervor were quickly removed from the audience, and inordinate displays of revival fervor were discouraged. The Simultaneous Campaign argued that the "true" results of the revival were not manifested in outbursts of emotional fervor, but in correct social behavior. Female evangelists assumed more visibility and authority in revival outreach, yet the label of "evangelist's wife" at least symbolically marked her subordinate role. Thus she was able to provide a domestic counterpoint to the businesslike orientation of the movement without threatening men's need for rationality and control.

The campaign's rational side was also designed to appeal to men. The Laymen's Evangelistic Council adopted its own organizational slogan to herald the campaign—"To Win Men to Christ—The King's Business." The *Record Herald* noted, "The Chapman-Alexander campaign is specifically directed to arousing men of Chicago." Targeting men (winning them to Christ) meant the evangelists had to make the product (the Gospel) more palatable to males and win them back to domesticity. But by 1910 modern masculinity continued to trouble revivalism's domestic equation. This decidedly less moral masculinity visibly manifested itself in contemporary urban life, particularly with the prostitution issue. The growing visibility of vice in urban America clarified the decline of godly manhood and caused the 1910 revival to work to rein in modern manhood with its "campaign

64. Marsden, *Fundamentalism and American Culture,* 59–62.
65. *Chicago Tribune,* October 20, 1910.

against vice."[66] Eradicating male sin and its evil effects meant not only calling men to live responsibly but also restoring the gender balance to the domestic order. Woman's redemptive authority must be asserted to bring men back to the faith. His recognition of and return to the purity of woman represented man's hope for salvation.

Maternal Theologies

Like his predecessor D. L. Moody, J. Wilbur Chapman explained the revival Gospel in terms of pious women and evil men. The city's sins were embodied in the public character of men, revivalism's "wayward sons" and husbands, while salvation rested with woman's domestic and feminine qualities. The campaign evoked motherhood, along with its submissive and sacrificial qualities, as the essence of spirituality and equated the qualities of motherhood with Christ. At the Evanston Tabernacle, J. Wilbur Chapman preached numerous sermons on motherhood to illustrate the Mother-Christ model. "Sin against your mother, and she will forgive you; no matter what you do, no matter how far away you wander from the right path, she is waiting at the gate there to receive you on your return. The sweetest name of mortal tongues is Jesus, Jesus, Jesus. Next to that stands Mother—blessed Mother." At another gathering, one of the revival's numerous meetings for men, Chapman pleaded with his male listeners for their unconditional surrender to Jesus, "your mother's Jesus."[67]

Like the earlier World's Fair campaign, revival narratives depicted salvation as the wayward son's return to a waiting mother, a reunion between mother and son, or wife and husband, and the restoration of domestic harmony. Chapman's sermon on "Forgiveness" equated this theological concept to the experiences of a young man who returned home after long years away. "His mother met him at the door," Chapman said. "There was no talk of forgiveness. She put her arms about his neck, and he knew that he had been forgiven for all the sorrow and distress he brought to her." One of the campaign's most popular songs, "Memories of Mother," evoked a similar Christology:

66. Chicago *Inter-Ocean*, October 17, 1910; *Chicago Record-Herald*, October 21, 1910. The letterhead on the stationery of the Laymen's Evangelistic Council described the organization as "A Business Men's Movement," 1907; Chicago *Inter-Ocean*, October 23, 1910.
67. Chicago *Inter-Ocean*, November 1, 7, 1910.

My mother's hand is on my brow,
Her gentle voice is pleading now.
Across the years so marred by sin,
What memories of love steal in.

The memories of bygone years,
My mother's love, my mother's tears,
The thought of all her constant care,
Doth bring the answer to her prayer.

I'm coming home by sin beset,
For Jesus loves me even yet,
My mother's love brings home to me
The greater love of Calvary.[68]

In the same sermon, salvation is embodied in a mother as she takes her wayward boy to "his old room that she had kept for him through the years. And
she put him to bed and pulled the covers up and tucked them about his
neck." Chapman concluded by noting that the "boy slept that night peaceful
and happy in the belief that his mother had forgiven him. O, men and women
such happiness is in store for you now if you will only accept Christ."[69] A
mother's love initiated salvation; the male's response to her nurturing love
completed it.

The final goal of salvation was domestic unity in the present and in eternity. "The home is the sanctuary of the nation," Chapman said. "If the home
is right our men and women will be right, our city will be right, and our
nation will be right." Revivalists attributed much of the urban sin and disorder to failures in the home and called again for a return to godly women
and men assuming their proper places in the home. Domestic harmony also
served as the model for eternal life. In the middle of November, Eva Booth,
commander of the Salvation Army in the United States and an independent evangelist, joined the Simultaneous Campaign. Booth preached to
seven thousand listeners and concluded her sermon with a description of
the death of her mother. The matriarch's dying words, Booth related emotionally, were "Home, Home, Home at last." In line with the middle class's

68. *Chicago Record-Herald*, October 27, 1910.
69. *Chicago Tribune*, October 21, 1910.

perception of the home as a place of retreat and rest, the revivalist understanding of heaven and eternal life was also embodied in domesticity.[70]

The campaign's reiterated sentimentalized, domestic narratives were
designed to draw men to domesticity and to restore the godly balance. This
appeal tapped into the anxieties of middle-class men who because of rapid
industrial change were feeling uncertain and unsure, particularly about
their work lives.[71] Having been raised to anticipate a future as independent
and self-employed workers, they now found themselves trapped inside
bureaucratic corporations. Having lost an economic life governed by moral
values, men looked for a morally responsible identity that was distinct from
the feminized religiosity of their mothers yet complicated by a fear of not
measuring up to their more stable fathers.

Revival narratives were equally prescriptive for women, who were dele-
gated to the roles of wife and mother, a moral shadow of perpetual patience,
a life of "sitting quietly," passively waiting for males to recognize and
return to their virtue.[72] This idealized and sentimentalized view of women
gave them influence in revival activism, justifying various ministries and
their expansion into society. But again, it was a symbolic representation, a
symbol that was undercut by the reality of women's work in revival and in
their broadening role in society in general. Revival narratives portrayed sacrificial wives and mothers bringing repentant men to their knees, yet it was
a model that depended not upon actual power or equality with men, but
upon acquiescing to their control. Revivalism's assertion of true womanhood converted men but at the same time sustained a model of submission.

Virginia Asher's ministry, and, in particular, her adamant promotion of
motherhood to workingwomen, symbolizes this contradiction within revival
rhetoric and practice. Virginia and William Asher were married in 1887.
Asher's biographer notes that the couple was able to have one baby that died
at birth. After the child's death the biographer writes, "the great mother-
heart of Mrs. Asher took on the world of lost souls and mothered them with
divine love."[73] Motherhood was, in many ways, a total abstraction to Asher.

70. Chicago *Inter-Ocean,* November 10, 1910; *Chicago Record-Herald,* November 13,
1910; Colleen McDannell and Berhard Lang, *Heaven: A History,* 228–75.
71. Filene, *Him/Her/Self,* 69–80.
72. Chicago *Inter-Ocean,* November 1, 1910.
73. Sanders, *The Council Torchbearer,* 6.

Yet, as a career revivalist, and as someone who spent the majority of her life in public ministry, Asher was a primary spokesperson for revivalism's maternal theology.

Rituals of Domestic Persuasion

Various rituals of the Simultaneous Campaign, both in the central meetings and in other outreaches, reinforced the power of womanhood and its domestic center. One significant ritual was Chapman's reading of personal letters that he solicited from the people of Chicago. Letter reading enabled the revivalist to establish rapport with his audience and to offer moral solutions to everyday problems. During this nightly ceremony, revivalists created "liminal space" within which participants came together and formed consensus around domestic ideals. Most frequently, the letters read by Chapman in a central meeting contained extensive narratives of the damning exploits of a husband or son, followed by a prayer request for the lost male. After reading each account, Chapman prayed with the entire assembly. Prayers often prompted another mother to stand and plead for her own "wayward son."[74]

This letter-reading ritual created a public forum for indicting men, often clarifying in graphic detail the sins of bad men, while, at the same time, accentuating the mother's strategic role in bringing them back to morality. In addition to the letter-reading ritual, entire services throughout the campaign were organized specifically around the theme of motherhood, and Chapman regularly asked audiences to either stand or wave white handkerchiefs in honor of their Christian mothers. Affirming motherhood was also incorporated into an individual's commitment to Christ. Revival converts were asked to promise, "because of a sweet faced Christian mother, to live as nearly as I can, as God would have me to live."[75] Recognition of a mother's love simulated a conversion experience itself.

Domesticity was also embedded into revival outreaches, particularly the evangelistic work of Virginia and William Asher. Because of their ministry at the Duluth Bethel, the Ashers were considered primarily saloon evangelists. The timing of the campaign in anticipation of the upcoming saloon referendum, however, meant that saloon owners received the revival couple

---

74. Chicago *Inter-Ocean,* October 20, November 26, 1910.
75. Ibid., November 1, 1910.

less than hospitably. Threatened by an inevitable moral attack, saloon operators refused to give the enemy (Virginia and Will Asher) access to their terrain. So instead, the Ashers shifted their outreach to "systematic campaigns
in the 'red light,' slum, and factory districts of Chicago," all public places
sorely in need of the Gospel. These sites provided the backdrop to the
Ashers' gendered Gospel of redemption. Their revival message went out to
"the people who do not believe they are wanted at a revival. The ones who
have lost hope for redemption."[76]

The Ashers' first outreach in the Chicago campaign took place in the
First Ward on the Levee. The Ashers went to the DesPlaines Street Station
jail to speak to the prisoners. William Asher immediately focused his attention on the sins of masculinity. "You men have given the Devil, the World,
the Flesh, Booze, and other things belonging to the Devil a fair trial and
He has not made good with you. . . . Why don't you chuck the devil over-
board and come over to the other side?"[77] Following the short sermon,
Virginia Asher unfolded her autoharp and, in her clear contralto voice, led
the prisoners in a variety of hymns. As always, Virginia Asher's quiet rendition of "My Mother's Prayer" induced an emotional response. On
November 2, this hymn filled the cells of inmates at the Chicago Avenue
Station:

MY MOTHER'S PRAYER

I never can forget the days
I heard my mother kindly say;
"You're leaving now my tender care,
Remember, child your mother's prayer."

My mother's prayer.
When'er I think of her so dear,
I feel her angel spirit near,
Her voice comes floating on the air,
Reminding me of mother's prayer.[78]

Men's emotional response to Virginia Asher's sentimental message suggests that evoking motherhood did tug at the consciences of the incarcerated

76. *Chicago Daily News,* October 15, 1910; *Chicago American,* October 20, 1910.
77. Chicago *Inter-Ocean,* October 27, 1910.
78. *Chicago Examiner,* November 2, 1910; Sizer, *Gospel Hymns,* 119–25.

prisoners. Upon hearing "My Mother's Prayer," one prisoner, Albert H. Smith, sobbed, "If I could be a child once more, and have my mother always near, I'd lead a different life. I'd never be here to-day," he said. Other prisoners also cried, one telling about the death of his mother. The prisoners' responses also suggest that the turn-of-the-century masculinity entailed more than bringing men under control; it was also an internalized conflict within each man. Histories of nineteenth-century families have noted that the childhoods of most turn-of-the-century males included an emotionally and physically distant father who, due to the social and economic conditions of the nineteenth century, spent large portions of time away from the family. A strong maternal presence compensated for paternal distance and absence. By the early twentieth century, however, modern masculinity implied separation from this female nurture in order to achieve both modernity and success. This requirement for separation produced anxiety that hinged on a male's attachment to his mother. "The crowds that attend these Chapman meetings," wrote one Chicago editorialist, "have mothers and grandmothers who were steeped in the Religious Feeling. And when the revivalist goes after it he is not disappointed. It is there." Society called for males to break ties with the feminine in order to be men, yet revivalists were calling them back to female virtue. Such contradictory demands could not help but produce uneasy consciences. "There are thousands of men in Chicago whose heads rest uneasy upon their pillows. . . . They have no peace night or day. They have sinned and they know it. They try to look the world boldly in the face. They smile with cynical smile, but their hearts are heavy."[79]

Male anxiety was only heightened by dependence upon women for sexual control and purity. In his struggle between celibacy and "sowing his oats," the godly male needed the passionless, virtuous woman to restrain and preserve his own sexual purity. Like D. L. Moody, J. Wilbur Chapman frequently spoke to men on the topic of "Sowing and Reaping" and used such narratives to reinforce the results of male impurity and excess. One of his many narratives detailed a mother who sent her son to St. Louis to search a hotel register for a record of her husband's fling with another woman. Chapman concluded the narrative, "That boy found his father's name there on the register—and he found the name of the woman who was

79. *Chicago Examiner,* November 2, 1910; Ryan, *Cradle of the Middle Class,* 232; Degler, *At Odds,* 77; Griffen, "Reconstructing Masculinity," 190; Dr. Frank Crane editorial, *Chicago Evening Post,* October 26, 1910; Chicago *Inter-Ocean,* October 21, 24, 1910.

with him. The son went to his own room and blew out his brains. When the father learned of the tragedy he too killed himself. And then the trusting mother followed her loved ones into eternity—a suicide. That father had sowed the wind and reaped the whirlwind."[80]

As in past revivals, the message to men was one of sexual control grounded by his relationship to a godly woman. Chapman preached, "Woman is men's salvation or his ruination. Life, society, Christianity, in a sense depend on her. Make her God-like and you make man God-like." Ultimately, the virtuous wife and mother held the key to the purity of her husband and family. In response to Chapman's "Sowing and Reaping" narrative, "a man broke from his seat, with unsteady steps made his way to the front and threw himself on his knees with his face in his hands. Others followed, young and old." By the close of the meeting thirty-five hundred men out of the five thousand in attendance stood "to declare themselves for Christ, and to forsake sin."[81] Such a widespread response reflected the depth of man's moral plight and his need for virtuous women to absolve it.

Convert Chicago through Its Women!

Even as the campaign used appeals of motherhood and the promise of domestic unity to reach men, revivalists emphasized that women must uphold their morally righteous side of the gender equation. "Thousands of women have failed to realize the sacredness and the greatness of their position in the future welfare of the city and its men," Helen Alexander preached. "Arouse the Chicago women to a view of their responsibility and you have achieved half the object of the revival."[82] The Simultaneous Campaign did not limit its preaching to men but sought out women of all classes with a message of true womanhood and domesticity.

Revival narratives acknowledged class differences by directing certain messages toward specific status groups. The revival supposed "there is a different Christian lesson for each woman in Chicago, but there are certain lessons for certain classes." Revivalists were quick to chastise the upper class in particular for their failure to look out for their lower-class sisters. The campaign

80. Chicago *Inter-Ocean,* October 24, 1910.
81. *Chicago American,* October 25, 1910; *Chicago Tribune,* October 24, 1910; Chicago *Inter-Ocean,* October 24, 1910.
82. *Chicago American,* Home Edition, October 25, 1910.

Four Charming Matrons Who Are Earnestly Aiding Their Husbands in Big Revival Meeting

Left to right, those shown are: Mrs. William Asher, Mrs. Charles M. Alexander, Mrs. J. and Mrs. Edith F. Norton.

Chicago Examiner
October 30. 1910

"Four Charming Matrons." Emphasizing the marital status of female revivalists deflected attention away from their independence. *Chicago Examiner,* October 30, 1910.

assumed a type of "trickle-down" outreach; effective evangelism must first infiltrate the upper echelons of the social order before it could be transmitted to the lower classes. Virginia Asher outlined this imperative: "We must reach the women 'higher up' in Chicago if we would have a city wide success in our work. . . . If you would reach the working girl of Chicago, you must first convert the society woman." The revival used Helen Cadbury Alexander's high status to convince upper-class women to shoulder their social and moral responsibilities. Mrs. Alexander was described as the "good angel" of the campaign. "She never hesitates to meet the lowliest of the low on common footing, and she sees the divine in the poorest of the poor." Other accounts of Mrs. Alexander describe her poignant appeals, her willingness to kneel prayerfully in the sawdust, but most importantly, her abandonment of social station in Britain for the sake of ministering to lower-status groups.[83] This was the correct model for elite behavior.

If Helen Alexander was the ideal elite, other women of high status failed the test, especially in terms of their leisure-time activities. Revivalists publicly chastised elites for their "enervating idleness" that violated middle-class norms of respectability and abrogated their moral responsibility. One Chicago headline read: "6,000 At White City Hear Rich Arraigned," then went on to criticize Chicago's society women "for whatever is not right in the lives of the city's working girls . . . when society women smoke cigarettes and drink it is only natural that the girls and women of other classes do the same thing."[84] Such criticisms extended to all types of personal behavior—use of leisure time, fashion consciousness, and childbearing. In an article entitled "To Women Who Prefer Poodle Dogs and Dolls to Children," J. Wilbur Chapman moralized:

> Just a word with you women who wear top heavy heads of false hair, who carry dressed dolls in your arms when you fare about the Loop on shopping expeditions, who balance hideous wastebasket hats on your already overloaded pates—just a word with you about the home. What sort of homes have you? What sort of children have you, if you have any? What sort of brains have you, if you have any?[85]

In each of these areas women of good moral standing and their families trumped frivolity. For the sake of societal order, revivalists urged elite women to reject pleasure and return to the values of domesticity.

Revivalists also criticized those middle-class women who emulated the behavior of their social betters. Middle-class women also shopped, fixed their hair, and had fewer children, but these women represented the bulk of revival supporters. Revivalists needed to remind them of their responsibilities without alienating their invaluable support. Speaking to a congregation at the Epworth Methodist Church, Virginia Asher reminded her audience, "If the church members would do their duty there would be fewer girls and

83. Chicago *Inter-Ocean,* October 25, 1910; *Chicago Daily News,* October 28, 1910; *Chicago Examiner,* October 30, 1910; Davis, *Torrey and Alexander,* 117–18, 123.

84. *Chicago Daily News,* October 28, 1910.

85. J. Wilbur Chapman editorial, *Chicago American,* November 7, 1910.

women in the 'red-light' district of Chicago." Asher also called for sympathy toward lower-class working girls. "If a woman repents and tries to be respectable the church people are the first to point the finger of scorn and set their busy tongues wagging about her," she said.[86] Asher argued that following these social mandates could erase the status differences that sharply divided the city. Moral adherence in effect would minimize, if not erase, class divisions, and it would create consensus. Revivals discounted class distinctions with rituals that purportedly put all participants on an equal basis and drew individuals into a moral unity. Newspaper accounts of the various assemblies took pains to describe the diversity of the revival crowd: "Handsomely gowned women touched elbows with men in working clothes; society matrons and maids sat side-by-side with shop girls and workers in factories." Regardless of the specific tack that revivalists took with regard to status, however, one theme remained consistent: women were becoming a largely unruly force. Attacking women's excesses exploited class-based consciousness even as it neatly "erased" the obvious middle-class commitment and entitlement from which the revival message was being spun.

Reaching Out to Working Girls

Part of the Simultaneous Campaign's extensive outreach to the city included working girls. The potential unruliness of these young women caused the revival to try to "teach" them the same social rules that were required of their "betters." Most of the outreach to working girls took place in factories during lunchtime breaks. Virginia Asher was given access to factory floors where she set up her organ and gathered workers around her for a short sermon and song. As female revivalists canvassed Chicago industries filled with young overworked women, their message was first one of sympathy. Like many other reformers, Asher and other revivalists portrayed the vulnerability of working girls, their innocence, and their isolation from domestic protection. These women were lost and alone, victims of the industrial system and men. Preaching to the two hundred girls in the "chipped beef" room of the Armour meatpacking plant, Asher argued, "Mere position in life cannot prove a hindrance to any one. There is room in the kingdom of God for every girl in the world. It makes no difference

86. *Chicago Tribune,* October 19, 1910; *Chicago Daily News,* October 28, 1910.

who or what you are, you can live a good life if you want to do so." Asher's message to the workers of the Kirk Soap Company was the same: "The working girl of this city needs sympathy more than anything else. If she knows that the world is in sympathy with her struggle it aids her in carrying on the battle." But revivalist sympathy came with a strong dose of normative domesticity. "Girls," Asher said, as she shook their hands, "don't forget the message. You need to live better lives, to make better wives, and to be mothers such as Christ desires."[87] Revivalists saw working women as innocents forced to yield to the whims of men, unable to live up to their true female potential as wives and mothers, and therefore deserving of pity.

While revivalists emphasized the naïveté of the young women, the workers themselves realized that revivalist sympathies could be directed toward a more tangible goal of improving their working conditions. After reading about the campaign's outreach to Chicago's working women, the Woman Employees of the Postal Service sent J. Wilbur Chapman a lengthy letter asking him to speak out against Sunday and night work. "We are obliged to toil incessantly," the women wrote. "When work is over we are so tired that some of us are easy prey to temptation. Others of us fail to attend church or places of entertainment that might better us, and we feel that we are slipping. Could you help us?" This letter was included in one of Chapman's letter-readings at the White City Casino. After reading the letter aloud in an evening meeting, Chapman publicly pledged to use all his influence to improve conditions for the postal workers.[88]

A similar scenario played out with the campaign's support of the 1910 Garment Workers' Strike. Even though Third Awakening revivalists had historically opposed any type of labor activism, revivalist sympathy for the plight of working girls moved the Evangelistic Campaign to support garment workers in their struggle for recognition and workers' rights.

On Strike or On the Levee?

By 1910 the men's clothing industry employed more than thirty-eight thousand individuals. Sixty-five percent of those workers were foreign-born,

---

87. *Chicago American,* November 21, 1910; Chicago *Inter-Ocean,* November 12, 1910; *Chicago American,* October 20, 1910.

88. *Chicago American,* October 26, 1910; Chicago *Inter-Ocean,* October 27, 1910.

and half were women. Women in the garment industry worked very hard, bending over a sewing machine or an iron for ten to twelve hours each day for a subsistence wage. Not only was their work difficult but they also were resented by the male workers, who tended to see their cheap labor as a threat to their own tenuous positions. This resentment ran so strong that male laborers refused to allow women into their unions. Factory owners were also hostile to female unions because any type of organization threatened their source of cheap labor and their profits. In spite of these obstacles, however, some of Chicago's female garment workers organized, and in the fall of 1910 the workers in Number Five Shop of the Hart, Schaffner and Marx Company responded to an arbitrary reduction in the sewers' piece rate by walking off the job. Initially, the sewers appealed to the United Garment Workers for support, but the union's largely male membership refused to take the strike action seriously and crossed the picket lines at Hart, Schaffner, and Marx.[89]

Rebuffed by the United Garment Workers, the strikers then appealed to the Women's Trade Union League, whose membership included both working girls and middle-class reformers committed to protecting women by improving their working conditions and wages. With the support of the WTUL, the striking women generated increased publicity and support for expanding the strike. By mid-October, at the start of the Simultaneous Campaign, eight thousand workers were on strike. On October 27, the United Garment Workers reconsidered the women's demands and agreed to support a general walkout that put close to thirty-five hundred workers off the job.[90]

Union activists tried to soften intransigent employers with middle-class support for the strike and, somewhat surprisingly, they found it at the Simultaneous Campaign. At the Chicago Opera House on October 23, J. Wilbur Chapman urged a crowd of two thousand businessmen to "lend financial aid, prayers, and civic influence to aid these toilers who are without employment, and without adequate funds to provide the barest of necessities . . . Help these suffering girls and women." After the revival meeting, the WTUL distributed strike pamphlets.[91] But the campaign's unusual backing of the strike cannot be seen as advocacy for worker rights

89. N. Sue Weiler, "Walkout: The Chicago Men's Garment Workers' Strike, 1910–1911," 238–49; Meredith Tax, *The Rising of the Women: Feminist Solidarity and Class Conflict, 1880–1917*, 91–92.

90. Barbara Wertheimer, *We Were There: The Story of Working Women in America*, 323.

91. Chicago *Inter-Ocean*, October 23, 1910.

or for labor reform; rather, the campaign supported the strike in order to protect young women, an agenda that fit well within their ideals of womanhood and domesticity. In many ways, revivalist sentiment paralleled the sympathy expressed by the WTUL's middle-class membership. Throughout the strike, the league's middle-class supporters emphasized the poverty of the strikers, their youth, and the way they were victimized by the employers and the state. Middle-class members of the league, like the Simultaneous Campaign, were not interested in reevaluating class relations; instead, they hoped to act as a somewhat benevolent elite speaking on behalf of the working-class masses.[92] The WTUL's middle-class understanding of the strike was assumed by the Chapman campaign—these were helpless working girls who needed a helping hand. Revivalists came out in support of a strike that would continue for four and a half months.

The revival's support of the strike was only the first step in what labor activists hoped would be an even wider Protestant endorsement of the strike. On November 15 a committee composed of James Mullenbach, superintendent of the Municipal Lodging House, Ellen Gates Starr of Hull House, and Agnes Johnson appealed to J. Wilbur Chapman and to the Laymen's Evangelistic Council for their support. Chapman agreed to ask Chicago ministers to pray for a "betterment of conditions for the working girls" and to interest Chicago businessmen in the cause. Although there is no documented evidence that prayer contributed to a labor settlement, the campaign endorsement did enlist strike support from several Presbyterian churches and the Moody Church contributed funds to the strike relief effort.[93]

The strike issue allowed the Simultaneous Campaign again to try to subsume class tensions within its moral regime. As opposed to seeing the strike as owners against workers, revivalists portrayed the strike in moral terms, a way to reinforce its hope of creating a "better manhood and womanhood." For some advocates of the strike, workers on picket lines affirmed capitalist exploitation and class divisions; for revivalists, young women on strike represented the cost of leaving domesticity—upsetting the moral balance and putting women at the mercy of industry. "Thousands of working girls fall from the right life because their daily work is so long and tedious that they are not strong enough when finished with their toil to withstand temptations which

92. Tax, *The Rising of the Women,* 110–14.

93. *Official Report of the Strike Committee, Chicago Garment Workers' Strike, October 29– February 18, 1910,* Women's Trade Union League.

beset them."[94] Through the strike revivalists reinforced the notion that apart from domesticity women faced daily temptation and walked in a minefield of potential sin.

As the strike wore on, the temptations that confronted workers became more intense as they faced hunger and homelessness caused by their unemployment. The greatest fear of revivalists was that these deprivations, on top of an already dire situation, would break a young woman's moral will and cause her descent into prostitution. "Long hours of hard work," Chapman said, "break down girls morally as well as physically and make them easy prey to designing men." Although the horrific tales of the white slave trade were somewhat exaggerated, numerous investigations into Chicago vice confirmed that poor wages and working conditions did create the tenuous line between working girl and prostitute.[95] Such reports frequently compared the meager weekly wages of a working girl to the daily take of a prostitute and affirmed that a young woman could make much more on the streets than in a factory or department store.

In one way the campaign's concern with prostitution reflects Chicago's preoccupation with this issue, and demonstrates how revivalism homed in on issues that were already capturing the city's attention. In another way, the prostitution issue reflects revivalism's longstanding alliance with Social Purity and its efforts to promote chaste women and men. In yet other ways, however, the publicity swirling around prostitution challenged the moral aspirations of the campaign and the alliance between Protestant faith and capitalism. Prostitution presented obvious evidence that industrial capitalism in effect was not sustaining a moral society. "The materialism of our age is the destruction of the ethics of Christianity. The loss of Christ's moral code is the loss of virtue," Chapman said. The ongoing investigation by the Chicago Vice Commission demonstrated that capitalist principles in fact now dominated the vice trade. With profit-oriented, businesslike efficiency, capitalism was selling its daughters into sex slavery. Chicago manufacturers and retailers, standing on the ideals of individual initiative, private property, and profit, obstinately blocked unionization and refused to pay its workers a living wage.[96] As a result, the prostitution business prospered alongside the

94. *Chicago American,* October 20, 1910; *Chicago Daily News,* October 26, 1910.

95. *Chicago American,* November 14, 1910; *Chicago American,* November 14, 1910; Rosen, *Lost Sisterhood,* 133.

96. Rosen, *The Lost Sisterhood,* 133; *Chicago American,* November 2, 1910; Weiler, "Walkout," 242; Meyerowitz, *Women Adrift,* 15–19.

more legitimate capitalist industries that exploited workers for the sake of corporate profits. Like the vice investigators, revivalists wanted to abhor the trade and its businesslike organization, but were much more reticent to criticize the economic system that encouraged it to flourish.

Prostitution also raised the question of capitalism's impact upon the family. Young women in the streets were visible reminders of the other economic factors that caused women to enter the trade; a breakdown in kin networks, or abuse, divorce, or death could economically devastate a family and push a daughter or sister out of the home and into prostitution. Prostitution clarified that both individual women and their families were threatened by capitalist exploitation. This threat was not limited to the working class; vice was also knocking at the doors of the middle class. Chicago's Levee, its "red-light" district, was not just expanding geographically; venereal disease was spreading into middle-class homes. Just as the WCTU argued that liquor corrupted the male drinker and disrupted domestic harmony, the Social Purists now argued that vice, "the twin evil of the liquor traffic," was spreading disease. The irresponsible behavior of unfaithful husbands threatened the health of their own wives and their offspring. These "twin evils," alcoholism and venereal disease, were referred to respectively as "social murder" and "social suicide," and both, according to Helen Hood, president of the Illinois WCTU, were headquartered in Chicago.[97] These domestic ruptures challenged revivalism's middle-class religiosity and its presumption of domestic influence. The Simultaneous Campaign's "crusade against vice" became a battle not only to protect women from the ravages of the public sphere but also to defend the sanctity of the home itself. With the Garment Workers' Strike as a backdrop, revivalists argued that when women left the domestic sphere they left its virtuous protection behind and opened themselves to exploitation. Loss of virtue, they argued, ultimately led to the reification of women and the sale of sex as a commercial product.

Absent from revival rhetoric, however, was the fact that many of Chicago's working girls were not being pushed from the home. Some working girls, desperate to escape abusive homes or to avoid the isolation and boredom of domesticity, actively chose to leave. Despite revival narratives emphasizing the plight of the working girl, many in fact intentionally set out in search

97. President's Address, Report of WCTU of State of Illinois, 52; David J. Pivar, "Cleansing the Nation: The War on Prostitution, 1917–21," 32.

of a life without parental or spousal supervision.[98] The independent life initiated by many working girls was disconcerting to middle-class social norms and particularly threatening to revivalism's moral balance. A working girl's individual initiative and independence added one more question to the barrage of issues being raised by the swelling divorce rate and declining fertility numbers. Revivalist faith dictated that the home was the salvation of the city and a defense against its evils, but now woman, the very heart of the moral order, could not wait to forsake her responsibility for the city life.

Working girls challenged domesticity because for them the city was not a bed of sin, but an opportunity for employment and excitement. Yes, this new life included the inevitable hard work and long hours, but it also included the freedom to engage in urban culture and to enjoy its nightlife of movie theaters and dance halls. Relieved of parental supervision and domestic duties, working girls, with their small but independent wages, carved out new lives defined by an open and sexually conscious style of living. Despite revivalist rhetoric to the contrary, Chicago's working girls were not solely the victims of the anonymity and alienation of urban life; they were also the beneficiaries, emerging as agents of sexual freedom, not restraint.

The thin line that separated the working girl from the prostitute troubled revivalists. Honest working girls warranted revivalist sympathy, but the possibility that young single women were having sex for either fun or money presented a more profound challenge. Such women could no longer control the disruptive male libido; in fact, they proved that they had libidos of their own. With female sexuality no longer in check, woman's place in the moral order was increasingly suspect. Many shifted blame onto the women themselves. Social Purists became quite adept at accusing prostitutes of selling themselves for finer clothes or a better standard of living. Others blamed prostitution on "some abnormal sex formation that induces a woman to drift into the promiscuity of a prostitute's life." However it was explained, this unruly feminine force upset the sexual equation of marriage and overturned its domestic apple cart.[99]

98. Meyerowitz, *Women Adrift,* 13–19; James R. McGovern, "The American Woman's Pre–World War I Freedom in Manners and Morals," 315–33.

99. Clifford G. Roe, *Panderers and Their White Slaves,* 109; J. H. Greer, *The Social Evil and the Remedy,* 51–52; Daniel Scott Smith, "The Dating of the American Sexual Revolution: Evidence and Interpretation," in Michael Gordon, ed., *The American Family in Social-Historical Perspective,* 426–38; Lewis A. Erenberg, *Steppin' Out: New York Nightlife and the Transformation of American Culture, 1890–1930.*

The Simultaneous Campaign's overt "sympathy" toward working girls and prostitutes frequently translated into implicit coercion, the urgent need to win women back to their proper places in the home or in the moral order. Throughout most of the nineteenth century, evangelical religiosity walked lockstep with middle-class ideals of individualism and self-help. When women entered the industrial economy and began to live out these ideals, however, they undercut domesticity, the bedrock of middle-class morality. Sympathy for working women was revivalism's only viable response. Any other response would in effect recognize woman's growing independence and would strike at the center of fundamentalism's gendered faith. The Simultaneous Campaign wanted to ally itself with women workers, but their domesticated moral standard forbade movement beyond its parameters.

As the Simultaneous Campaign sought to "win men to Christ" with ritualized appeals to the sanctity of motherhood, this same Gospel was losing its potency with women for whom this domestic ideal was no longer relevant. A rising divorce rate, the decline in childbearing, and the increased visibility of independent women did not bode well for domesticity's moral mission. As a result, the campaign heightened its rhetoric, admonishing elites for not living up to their social responsibilities and imploring working girls to realize their true occupations as wives and mothers.

The "Greatest Revival in Chicago's History"

By the first of November, the fervor aroused by the Simultaneous Campaign caused the *Inter-Ocean* to conclude, "Chicago is in the midst of the greatest religious revival in the city's history."[100] Such enthusiasm created the need for revival replacements. The revivalist Billy Sunday as well as two prominent rescue mission organizers, Melvin Trotter and Harry Munroe, came to Chicago to assist the Simultaneous Campaign. Mrs. E. M. Whittemore, an evangelical elite committed to the rescue and rehabilitation of New York City prostitutes and founder of the Door of Hope Mission, also came to aid the revival effort.

Whittemore heightened revivalism's moral rhetoric by appealing to her listeners with stories of her work with what she termed the "fallen sisters." One of Whittemore's most effective narratives told of a prostitute named

100. Chicago *Inter-Ocean*, October 30, 1910.

Delia, nicknamed the "Blue Bird of Mulberry Bend," one of New York's most infamous vice areas. According to Whittemore, Delia, or "Blue Bird," was a "leader of a gang of crooks, a drunkard, and an opium eater. Her soul was stained with every sin in the decalogue." Whittemore's saccharine narratives mirrored many of the other stories of "fallen" women that circulated throughout the revival.

But Delia's story represented more than a "fallen woman": she was also a "leader," which implies female agency, independence that took her far outside the domestic boundary. After Delia is converted through the work of the Door of Hope, she gives "her entire time and energy to the work of reclaiming lost souls." Delia's repentance changes her behavior; nevertheless Delia must pay for her sins and, like many of the other prostitutes in Whittemore's stories, she dies a slow and excruciating death. The "Blue Bird of Mulberry Bend" had violated the domestic rules, and even though she repented, she still had to pay for her sins in kind. Delia's story illustrated that females paved the way to salvation, but for those women who strayed from the moral path, the penalty was severe. In an editorial in the *Chicago Tribune,* J. Wilbur Chapman affirmed this message to women: "Christ's attitude towards vice has always been one of sternest rebuke, but his sympathy with the precious has been indescribably tender."[101]

Even though prostitution and the outlawing of vice were dominant issues of the revival, the Chapman-Alexander campaign did not organize a Gypsy Smith–style invasion of the Levee district. In the closing days of the crusade, the revivalists made a less publicized trip to the vice district. On November 25, Mabel and J. Wilbur Chapman and a number of other evangelists, including Virginia Asher and Ernest Bell from the Midnight Mission, went to the red-light district. On the Levee, Chapman stopped three times to preach to men on the street. His message to the men was summarized in the sermon title—"The Wages of Sin Is Death." The group then entered the Everleigh House to lead a short revival service.

The Everleigh House was Chicago's most sophisticated and celebrated brothel. Minna and Ada Everleigh, two entrepreneurial sisters, created the establishment and widely publicized its cultural allure, which included a music room, library, art gallery, and grand ballroom. The Everleigh House also boasted of its more licentious pleasures: brass beds inlaid with marble,

101. *Chicago Examiner,* November 4, 1910; Rev. F. A. Robinson, ed., *Mother Whittemore's Record of Modern Miracles; Chicago Tribune,* November 18, 1910.

and a gold fountain that spouted jets of perfumed water. There was no disguising the international reputation of this brothel and its privileged political status maintained by substantial financial contributions to the Levee's aldermen, "Hinky Dink" and "Bathhouse John." For the evangelists of the Simultaneous Campaign, no other location in Chicago symbolized more distinctly the sins of urban life. The campaign's ritualized "invasion" of the Everleigh House publicly confronted the exploitation of woman, the sins of uncontrolled manhood, and their corrupt alliance with municipal government. Twenty young women gathered in the ballroom of the Everleigh House to hear Chapman's sympathetic message that described "a loneliness unspeakable" when "there will be no friend on earth to whom you can turn." Chapman concluded, "I want to leave you with this message, that no matter how low you may sink, no matter how deep your sin. You will always find a friend in Jesus." After Chapman's speech, Virginia Asher closed the service with "My Mother's Prayer," and, having sown the seeds of domestic faith, the group quietly left the brothel.

Women and men alike heard the revival message. Newspaper accounts reported that the revival response was more ambiguous than the revivalists would perhaps have wanted. "There was no scoffing on the part of the few who stopped to hear the singing, and when he prayed the men of the street stood with bowed and uncovered heads." In the Everleigh House the garnet-colored electric lamp cast a weird, mystical light over the strange spectacle of a service. "There were no tears" from the women of the Everleigh House, "neither were there any smiles. The stillness of death pervaded the richly furnished parlor."[102] In spite of revivalist sympathies, a level of paternalism pervades this encounter, a moral positioning that again was thought, at least by the revivalists, to override all class and cultural differences. From the perspective of the "habitues of the underworld," however, the voyeuristic tone used to describe their workplace would seem to strengthen the divide between these women and the more conservative readers of these newspaper accounts.

102. Alson J. Smith, *Chicago's Left Bank*, 146; Asbury, *Gem of the Prairie*, 249–54; Wendt and Kogan, *Lords of the Levee*, 283–86; Chicago *Inter-Ocean*, November 26, 1910; *Chicago Record-Herald*, November 26, 1910.

The Politics of Revival

The Simultaneous Campaign had much less sympathy when it came to city hall. In the political arena the campaign hoped that its moral message would mean a vote against vice and liquor in the upcoming election on November 8. Other organizations had a similar intent. The Law and Order League, under the watch of A. B. Farwell, led the saloon referendum battle and hired University of Chicago students to canvass Chicago's eighty precincts in search of possible vote fraud. To no one's surprise, the students discovered thousands of illegal voters on the city's rolls. On election day, Chapman editorialized about a Christian's political duties, "If politics is dirty it is due to the political barnacles who have fastened themselves on the vitals of the city. It is your Christian duty to drive them into retirement or into jail with your vote and your personal effort, and then you will have clean politics and a clean city." Chapman's appeal to clean up the city struck a chord with Republicans disillusioned with the current mayor, Fred Busse. The Busse administration had mismanaged Chicago's utility funds, and instead of cleaning up city hall as promised, Busse's mayoral term was marred by more Democrat-like graft.[103]

On October 30, the Democratic Party sent a citywide letter to registered Democrats and to independent Republicans. The letter, somewhat ironically, urged all to "teach the Republican Party a lesson" and to "turn the rascals out." Frustration with Busse's boodling, plus the saloon-closing referendum, brought Republican voters to the polls with a strong moral agenda. On election day, the *Inter-Ocean* reported "thousands of members of the great evangelistic army of laymen engaged in the crusade against vice in Chicago spent much of their time in the vicinity of the polls. 'Vote as Christ would have you vote,' was their slogan."[104]

Despite what Protestants saw as the righteousness of the Republican cause, their electioneering did not succeed in closing down either Chicago's liquor or vice trade, although it did oust Fred Busse. "It was the Republicans who manned the guillotines yesterday," the *Inter-Ocean*

103. Clayton, "The Scourge of Sinners," 68–77; *Chicago American,* November 8, 1910; Chicago *Inter-Ocean,* October 30, 31, 1910; see also the front-page political cartoon, *Inter-Ocean,* November 8, 1910, September 20, 1910, November 1, 1910.

104. Chicago *Inter-Ocean,* October 30, November 9, 10, 1910. The Republican majority of 77,000 in the 1908 election was converted in two years into a Democratic majority of 35,000.

announced. "The Democrats got out their vote, and the Republican voters, taking advantage of the first opportunity to lambaste the hyphenated ticket (Mayor Busse-Governor Deneen), rolled up the pluralities." The morality vote by Republicans succeeded in punishing Mayor Busse, but brought the election victory to the Democrats. Busse's defeat revived a mayoral legacy— Carter Harrison II. Harrison, like his father who presided over the 1893 World's Fair, captured the ethnic vote and held it. His election as mayor guaranteed the continued tenure of Democratic aldermen, including those from the infamous First Ward.[105]

The defeat of the Republican mayor, however, was quickly overshadowed by the publication of the city's Vice Report. In June 1911, eight months after J. Wilbur Chapman's Simultaneous Campaign, Chicago's Vice Commission issued its findings. Many of the issues "officially" raised by the report had been publicized by the various outreaches of the revival campaign. The commission's most startling finding was that prostitution was now a big business. Dr. A. W. Harris, president of Northwestern University and a member of the Vice Commission, noted, "There is some indication that it (the vice trade) is feeling the influence of the centralizing methods characteristic of other lines of business." The report estimated that the trade yielded a $15 million annual return from the city's 1,020 resorts, 1,880 keepers and madams, and between 4,000 and 5,000 prostitutes, most of whom lived in the First Ward.[106]

The Vice Report also reaffirmed the trade's victimization of women. Like earlier Social Purity pronouncements, prostitutes were portrayed as victims of a now highly organized vice industry. But the Chicago Report, like numerous vice reports published in other cities, also highlighted the increased physical danger of prostitution, particularly to the unsuspecting middle-class wife who was threatened with venereal disease. "Prostitution is pregnant with disease," the report began, "a disease infecting not only the guilty, but contaminating the innocent wife and child in the home with sickening certainty almost inconceivable." The increased awareness and publicity about the health risks of prostitution shifted Social Purity into a Social Hygiene movement. The discourse of Social Hygiene, detailed with the symptoms of venereal disease—"sterility, insanity, paralysis, the

105. Buenker, "Dynamics of Chicago Ethnic Politics," 176.
106. Address by Dr. A. W. Harrison, "Work of the Chicago Vice Commission," *City Club Bulletin* 4 (January 1911–December 1911), 123.

blinded eyes of little babes, the twisted limbs of deformed children, degradation, physical rot, and mental decay"—focused primarily on sexually transmitted diseases. For middle-class readers of the report, such descriptions confirmed that the dangers surrounding prostitution, at least for the middle class, had become more physical than moral.[107] As the city's population expanded outward, the trade could no longer be contained within segregated areas, and that raised the possibility of disease spreading into outlying residential neighborhoods and homes. Unlike earlier opponents of vice who saw prostitutes as the violated victims of evil men, this report now described women as transmitters of disease that infected innocent wives, children, and middle-class domesticity. For its middle-class readers the Vice Report confirmed "scientifically" what the Simultaneous Campaign had preached—business interests consumed working girls, broke down their moral will, and led them into sin. Perhaps more importantly, the report also established that some prostitutes were "guilty," publicizing again that some women were not mere innocents; their presence threatened the domestic center of the social order.

The gravity of the Vice Report cut to the heart of Mayor Harrison's political realism. Harrison realized that he must respond to the report while at the same time holding onto his Democratic support, particularly in the First Ward.[108] Following the report's publication, the mayor ordered sporadic raids on the Levee, temporarily pushing prostitutes out of their Levee environs and into other parts of the city. These meager efforts by the mayor only briefly pacified the clamor to completely shut down the trade. Herbert Asbury, a New York writer and editor, observed that the Vice Report "completed the shift in public opinion," and that "throughout the summer of 1911 Chicago was filled with the fires of reform."[109]

107. Wendt and Kogan, *Lords of the Levee,* 294; Vice Commission of City of Chicago, *The Social Evil in Chicago,* 25.

108. Charles Edward Merriam, *Chicago: A More Intimate View of Urban Politics.* 18. Merriam would later describe Harrison as a "political realist" who "does not follow the lead of reform but does not antagonize them."

109. Asbury, *Gem of the Prairie,* 295; the "shift in opinion" may also be explained by a leaflet distributed by the Illinois Vigilance Association. The leaflet noted: "Chicago property owners in some of the best residential districts have lost many millions of dollars in property values because vice was tolerated in the proximity of their homes." "Protect Your Home, Property Values Injured by Immoral Neighbors," Illinois Vigilance Association, 1908.

The Vice Report strengthened the cause for all Social Purity groups and their Protestant leaders—the Law and Order League, the Sunday Evening Club, and the Vigilance Association. In October 1911, efforts to close the Levee again received a boost, this time from an unlikely source. Mayor Harrison, already under pressure from the anti-vice forces, was handed a colorful brochure emblazoned with all of the attractions of the Everleigh House. The publicity surrounding the brochure uncomfortably wedged Harrison between his allegiance to the First Ward and the growing outcry for public decency. In spite of a twenty-thousand-dollar bribe offered by the Everleigh sisters, Harrison was pushed toward outlawing the trade. On September 29, 1912, three days before the closing of Chicago's red-light area, ten thousand opponents of vice marched down Michigan Avenue to appeal for a "clean Chicago." The Chicago *Inter-Ocean* noted that persistent rain "failed to wilt the ardor of several thousand of Chicago's Anti-Vice forces, who changed Michigan Avenue's wonted refrain of tooting automobiles to reverberating gospel hymns." Within two years of the Simultaneous Campaign, Mayor Harrison shuttered the Everleigh House, closed the Levee, and outlawed prostitution in the city. Chicago's vice trade was criminalized and essentially pushed underground. It was rumored that the infamous Everleigh sisters, along with the best of their furniture, set up shop on Riverside Drive in New York City where "they played their gold-plated piano, served champagne and planked shad to guests who came visiting, and to recall, as old roués will, the past in Chicago. And it was agreed most of the guests now had more toes than teeth."[110] The era was over.

Recapping the Simultaneous Evangelistic Campaign

Chapman's Simultaneous Campaign again evidences revivalism's willingness to adapt to modern times. Like D. L. Moody's revival, the 1910 revival shows revivalism's willingness to use the tools of modernity to spread its message. Taking their message outside what were seen as the cloistered walls of a church, evangelists were able with some savvy to tap into the publicity generated by the Garment Workers' Strike and the city's

110. Chicago *Inter-Ocean,* September 29, 1912; Reckless, *Vice in Chicago,* 3; Wendt and Kogan, *Lords of the Levee,* 294–99; Stephen Longstreet, *Chicago, 1860–1919,* 300–301.

outrage over prostitution to generate increased enthusiasm for the campaign. They also communicated the message with some skill, organizing and moving throughout the city into places of entertainment as well as the workplace. This outreach was modern because not only did revivalists go to contemporary sites but also the organization and execution of the revival was businesslike and rational, appealing to society's shift toward consumerism. Part of its appeal was also because of the revival's eagerness to place and publicize women as propagators of their message.

At the turn of the century, America saw the emergence of the "new woman": educated, middle-class, single women who forged careers for themselves in urban reform. Women such as Jane Addams and her colleagues Florence Kelley, Alice Hamilton, and Julia Lathrop, leaders in a "women's dominion of reform," were deeply rooted in the Protestant tradition.[111] Protestantism encouraged "new women" to create public expressions of domesticity that led to settlement houses, social welfare, and eventually municipal reform. "New women" did not openly defy middle-class gender ideals, but they clearly made use of these ideals to establish careers that were independent of home or family.

In some respects, one may view the female revivalists, so visible in the Simultaneous Campaign, as fundamentalism's "new women" as well. They too represented the increased educational and practical experiences that Protestant women gained at the turn of the century. As they adapted to woman's newfound place in the city, fundamentalists and their revivalist spokespersons strategically placed women in factories, amusement parks, and even brothels to reach other modern women. This led to a growing visibility and influence for the women within revivalist circles. Virginia Asher, Helen Alexander, Mabel Chapman were clearly a presence in the revival, symbolizing the empowerment of women.

Revivalists, however, held to an unbreakable bond between domesticity and morality and saw the two in tandem as a religious principle to be defended. Female evangelists such as Virginia Asher and Helen Alexander extended this notion of domestic morality, a model they perceived as highly beneficial not only to women but also to the continuation of the faith. The Simultaneous Campaign's insistent portrayal of these women within the context of marriage allowed women to wield female influence, but without actually challenging male dominance. Their presence in revivals established

111. Kathryn Kish Sklar, "Protestant Women and Social Justice Activism, 1890–1920."

an appropriate balance between emotion and reason, upheld the stability of the family, and enabled sexual purity to be sustained.

At the same time, revivalists used gender ideals to personalize both the evils they confronted in the city and the righteousness they hoped would overcome these evils. Revivalism's moral standard was rhetorically and ritually defined by gender roles that they saw as essential to communicating the Gospel message. Like preceding revivals, the Simultaneous Campaign reasserted traditional gender roles and categorized as "sinful" those individuals or groups that did not abide by them. Acceptance of these roles was seen as spiritually right and as a counterbalance to the broader social developments fundamentalists feared were undermining the feminized and familial basis of Protestantism. The problem was that these gender roles were no longer clear-cut; they were in fact losing their potency. For men, the goal of being a modern man challenged his earlier domestic assignment, and many women were no longer willing to abide by domestic constraints. The symbols of revivalism's "good" and "evil" had been ritually constructed around gender ideals, symbolic constructs that revivalism endowed with deep religious meaning. By 1910, however, these constructs were losing their social relevance.

Revivalism's public defenses of this ideal reveal the contradictions within its moral message. The model of the virtuous but submissive female ameliorating the potential sins of the evil male was quickly losing credibility, especially with women who had experienced a taste of independent life. In alliance with the Social Purity movement, the plight of the working girl and the prostitute could arouse revivalist sympathies for their loss of domestic virtue, but it was equally clear that increasing numbers of women were choosing to bypass this moral standard. Virginia Asher, in her appeal to prostitutes at the Everleigh House, urged women themselves to acknowledge and accept the religion of motherhood and domesticity. But as more and more women of all social classes increasingly ignored domestic dictates and pursued independence, the revival Gospel shifted toward a much stronger assertion of domesticity with a masculine twist.

CHAPTER 4

"I'll Never Be an Angel If I Haven't Manhood Enough to Be a Man!"

THE 1918 BILLY SUNDAY REVIVAL

In March 1918 Billy Sunday came to Chicago for a ten-week revival. Sunday's sensational New York City campaign in the spring of 1917 followed by revivals in Los Angeles, Atlanta, and Washington, D.C., brought the revivalist to Chicago as a religious célèbre. The 1918 Chicago revival, however, would be Sunday's last revival in a major urban area. The campaign replaced J. Wilbur Chapman's simultaneous model with a highly centralized evangelistic machine complete with a lakefront tabernacle and trained professional staff. Like the revivalists that preceded him, Billy Sunday brought the tools of modernity to the front line in battling Chicago's sin. Highly centralized and hyper-masculine, the Sunday revival nevertheless maintained revivalism's mandate for domestic balance. But Sunday's portrayal of sin tilted the moral schema toward men and elevated a domesticated masculinity as the epitome of righteousness. Strongly influenced by the rhetoric of the Anti-Saloon League and the Social Hygiene movement, revivalist morality found its virtue in man's nature and agency and, as a result, by 1918 the sins of the city shifted into the female camp.

The earlier revivals of Dwight L. Moody and J. Wilbur Chapman had navigated the shifting gender terrain at the turn of the century. Domesticity within the Moody and Chapman revivals had balanced masculinity with femininity and promoted the godly woman as the antidote to the sins of uncontrolled men. The Billy Sunday revival retained the domestic balance, but men increasingly claimed the moral high ground. Earlier revivals placed morality in the hands of women, who served as buffers and antidotes to the degrading forces of the industrial economy. Now, shifting the moral power to men signaled a stronger reconciliation between faith and the business of corporate consumer culture. Revival rituals were increasingly orchestrated, and in the rhetoric of revivalism men became "angels" and women became "frizzle-headed sissies"; repentant male sinners could no longer "come home"; instead they were told to "be a man!"

Just as revivalism's earlier promotion of virtuous womanhood had sustained suspicions about the "respectability" of black women and men, Sunday's promotion of white masculinity also cast implicit class and racial aspersions. Sunday's ongoing emphasis upon domesticity perpetuated white middle-class standards that, even if unintentional, celebrated the separateness and superiority of whiteness. Revivalism's popularization of white domesticity played well within the broader changes in America society as it more rigidly institutionalized and enforced segregation in the second decade of the twentieth century.

At the same time, however, revivalism's mandate to save individual souls and sustain its moral regime motivated Mr. Sunday to reach across racial lines for the cause of Prohibition. For the sake of this moral goal, middle-class blacks and whites rallied around the common cause of outlawing alcohol. But the now-masculinized domesticity of revivalism undercut that same racial unity. In the end, the 1918 moral outreach appears to have less to do with the establishment of religious inclusivity than with the cultivation of its social and racial boundaries.

Chicago's Divided Demography

In 1918 Chicago was more deeply divided in terms of race, ethnicity, and status. When World War I erupted, Chicago industries needed workers to fill wartime jobs. In response, thousands of African Americans joined the Great Migration out of the South, moving into Chicago and other northern cities. Between 1910 and 1920 the city's African American population grew by 148 percent. The migration triggered significant changes within the black community itself. In the first decade of the twentieth century an economically stable middle class had emerged that was fueled by opportunities in business, the professions, and politics. This new middle class favored black-only economic and social institutions in contrast to Chicago's older, more integrationist black elites. The Great Migration, however, meant greater numbers of poorer blacks arriving from the rural South, whose lifestyles accentuated the status differences between the newly arrived and their social "betters." In particular, the middle class viewed the recent arrivals as threats to their own social responsibility and stability. Of particular concern were the leisure-time activities of the newly arrived migrants who found community in saloons and entertainment in petty gambling. Participation by poorer blacks in what were viewed as "immoral" activities by their black "betters" seemed to validate white criticism that all blacks lacked moral discipline and social control. The new middle class worked actively within black churches and reform organizations to eradicate such "immoralities" and to validate their own respectable status. They played an important role in welcoming new migrants to the city and in many instances provided social services to them.[1]

Efforts to integrate new arrivals into the city and to uphold middle-class norms, however, proved difficult. While the city's industries may have needed black workers, Chicago whites were less than eager to welcome the new arrivals. In 1917 the Chicago Board of Real Estate selected a committee to outline a segregation plan designed to curtail black incursions into white neighborhoods. The committee's work realigned the city's residential boundaries and crowded the vast majority of new African American arrivals into the city's Black Belt.[2] Middle-class blacks also held a tenuous position in Chicago society. Most whites still deemed even middle-class blacks as inferior and lacking "respectability," and as a result discrimination, rooted in both status and race, became even more explicit.

Ethnic differences also continued to divide the city. Chicago's changing demographics caused many white, native-born Chicagoans to move, creating an even greater divide between its native-born "better" class that lived in the suburbs and its largely ethnic working class that remained in the central city. In 1910, at the time of Chapman's Simultaneous Campaign, the foreign-born and their children dominated Chicago's population. Along with black workers, immigrants who were also looking for jobs continued to flood the city after 1910. The influx of "new" immigrants and African

1. Alan H. Spear, *Black Chicago: the Making of a Negro Ghetto,* Table 1: "Negro Population of Chicago," 12, and 71–89; Grossman, *Land of Hope,* 129–31, 140, 156; Knupfer, *Toward a Tenderer Humanity,* 30–36.
2. Thomas Lee Philpott, *The Slum and the Ghetto: Immigrants, Blacks, and Reformers in Chicago 1880–1930,* 163–65.

WISDOM.—O man! Behold, standing before thee, him whom thou needest most beware.

The best fighting is against yourself.—Arab Proverb.

"Wisdom—O Man!" *Ram's Horn,* January 2, 1895.

Americans spurred a smaller but equally significant migration of white middle-class Chicagoans to outlying suburbs. Between 1910 and 1916 the population living in Chicago proper (within four miles of State and Lake streets) remained stable at around one million residents. The population living in the area four to seven miles outside the city, however, jumped from 460,000 to 1,076,000, and the population in the area seven to ten miles outside the city increased from 180,000 to 332,000. "Better" families who had once inhabited the inner city now migrated to the west (Oak Park, Riverside, and River Forest) and to the north (Evanston, Wilmette, Kenilworth, Winnetka, and Lake Forest). One observer noted, "It was, indeed, no longer a city at all, in the nineteenth century meaning of the word. By the second decade of the twentieth century Chicago was more of a mart than a metropolis, a city abandoned by the well-to-do."[3]

Chicago elites, often referred to as the "Prairie Avenue Set," made the most dramatic move. This wealthy clique included the industrial, meat-packing, and mercantile magnates of the city who originally resided along the South Side's prestigious Prairie Avenue. In the late nineteenth century, as the Levee expanded southward and the unsavory odors of pollutants filled the air, these elites began to build along the "Gold Coast" on the near North Side or beyond. When they moved out, they sold their homes at cut-rate prices, causing property values on Prairie Avenue to plummet. One residence, for example, that in 1870 cost $150,000 was sold in 1909 for $36,000. The luxurious homes of the "Prairie Set" were transformed into apartments quickly populated by workers from the nearby industries. Newly arrived blacks also moved into areas directly to the west of Prairie Avenue. The boundary between these black and white ethnic neighborhoods was decided by a rapidly developing color line.[4]

The city's changing demography presented both internal and external challenges for Chicago Protestants. Internally, Protestants aligned themselves theologically into either modernist or fundamentalist camps. While more conservative Protestants tended to leave mainline denominations for doctrinal reasons, downtown Protestant churches watched as many of their congregants moved to outlying suburbs for less religious reasons. Chicago's First Presbyterian, located at Clark and Lake Streets, was the city's oldest

3. Mayer and Wade, *Chicago: Growth of a Metropolis*, 252. Wayne Andrews, *Battle for Chicago*, 240–41.

4. Mayer and Wade, *Chicago: Growth*, 252.

Presbyterian church. The church found itself caught in the middle of Chicago's shifting population. "In the growth of the city it was found that the location was not good," one church bulletin noted. "The encroachments of business had made necessary the removal of many families, whose homes had been for years in the immediate vicinity of the church."[5] Other churches experienced similar transitions. The Second Presbyterian Church on Michigan Avenue was one of Chicago's most socially prestigious institutions, with many members from the "Prairie Avenue Set." By 1919, Second Presbyterian's neo-Gothic edifice, originally constructed in 1874, was decorated with fourteen Tiffany windows that had been donated by various wealthy parishioners. The church stood as a monument to Protestant dominance, and particularly to the preeminence of Chicago as a Presbyterian city. Like other downtown churches, however, its prestige could not shield it from the encroaching Levee nor from the pollutants of nearby tanneries and rendering factories.[6]

At the turn of the century, Second Presbyterian's "Prairie Avenue Set" began to disperse to more desirable parts of the city, initiating a transformation that continued for the next two decades. On May 1, 1918, the elders of the Second Presbyterian Church retired some eighty-five members for continued nonattendance. At the same meeting, however, there was tangible evidence that the mission outreaches of the church had paid off: the elders accepted seventeen new members from the Italian Christian Institute. The replacement on the church register of Anglo-Saxon names like Davis, Russell, Morris, and Reynolds with those like Galano, Martignetti, and Paola was symptomatic of the ethnic transition occurring in numerous downtown churches.[7]

The migration of African Americans brought greater racial separation on the religious front as well. Although many Chicago churches were already segregated, Moody Church, founded on D. L. Moody's more inclusive tendencies, had maintained its integrationist position. In 1916, however, the church reversed its policy. In that year, Paul Rader, pastor of the Moody Bible Church and a noted fundamentalist spokesperson, announced that

5. *Miscellaneous pamphlets,* First Presbyterian Church of Chicago.

6. Andrew Stevenson, *Chicago: Pre-eminently A Presbyterian City;* Erne R. and Florence Frueh, "Stained Glass Windows at the Second Presbyterian Church," 210–217.

7. *Session Records,* May 1, 1918, vol.5, February 5, 1911–September 23, 1920, Second Presbyterian Church.

African Americans were no longer welcome at the church.[8] "After thirty years of attending the Moody Church, corner of LaSalle and Chicago Ave., which has been one of the greatest factors of religious uplift and civic betterment of Chicago among all races and nationalities and which D. L. Moody made famous through his great work, the evil of the color line has reached its doors," a black community newspaper noted. Arguing that African Americans already had their own churches to attend, the paper quoted Rader as saying, "Negroes should attend their own. At any rate, they are unwelcome at the Moody Church. . . . They cannot use the Negroes any longer and permit them to be crowding the white people out."[9] Certainly by 1916 Chicago had numerous black churches, but the point is that Moody Church's traditionally more tolerant attitude toward African Americans had succumbed to the growing paranoia and racism of whites.

The line between Chicago Protestants and Catholics also hardened. As Chicago's immigrant numbers swelled past those of the native-born, Catholics significantly outnumbered Protestants. The 1916 Census of Religious Bodies revealed 720,000 Roman Catholics in Chicago, as compared to 60,000 Lutherans and 30,000 members each in the Methodist Episcopal, Presbyterian, Baptist, and Jewish faiths. As sociologist Kevin Christiano has noted, the growth of heterogeneous urban populations led to greater cultural conflict that, in turn, heightened religious turmoil. Emerging out of this turmoil, Christiano argues, came an obvious Catholic presence, as well as a "lean and organized Protestant opposition."[10] Despite theological differences between fundamentalists and liberals, the dominance of an "alien" (i.e., Catholic) faith, alongside the city's other challenges to its moral order, drew Protestants together.

Protestant unity is evidenced in the widespread support Billy Sunday garnered for his revival. While some Protestants voiced their reservations about the Reverend Sunday's "happy-go-lucky air of equality with the Master" or his "lofty scorn toward fellow Christians," most Protestants, whether fundamentalist or liberal, considered the moral ramifications of a Billy Sunday revival along with the media bonanza it would provide and

8. *Christian Workers Magazine,* May 1915, vol.15 (1914–15).

9. Chicago *Illinois Idea,* May 15, 1915.

10. "1916 Census of Religious Bodies," in Loretto Dennis Szucs, *Chicago and Cook County Sources: A Genealogical and Historical Guide.* Kevin J. Christiano, *Religious Diversity and Social Change in American Cities, 1890–1906,* 148–149.

willingly joined the revivalist camp.[11] As a part of this "lean and organized" Protestantism, many churches threw their support to Sunday, banking once more on revival's potential for moral intervention.

The Politics of Moral Activism

By the second decade of the twentieth century, Progressive reform and political partisanship were in full swing. As Democrats and Republicans battled to control municipal government, each lifted its own banner as the party of decency and portrayed the other as the epitome of corruption and evil. Chicago politics were even more conflicted by the U.S. entry into World War I. In 1917, a year before the Billy Sunday revival, President Woodrow Wilson took the nation to war, a decision that pitted ethnic groups loyal to the Central Powers against those whose loyalty rested primarily with Great Britain.

Many of the same moral issues that led Protestants to support revivalism kept them within the Republican Party. The fact that Chicago Catholics, who were mostly Democrats, outnumbered Protestants did not guarantee Catholicism's dominance in the city, nor did it grant political control to the Democratic Party. Rather, a slugfest played out between what city alderman Charles Merriam described as a "Catholic-labor-foreign complex as over against a Protestant-capitalist-native American complex."[12] In many of these battles, Protestant moralists shared common ground with Progressive reformers, particularly in their desire to clean up city politics.

The momentum for a municipal housecleaning had been boosted by Illinois's ratification of female suffrage in 1914. In Illinois, the arguments for the woman's vote had been determined largely by status. Working-class women saw the ballot as part of a larger agenda to improve their lives as working women, while middle-class suffragists saw the vote as a way to protect the home and to bring maternal values to the political arena. The middle-class rationale, based on expanding female moral influence, coincided with fundamentalism's domestic ideal. Some fundamentalists saw giving an independent political voice to women as a threat to the family,

11. *Christian Worker's Magazine,* August 1915, vol. 15 (1914–15).
12. Merriam, *Chicago: A More Intimate View,* 129–130.

Mr. and Mrs. Billy Sunday leaning off the steps of a railroad car. The celebrated arrival of Sunday in Chicago initiated the media bonanza that surrounded the event. *Chicago Daily News,* Chicago Historical Museum.

but many others, including the Woman's Christian Temperance Union and the National Women's Suffrage Association and Billy Sunday, supported the women's vote because it could direct the domestic influence of middle-class women into urban reform. The women's vote would further activate middle-class values by offsetting the male ethnic vote, particularly its support of saloons. "I have always thought," Billy Sunday said, "that it was a queer law that would let a whiskey-soaked old ward-heeler vote and keep a bright, snappy woman away from the polls. One of the principal reasons that I am in favor of women's suffrage is because the opposition has crawled out of the saloons and breweries." The revival's support of Prohibition allied with its suffrage support. Sunday asked an audience to "join with me in a battle for two great victories, the elimination of booze and the elimination of the vicious doctrine that woman is lower than man and possibly a little higher than the animals."[13] By protecting woman's place in the domestic order, suffrage, like prohibition, promoted a moral society. For many fundamentalist supporters, the women's vote would enfranchise their domestic influence, not their personal independence.

This revivalist argument, which paralleled the suffrage mainstream, was quite different from feminism, which stood for female individualism and self-development, not self-sacrifice or submission to family interests.[14] Feminists supported women's rights based on sex equality and rejected the ideology of separate spheres, which feminists saw as oppression, not uplift for women. Feminists were much more interested in equality and independence than in carrying traditional gender roles into the voting booth. The emerging critique and its feminist demand for equality between women and men was, of course, antithetical to fundamentalism and its hope that the women's vote would give more clout to their attacks on public immorality.

Women's role in the election of Republican William Hale Thompson, who was mayor of Chicago during the Billy Sunday campaign, clarifies the more conservative, reform expectations of many of Chicago's middle-class women. The 1915 election offered the first opportunity for Chicago women to cast ballots in a municipal primary, and Republican women seemed determined to use their vote for reform. In the February 1915 primary, "Big Bill" Thompson understood the potential of the woman's vote, promptly seizing the reform mantle and promoting himself as the "decent" candidate. His campaign song, "We want a cleaner city where the good can thrive and shine," appealed to the reformist zeal of Republican women, and their vote brought Thompson the primary win.[15]

13. Steven M. Buechler, *The Transformation of the Woman Suffrage Movement: The Case of Illinois 1850–1920,*161; Aileen Kraditor, *The Ideas of the Woman's Suffrage Movement, 1890–1920,* 249–264; Nancy Cott, *The Grounding of American Feminism,* 30. De Berg, *Ungodly Women: Gender and the First Wave of American Fundamentalism,* 50–54; Bendroth, *Fundamentalism and Gender,* 47. DeBerg, *Ungodly Women,* 32–33. Buechler, *Transformation,* 117–121. For suffrage opposition "Woman Suffrage—A Reform, But Unto What?" *Christian Worker's Magazine,* October 1916, 112–113, and "Sex Relations in Church and State," *Christian Worker's Magazine,* July 1917, 942–946. Miscellaneous Campaigns, Scrapbook 6, William Ashley and Helen Amelia Sunday Papers; Jack S. Blocker, Jr., 'Separate Paths: Suffragists and Women's Temperance Crusade," 460–76; *Chicago Tribune,* March 10, 1918.

14. Aileen Kraditor, *The Ideas of the Woman Suffrage;* Cott, 39.

15. Douglas Bukowski, "Big Bill Thompson: The 'Model' Politician," in Green and Holli, eds., *The Chicago Political Tradition,* 62.

Thompson's primary victory, however, may also be attributed to the divisive impact of world conflict. When the European war erupted in 1914, the United States had vowed to stay out of the conflict. Despite U.S. neutrality, Chicago's ethnic and religious loyalties were sharply divided on the war; many immigrant groups, siding with their countries of origin, supported the Central Powers, while the native-born population allied with England and France. In a city that included the sixth-largest urban German population in the world, as well as the second-largest Bohemian, Norwegian, and Polish populations, Chicago's diversity made for a hotbed of ethnic tensions. The 1915 mayoral contest exacerbated these tensions; "Big Bill" Thompson, having won the Republican primary, touted his "decency" along with his native-born Protestantism. His Democratic opponent, Robert M. Sweitzer, promoted his Catholic and pro-German sentiment. Neither candidate had any compunction about exploiting these differences for political advantage; Thompson issued secret circulars attacking Sweitzer's Catholicism, while Sweitzer accused Thompson of vowing to drive Catholic teachers from the schools. Thompson fought back by contrasting his native-born, Protestant, and reformist stance with Sweitzer, who was portrayed as the embodiment of the Catholic-foreign element. Coming back at Thompson and trying to solidify his German support, Sweitzer then circulated a "German Fatherland" letter that informed a German-only audience, "You, your relatives and friends can be of great assistance to Germany and Austria next Tuesday by electing Robert M. Sweitzer."

Intended only for Chicago's German voters, the letter nevertheless found its way into the city's Polish and Czech neighborhoods. When these populations got wind of the letter they were outraged by Sweitzer's implicit support of German oppression against their homelands. The ethnic enmity ignited by the "Fatherland" letter, in addition to the moral indignation provoked by Sweitzer's bawdy preelection parade, appeared to seal Thompson's "decency" campaign.[16] When the final vote was counted, the majority of Chicago's women and the population as a whole voted for the Republican Thompson. By ousting the Democrats from City Hall, many, especially female voters, thought they had initiated a new phase of reform.

One observer, however, was perhaps more realistic: "The world was whirling into hell, while the city of Chicago was suffering from its same old

16. Bukowski, "Big Bill Thompson," 63.

diseases—lazy government, crooked police, stupid smoke-inspectors, dirty streets, and litters of garbage."[17] The words of Charles Merriam, one of Thompson's chief critics, were similarly pessimistic. "With the War, calamity descended upon the city. The spoils system swept over the city like a noxious blight, and the city hall became a symbol for corruption and incompetence. . . . Chicago descended to the lowest depths in its history, as the civic idealism of the community was for the moment put to rout." Merriam's dismay with Thompson's victory was later confirmed by many who noted that "Big Bill" was even more inclined toward machine politics than his political opponents had been.[18]

When America actually declared war, the city's political contention escalated. While European nation-states battled on the Western Front, their Chicago-based copatriots also clashed, and city politicians played both sides to their own advantage. Mayor Thompson, who had now set his sights on the U.S. Senate, assumed an ambivalent stance toward the war, cautiously evaluating what taking sides might mean for his political future. As a concession to the left, for example, the mayor permitted the People's Council for Democracy and Terms of Peace to meet in the city. The council was an antiwar group whose membership included radicals such as Crystal Eastman and the Socialist Victor Berger. When the council convened in September 1917, the Illinois state governor promptly ordered the Chicago police to disperse the convention.[19]

Billy Sunday also took advantage of the war to strengthen his cause with Chicago's native-born population. Despite his initial reticence to an American wartime commitment, Sunday eventually became one of the war's strongest supporters. The revivalist readily seized upon President Wilson's appeal to spread American individualism abroad and make the world "safe for democracy." The revivalist did not hesitate to dramatize his message with wartime headlines. "Grabbing souls from the devil is no more of a haphazard affair for Billy Sunday than grabbing Huns from Hindenburg is for Haig or Pershing," the media proclaimed. "Billy Sunday has the devil half licked before he starts to fight. His drive is organized and systematized long before he takes the field. His methods are those of

17. Lloyd Lewis and Henry Justin Smith, *Chicago: The History of Its Reputation,* 375–377.
18. Merriam, *Chicago: A More Intimate View,* 22; Bukowski, "Big Bill Thompson," 61.
19. Bukowski, "Big Bill Thompson," 66–67.
20. *Chicago Tribune,* March 6, 1918.

Flanders and the Campagne."[20] Wartime analogies amplified Sunday's Gospel, aligning America and her armed forces with the causes of purity and righteousness, while the Central Powers and the Kaiser provided a convenient embodiment of Satan. The revivalist's patriotic rhetoric against the German "Hun," particularly in Chicago, could easily be construed as an indictment of ethnic populations in general, and Germans in particular. War rhetoric also allowed the revivalist to go after his real target—the liquor interests. Bring on the saloon!

The "Morality" of Prohibition

For Billy Sunday and his supporters, cleaning up Chicago was integrally tied to shutting down its saloons. For conservative Protestants, the outlawing of prostitution left the saloon as the most visible evidence of Chicago's sins. Vice had been legally suppressed, but the city's thriving saloon business continued to rile ethnic and status tensions pitting native-born, middle-class Chicagoans against its foreign-born working-class people.[21] Like his revivalist predecessors, Sunday excoriated liquor as a threat to an individual's relationship to God, to the family, and ultimately to the nation as a whole. In the course of his revival career, Sunday had become a strong ally of the Anti-Saloon League, a national organization that had numerous state affiliates. The Illinois State Anti-Saloon League, which formed in 1898, was a powerful lobby at the state level and a strong promoter of Billy Sunday's anti-liquor potential in urban America.

Billy Sunday's anti-liquor argument paralleled that of the Anti-Saloon League and its masculinized attack on the liquor industry. Whereas earlier reform rhetoric by the WCTU argued for the protection of women and the home, the Anti-Saloon League and Billy Sunday's revival rhetoric focused primarily on liquor's detrimental influence on men and its threat to their self-control.[22] Condemning liquor also implied the superiority of white males over immigrants and African Americans.

---

21. Norman Clark, *Deliver Us from Evil: An Interpretation of American Prohibition.* Clark demonstrates that after the Civil War anti-saloon achievements were concurrent with "white slave" panic. Nationally, the Volstead Act (1919) that outlawed liquor followed on the heels of the Mann Act (1910) that prohibited prostitution.

22. James Timberlake, *Prohibition and the Progressive Movement 1900–1920,* 135; Eric Burns, *The Spirits of America: A Social History of Alcohol,* 147.

From early in the nineteenth century, fear of the immigrant fueled Prohibition sentiment among native-born whites. Anti-saloon forces had viewed foreigners with suspicion and distrust, fearing that immigrant workers were labor agitators or even Socialists. Nativist fears and class animosity easily turned into moral accusations. Foreigners, they alleged, had no self-control or moral compass. Since the days of D. L. Moody in Hell's Kitchen, middle-class Chicagoans had linked images of unruly, loose-moraled young men to saloons and then to unions and finally to anarchy. Whatever the cause of these nativist fears, there was "one sin that tied all of these depravities together . . . saloons run by foreigners were the taproot of every urban corruption." Prohibitionists, historian Eric Burns points out, were not inherently unkind or bad people. "They were simply people who did not know what to make of the unfamiliar . . . they did not hate the black man and the Serb, the Italian and the Pole, the Czech and the Croatian. They feared them, and it is not animosity that makes a person afraid; it is ignorance, a lack of knowledge, a narrow kind of living."[23]

Fear of the immigrant was also paralleled by racial fears; liquor, it was thought, unleashed the "bad" black man. A good portion of the success of the southern Prohibition movement was achieved at the expense of blacks. After the Civil War and the end of slavery, white southerners argued that blacks were not ready for freedom or the vote because they were not moral. Liquor was a major part of this southern argument to deny rights to blacks. Raising the stereotypes of the "black rapist" or "black primitive," whites justified oppressing blacks, often with lynching, on the basis that blacks were "depraved." "Liquor, lust, and lynching all ran together, especially in the dangerous cities," writes political scientist James Morone.[24]

In the last half of the nineteenth century, southern communities instituted local-option laws that brought the liquor issue before voters. In these elections, the newly enfranchised blacks often provided the swing vote. In communities where the electorate defeated local option, the Republicans, who were the minority party in the South, discovered a wedge issue with liquor; i.e., "the Democrats were soft on drunken Negroes." As a way of seizing the "moral" high ground and taking power away from the Democrats, the Republicans accused blacks of backing the liquor interests.[25] To further

23. Morone, *Hellfire Nation*, 292–302; Burns, *The Spirits of America*, 178.
24. Morone, *Hellfire Nation*, 297.
25. Andrew Sinclair, *Prohibition, the Era of Excess*, 29–35.

extend their political influence, Republicans insisted that in order to pass prohibition laws and to protect white women, the vote must be taken away from blacks. In short, liquor and its prohibition was a significant tool to disenfranchise the black voter.

The irony of the Republican tactic is that many blacks and in particular most black Christians favored temperance, but in southern politics black support for temperance was completely dissipated when whites successfully combined it with a move to disenfranchise African Americans. In the first decades of the twentieth century as Jim Crow was legalized, the Prohibition cause for both parties was tied to white male supremacy and race control. In 1914 Representative Richmond Pearson Hobson, an Alabama Democrat, introduced a Prohibition amendment to ban the buying and selling of alcohol. In his defense of the amendment (which failed to pass in 1914), Hobson argued: "Liquor will actually make a brute out of the Negro, causing him to commit unnatural crimes. The effect is the same in the white man, though the white man being further evolved it takes a longer time to reduce him to the same level." Connecting Prohibition and Jim Crow laws originated in the South but became a national phenomenon: "the white South cast its call for Prohibition in the timeless language of American moral fears: the depraved savage endangers us. Put that way, it reverberated across the rest of the nation." What had originally been southern arguments that liquor in the hands of a black male was "fuel for black lasciviousness" that turned the black male into a rapist spread nationwide and became an integral part of the belief in white supremacy.[26] As African Americans moved north in the Great Migration, white fears concerning their immoral, violent behavior and its link to alcohol spread into Chicago as well.

26. Gilmore, *Gender and Jim Crow,* 58–59, 249. Representative Richmond Pearson Hobson as cited in Burns, *The Spirits of America,* 179. In *Pressure Politics: The Story of the Anti-Saloon League,* Peter H. Odegard points out that the Anti-Saloon League propagandized the menace of the "drunken negro" to promote its cause. For example, in response to gin sold by Lee, Levy, and Company that was labeled with pictures of nude white women in seductive poses, *Colliers* wrote in its June 6, 1908, issue, "Is it plain now? The secret of many a lynching and burning in the South? The primitive negro field hand, a web of strong, sudden impulses, good and bad, comes to town or settlement on Saturday afternoon and pays his fifty cents for a pint of Mr. Levy's gin. He absorbs not only its toxic heat, but absorbs also the suggestion subtly conveyed that it contains aphrodisiacs. He sits in the road or in the alley at the height of debauch, looking at the obscene picture of a white woman on the label, drinking in the invitation it carries. And then comes . . . opportunity . . . Then follows the hideous episode of the rope or the stake" (page 62). Morone, *Hellfire Nation,* 299; Pegram, *Battling Demon Rum,* 126–28.

As the Eighteenth Amendment quickly passed through both the House of Representatives and the Senate in December 1917, Prohibition politics continued to play out in ways that were far from equitable for African Americans. Many African American spokespersons attributed the speed with which the amendment was finally approved to "moral" northern politicians who caved in to southern Democrats' ongoing efforts to disenfranchise blacks in return for getting a "thumbs up" on the Prohibition amendment. Shortly after passage of the Eighteenth Amendment by both the House and Senate, the *Chicago Defender* noted: "If that amendment should ultimately be ratified . . . it will be due to southern Democratic methods that have been adopted and enforced through the acquiescence if not approval of northern public sentiment to illegal and questionable methods that have been adopted and enforced by southern Democrats to suppress the Colored vote."[27] Prohibition legislation, designed to protect home and family, also justified Jim Crow segregation and supported the ongoing disenfranchisement of black Americans.

When Billy Sunday arrived in Chicago, momentum for Prohibition was building. The Eighteenth Amendment had successfully passed through the federal government and was now in the hands of the state legislatures for ratification. Mr. Sunday came to the city with impressive credentials for confronting and defeating the liquor interests. His past assaults on the saloon and his verbal lashings of the liquor interests had been highly successful in creating "dry" communities throughout the country. His revivals inspired anti-saloon activists nationwide and convinced them of Sunday's effectiveness in the Prohibition cause.

The effort to close Chicago saloons also coincided with Mayor "Big Bill" Thompson's need to satisfy his voting constituency and to fulfill, if even in a limited way, his campaign promise to promote civic decency. After his election in 1915, Sabbatarian and temperance advocates pushed Thompson to respect their position by closing the saloons on Sunday. Religious conservatives refused to back away from what they saw as taking the Lord's Day out of the hands of the saloonkeeper and giving it back to the nuclear family. By 1918, a variety of groups across the political spectrum had embraced this viewpoint. They too saw closing saloons on Sunday as a way to improve family life and to uplift urban America.[28] In Chicago, however, saloon closing

27. *Chicago Defender,* March 30, 1918.
28. Clark, *Deliver Us from Evil,* 93; "The Footprints of God in the Temperance

remained a particularly "hot-button" issue. Chicago's ethnic populations and her saloon-owning aldermen argued that saloons on Sunday were not immoral and that family togetherness could be just as warm in a community beer-garden as in the privacy of one's home. These proponents held to a "Continental Sunday," even though open saloons on Sunday directly violated Illinois state law.

By 1918, however, Prohibition activism was one of several factors that were at work against the saloon. First, Chicago's Vice Report firmly documented the alliance between saloons and the brothel. These findings badly tarnished the reputation as well as the political impact of saloon owners and operators. After the report's publication Carter Harrison II closed the Levee and ousted its residents. The forced exodus of prostitutes from the saloon made it much more difficult to attract customers and turn a profit. Second, saloons were local businesses, anchored in neighborhoods and highly dependent upon a local clientele for their business. In the first decades of the twentieth century, many of the saloons' original neighborhood patrons moved to suburbs where they no longer imbibed in saloons but indulged in the privacy of their own homes. These same suburbs oftentimes voted to keep their communities "dry" and free from associated vices such as gambling and prostitution. These votes made the creation of any new saloons in suburban settings highly unlikely. Third, a younger generation no longer held the same social attachment to the saloon as their fathers or grandfathers. Younger urbanites were drawn to new urban venues that took them away from the saloon and made it difficult to see the institution as the social center that it once was. Their exodus was helped by the car, which provided mobility and offered choices of entertainment and nightlife to young people within the expanding city. All of these factors challenged loyalties to the neighborhood saloon. As saloon patronage and profitability declined, the political effectiveness of its saloon-owner/aldermen was also significantly reduced. As a result, the now weakened aldermen were unable to override the "decent" Mayor Thompson who enforced state law and closed the saloons on the first Sunday of October 1915.[29]

Movement," *Christian Worker's Magazine,* August 1915, 747–50; Mark Haller, "Urban Vice and Civic Reform: Chicago in the Early Twentieth Century," in Kenneth T. Jackson and Stanley K. Sculz, eds., *Cities in American History,* 295; Alexis McGrossen, "Sabbatarianism: The Intersection of Church and State in the Orchestration of Everyday Life in Nineteenth-Century America," in David K. Adams and Cornelius A. van Minnen, eds., *Religious and Secular Reform in America: Ideas, Beliefs, and Social Change,* 133–58.

29. Haller, "Urban Vice and Civic Reform," 295. Clark, *Deliver Us from Evil,* notes that

For Chicago's "dry" forces, Sunday closings were not enough. They wanted to close all saloons permanently. In the vanguard of the city's Prohibition drive was the Dry Federation, headed by Philip Yarrow, a pastor of the Morgan Park Congregational Church. Yarrow described himself as a "simple minister, pledged to break down every pagan, immoral and obscene institution with which our world society is threatened." As superintendent of the federation, Yarrow consistently "plagued officials who were inclined to wink at the law which ordered saloons closed on Sundays." Yarrow's commitment also included Social Purity activism. He headed Social Purity's Illinois Vigilance Association, a position that he held until his death in 1954.[30]

The Prohibition and Social Purity causes stoked Chicago's moral flames, and the outbreak of World War I gave the anti-liquor forces even more fuel to close the saloon. Portraying indulgences in liquor and prostitution as unpatriotic and detrimental to the high ideals of the war allowed the Dry Federation and the Vigilance Association to win even more supporters to their causes. Under Yarrow's leadership, the Dry Federation appealed to moral Chicagoans who often held anti-German sentiments as well. After all, wasn't the United States at war with Germany and wasn't it Germans who drank all the beer? Prohibitionists argued that grain used by German breweries in the United States should be feeding the troops overseas and not fueling urban immorality.[31] Prohibition was a central topic in Billy Sunday's 1918 campaign. Just as J. Wilbur Chapman's Simultaneous Campaign had coincided with Social Purity's efforts to abolish prostitution, Billy Sunday stepped into the already polarized city assuming a militaristic front line against saloons. Supported by both the Woman's Christian Temperance Union and the Anti-Saloon League, Billy Sunday linked Chicago's saloon-closing crusade to his own revival-induced moral regime. It was no coincidence that the beginning of Sunday's Chicago revival on March 3, 1918, paralleled the start of yet another campaign for a "dry" Chicago. Banking on

---

by 1907 one hundred precincts in Chicago had closed their saloons (page 102). Asbury, *Gem of the Prairie*, 309–10; Duis, *Public Drinking in Chicago and Boston*, 288–93; Perry Duis, "The Saloon in Changing Chicago," 214–24.

30. *Chicago Sun*, August 4, 1946, Philip Yarrow clipping file.

31. Pegram, *Battling Demon Rum*, 144; Morone, *Hellfire Nation*, 307–13. George Lohman, the deputy city collector, predicted that Chicago's 6,053 saloons would be reduced to 5,000 after May 1. These closings were due to city council legislation prohibiting any alien or noncitizen to maintain a business within the city. *Union Signal*, April 25, 1918.

the fact that a Billy Sunday revival would raise anti-saloon sentiment, the Dry Federation initiated a citywide petition to place an anti-saloon referendum on Chicago's April 2, 1918, ballot, to be voted on four weeks into the Billy Sunday revival. The revival also coincided with the Prohibition Party's national convention that was held in Chicago in the second week of March.[32]

Against a backdrop of what promised to be a hard-fought referendum contest, Billy Sunday came to town. Like his revivalist predecessors Dwight L. Moody and J. Wilbur Chapman, Billy Sunday had strong ties to Chicago. Sunday's fame, however, came not through religion, but through the Chicago White Stockings, the city's professional baseball team. Sunday's skill and popularity on the ball field in the 1880s endeared him to many Chicagoans for whom baseball was becoming an urban obsession.[33] Sunday initiated his baseball career as a rookie in May 1883 when he was struck out four times by Boston Beaneaters' pitcher "Grasshopper" Jim Whitney. But in spite of an initial poor showing, Sunday went on to become a hard-driving, gutsy scrapper who set a White Stockings team record by stealing ninety-five bases in one season. Sunday also developed a reputation off the ball field as a heavy drinker, which was typical of many professional ballplayers. In 1886, Billy Sunday would certainly have qualified as one of Chicago's "restless" young men.

While in one of his drunken stupors, Sunday stumbled into a nightly outreach meeting at the Pacific Garden Mission. At the mission, the young ballplayer got religion, recounts Sunday biographer Elijah Brown. "The old gospel songs—the same his mother had sung in the little log cabin back in Iowa—caught at his (Sunday's) heart strings and set them vibrating in sympathy with memories of childhood days." Sunday eventually came back to the mission and met Sarah Clark, its head. Clark "talked to him like a mother, and with a wisdom given to her from above, led him to where he could see the light streaming from the cross." A godly woman brought Billy Sunday, like many other men of his generation, to Jesus.[34]

32. "Winners on the Athletic Field Have No Use for Booze, Says Billy Sunday," *Union Signal,* March 14, 1918; *Chicago Tribune,* March 3, 12, 1918.

33. Biographical data on Billy Sunday are found in McLoughlin, *Modern Revivalism,* 402–5; McLoughlin, *Billy Sunday Was His Real Name,* 1–7; Lyle W. Dorsett, *Billy Sunday and the Redemption of Urban America,* 5–60.

34. Roger A. Bruns, *Preacher Billy Sunday and Big-Time American Evangelism,* 40–44; Elijah P. Brown, *The Real Billy Sunday,* 38–39; Robert F. Martin, *Hero of the Heartland: Billy Sunday and the Transformation of American Society, 1862–1935,* 34.

Sunday was also deeply influenced by his wife, Helen Thompson, who was also a Chicago native. Helen Thompson Sunday was the daughter of William Thompson, the owner of a large dairy on the city's West Side. Her Scots-Presbyterian family background was very unlike her husband's orphaned and godless one. The Thompson family were longtime members of the Jefferson Park Presbyterian Church, Virginia and William Asher's home base. After his conversion at the Pacific Garden Mission, Billy Sunday joined the Jefferson Park Church, where he met Helen Thompson at a prayer meeting. After a three-year courtship (largely because of the elder Thompson's hesitation to allow his daughter to wed even a redeemed baseball player), Helen Thompson and Billy Sunday were married in 1888.[35]

Three years after his Christian conversion, Billy Sunday quit professional baseball to begin an evangelistic career with Chicago's YMCA. After two years of locating speakers for the noontime prayer meetings, fund-raising, and distributing tracts in local saloons, Sunday entered the revival arena as the advance man for J. Wilbur Chapman's Simultaneous Campaigns. In 1895 he struck out on his own and moved throughout the Midwest organizing revivals on what Sunday termed the "kerosene circuit," small towns without electricity.[36] Sunday's vaudevillian style and success at convincing individuals to "hit the trail" eventually led him to much larger urban venues.

Organized for Success

The 1918 revival reached a new level of corporate efficiency, an image reinforced in the spatial layout of the revival and its highly centralized format. Prior to the start of the revival, a large wood-frame tabernacle was constructed on the lakefront at the end of Chicago Avenue. The structure was located close to Chicago's public transportation, easily accessible from any of the Chicago streetcars via the Northwestern Elevated station. The tabernacle held

35. Billy Sunday and Virginia Asher met early in their careers when Virginia sang at the funeral of Helen Sunday's mother, presumably at the Jefferson Park Church. Later, because of the reputation of her work among factory women, Virginia Asher was offered a position on the Sunday staff. In addition, the Ashers and the Sundays each owned homes in Winona Lake, Indiana, where they resided when not on the revival circuit. Scrapbook 5, December 1913–February 1914, Billy Sunday Papers; William T. Ellis, *Billy Sunday, The Man and His Message*, 46–47.

36. Dorsett, *Billy Sunday*, 61–63.

The Sunday tabernacle was easily accessed via Chicago's public transportation. *Chicago Daily News,* Chicago Historical Museum.

fifteen thousand people and had numerous entrances and exits to enable crowds to move quickly in and out of the facility. A Billy Sunday Tabernacle zealously created liminal space in which to house its consensus-building rituals. The tabernacle was intentionally nonchurchlike in its design because, according to Sunday, churches "have fallen down on their job. . . . So far as the mass of people is concerned churches repel rather than attract." The tabernacle instead stood as a secular, populist symbol: "The big, bare, frame shack is borrowed directly from politics . . . there is nothing about any of it to suggest the church or any of its surroundings."[37] The tabernacle's political reference symbolizes revivalism's goals of endowing what was consciously constructed as political space with religious meaning and invigorating its Gospel with political relevance.

A subtle, but significant, difference existed between the Sunday revival and its predecessors. The churches, tents, and street corners of earlier revivals were replaced by one tabernacle that dominated Chicago's lake-

37. *Chicago Tribune,* February 17, March 3, 9, 1918.

front, and all activity was directed toward this center.[38] Although prayer meetings were held in homes throughout the city, the prayers were directed toward those who would attend tabernacle meetings. Very little of the revival was actually directed outward into the community; instead attention was drawn toward Mr. Sunday and his tabernacle. The Sunday organization also assumed direct authority over Protestant churches, requiring their financial support as well as a partial suspension of regular church activities to direct full attention toward the revival event. The weekly calendar of the Fourth Presbyterian Church, a denominational supporter, noted that "Next Sunday morning our regular eleven o'clock service will be combined with the Sunday Evangelistic Campaign at the Tabernacle."[39] Evangelizing in saloons and brothels, a central element of earlier revivals, was not part of the 1918 agenda; hence the entire format of the revival was more "respectable," as it separated itself from any reference to the brothel or saloon. Sunday replaced the more diffuse and inclusive "reaching out" into the community that had characterized earlier revivals with a highly structured "drawing into" the tabernacle, the locus of the revival's power.

Orchestrating a revival of this magnitude entailed significant planning and coordination. A Billy Sunday revival, observers noted, was "organized as efficiently as a large industry." Growing corporatism in the secular realm was mirrored in revival organization and a professional revival staff of "religious specialists." The revival staff was organized hierarchically with power emanating from the top. In describing the Chicago revival, the *Tribune* noted: "Accompanying Mr. Sunday were religious specialists, each of whom may be said to be the center of a campaign, although all directing their influence towards the big tabernacle of which Mr. Sunday is the central dynamic center."[40] In September 1916, two and a half years before the start of the revival, the Reverend James E. Walker, Billy Sunday's advance man, presented an outline of work to be completed in Chicago before the revival. The outline, drawn up by an executive committee that coordinated some fifteen areas of the revival, included finances, building, and transportation as well as specific areas of revival ministry such as prayer meetings, music, boys' and girls' work, personal workers, student work, and women's and

38. Ibid., March 18, 1918.
39. Martin, *Hero of the Heartland,* 50–53; Weekly Calendar, Fourth Presbyterian Church, March 3, 1918; McLoughlin, *Billy Sunday Was His Real Name,* 79.
40. *Chicago Tribune,* March 3, 10, 1918.

men's work. Each specific area was under the direction of a member of Billy Sunday's staff. Trumping the organizational savvy of both Dwight L. Moody and J. Wilbur Chapman, Billy Sunday's campaign was professionalized to the fullest. Sunday's "religious specialists" were employees, each paid a stipend on a campaign-by-campaign basis. In addition to travel and living expenses, most full-time revivalists earned between two and five thousand dollars for each major revival. The size of the staff fluctuated according to the size of the revival. Twenty "religious specialists" came to Chicago, making it one of the largest of Sunday's many urban campaigns.[41]

Sunday's revival machine garnered support from churches as well as civic organizations and corporations. Church support was vital, but the revival successfully mobilized other organizations toward the realization of revivalist goals. In the first days of the revival, the *Chicago Tribune* informed its readers: "Reservations to Be Made Only for Delegations Bearing Emblems," and delegations must "Wear a Badge to Get a Seat at Sunday's Talk." In response, fraternal organizations en masse, including the Masons, Odd Fellows, Elks, women's clubs, singing societies, and a variety of delegations from industries and department stores, filled the tabernacle nightly, creating the aura of a mass political rally. Revival organizers encouraged women who worked in downtown businesses to walk together to evening tabernacle meetings, thereby creating revival enthusiasm along with corporate loyalty. The *Chicago Tribune* noted, "Delegations' arrivals often create the greatest enthusiasm." Sunday appealed to the delegations themselves, replacing earlier references to individual attendees with allusions to their corporate identities. He endorsed products and encouraged America's consumption habits. Preaching to more than six thousand working women from a variety of Chicago industries, Billy Sunday intimated: "I have eaten Armour's and Swift's hams. Yes, and I have chewed Wrigley's gum, and I have purchased an electric toaster from Western Electric and house screens from Sears and Roebuck. I know you all."[42]

The tabernacle environment created liminal space where corporate values were honored and the spirit of capitalist competition prevailed. On March

41. Paper outlining plan of work presented September 13, 1916, by Rev. James E. Walker, Revival Files, Billy Sunday Papers. A comparison of salaries in the Buffalo, New York City, and Washington, D.C., campaigns, for example, shows a disparity of payments between the three events. Scrapbook 10, January 28, 1917, Billy Sunday Papers; McLoughlin, *Billy Sunday,* 109; *Chicago Tribune,* March 12, 1918.

42. *Chicago Tribune,* March 5, 27, 1918.

20, for example, eight thousand working women attended the tabernacle, a record-breaker that prompted Homer Rodeheaver, the revival's song leader, to initiate a singing contest between the workers from Carson, Pirie, Scott and Company and those from Marshall Field's. The corporate exuberance nurtured by a Sunday revival was particularly timely for Chicago's department-store owners. Downtown stores like Marshall Field or Carson, Pirie, Scott campaigned to make women's work in their stores appear less immoral and more uplifting. Surely a Billy Sunday revival with its parades of modestly dressed clerks would fit the bill. At other Sunday revivals large contingents of working women marched to the tabernacle with Bibles in hand. Some female workers entered the meeting place linked together with a daisy chain or carried banners that promoted their corporate logos.[43] Overall, revival attendance reinforced the positive good of corporations and their beneficial influence on employees.

A Billy Sunday revival also honored corporate loyalty by linking it to conversion, or "hitting the trail." Unlike earlier revivals where repentant sinners were separated out and privately encouraged to meditate on their sinful state, Billy Sunday called entire delegations to "hit the trail," meaning whole groups proceeded to the front of the tabernacle to shake the hand of the revivalist. Collective conversions, however, raised problems with fundamentalism's mandate for personal salvation. In response to this concern, the media were obligated to delineate between the two types of "trail-hitters": those who went to the front of the tabernacle to express the group's unified support of Billy Sunday, and the truly penitent.[44] In the actual enactment of the conversion ritual, however, it was difficult to delineate the real penitents from those who merely wanted to bask in Sunday's celebrity status.

Underlying the spectacular elements of the revival—the preacher, the crowds, the lights, the enthusiasm—were closely monitored control mechanisms that mirrored corporate organization. Marches, banners, songs, and daisy chains all served as tools to regiment participants and regulate the revival event. The order so evident in the Sunday revival was the logical outcome of Third Awakening revivals that from the beginning had been committed to making religion accessible and modern. The efficiency of the 1918

43. Ibid., March 20, 1918; Susan Porter Benson, *Counter Cultures: Saleswomen, Managers, and Customers in American Department Stores, 1890–1940*, 134–39; Brown, *The Real Billy Sunday*, 150–51.
44. *Chicago Tribune*, March 23, 1918.

The lights, music, and spectacle of the tabernacle. *Chicago Daily News*, Chicago Historical Museum,

revival was evident even before the revival started. Tabernacle preparedness included practice drills for ushers and a list of rules for the large choir. Female choristers were instructed: "Don't knit, don't giggle, don't flirt, don't get easily peeved. Be on time. Be regular." Within the meetings themselves, all distractions were strictly controlled. Women were told not to wear hats, and they were rebuked for fanning themselves if the tabernacle became too warm. Such activities were considered "putting on airs" and therefore inappropriate. Emotional outbursts from the crowd were either shouted down by Mr. Sunday himself or instigators were quickly removed from the tabernacle. On March 19, "the police were instructed to prevent crowding at the doors by keeping open a line through which holders of special tickets can pass."[45]

45. Ibid., March 3, 19, 1918; McLoughlin, *Billy Sunday Was His Real Name,* 127; February 15, 1915 (Buffalo), Scrapbook 6, Billy Sunday Papers.

In many cases it would appear that the 1918 revival's adaptation to corporate culture and its cultivation of controlled theatrics overwhelmed its
religion. Style was an important part of a Billy Sunday revival as the spectacular elements of the revival surpassed earlier revivalism's ability to engage
and entertain. Sunday's image, like that of a celebrated "movie star," dominated the revival. The revivalist unabashedly met and mingled with the
wealthy and famous, making no secret of his widespread support from the
nation's leading industrialists and entertainment personalities, and using
their successful images to enhance his own. The tabernacle spectacle—the
arrival of large delegations striding to their seats, music, and the theatrics of
Sunday himself—provided a thrill not unlike amusement parks, theater, or
the moving pictures that were becoming all the rage. Like Dwight L.
Moody's effort to compete with the attractions of the 1893 World's Fair,
Billy Sunday adapted the techniques of commercial entertainment to pitch

Regimenting revival rituals and crowds ensured a modern, well-run event.

religion. For example, in an obviously ironic twist on his Prohibitionist stance, Sunday endorsed a "Billy Sunday cocktail" made of cracked ice and water. The *Chicago Tribune* played along and extensively instructed its readers on the proper etiquette for drinking the "cocktail." After "quaffing the cocktail, pay the man, and walk out singing: 'Lips That Touch Liquor Shall Never Touch Mine,'" the paper read.[46] Such antics created a media bonanza. Sunday's style and symbiotic relationship with the newspaper media created a "modern" commercial phenomenon that was only enhanced by widespread advertising.

Billy Sunday's hold on the media, however, was paralleled by the media's use of Mr. Sunday. Newspapers quickly seized the revival's potential for

46. *Chicago Tribune,* March 3, 12, 1918.

their own profits and headlined the spectacular to raise their readership. The *Chicago Tribune* provided all-encompassing coverage of the revival, heralding the arrival of the Sunday staff in the city as well as daily news about revival staff and tabernacle activities. Newspapers also printed full-text accounts of Sunday's tabernacle sermons as well as pithy, prepackaged phrases—"Billy Sunday Epigrams"—that were excerpted from earlier sermons and reappeared in various urban newspapers. Such headlines as BILLY WRESTLES DEVIL—LANDING ON ALL FOURS provided interesting print and were used by the dailies to promote sales and circulation. Throughout the revival, advertisements in the *Tribune* featured a full-page picture of the revivalist with headlines, "Billy Sunday's Daily Message in Your Home—Through the Chicago Tribune." These advertisements were inevitably underscored with subscription coupons.[47]

The Man and His Message

Sunday's past career as a professional baseball player primed his audiences for his masculinized tabernacle performances, and his ritualized athleticism reinforced America's national craze for male fitness; Sunday's revival performance strengthened the essential relationship between being a man and being a Christian. In one of his "Epigrams," Sunday insisted that Old Testament patriarchs, for example, be remembered primarily for their manliness. "David didn't want Solomon to be an ol' woman or a sissy," Sunday said. "He wanted him to be a man with knotted muscles, and gray matter, and gasoline and sparker working right. David had vim, vigor, pepperino, and tobasco sauce in his blood instead of pink tea and ice water. Solomon knew what his father meant when he said, 'Son, be a man.'" "Nobody," Billy Sunday said, "can read the Bible thoughtfully and not be impressed with the way it upholds the manhood of man." His sermons used much of the same rhetoric of earlier revivals, but he modernized Protestantism's earlier ideal of Christian manhood to make it even more compatible with consumer-oriented capitalism. "It Takes a Real Man to Be a Christian," one headline read.[48]

47. Ibid., March 24, 1918.
48. *South Bend Tribune,* June 16, 1913, Press Clippings, Billy Sunday Papers. Similar epigrams were found in other newspapers that supported Sunday's revivals. *Baltimore News,* April 12, 1916, Press Clippings, Billy Sunday Papers.

Not unlike his revival predecessors, Sunday's model of male morality was defined by self-control. "When the Chickens Come Home to Roost," Sunday's sermon preached to men only, warned men against their "loose proclivities." The revivalist also "hammered away at matrimonial infidelity, all sexual immorality, drunkenness, profanity, bad treatment of wives and children, and cheating in business and irreligion." Sunday, however, reconfigured these somewhat outdated ideals based on a man's self-control and delayed gratification, into a new form of masculine restraint evidenced by virility and its compatibility with corporatism. In earlier Third Awakening revivals, man's potential for immorality was balanced or reined in by woman's moral influence, but Billy Sunday urged his male listeners to take control of their own lives. This was morality achieved by those who were "man enough" to seize the right. Sunday's diatribes on manly control also reinforced the superiority of white men over others, namely, foreign immigrants and blacks, who were disparaged precisely because they were perceived by whites to lack any control over self.[49] Billy Sunday's Gospel tipped the moral scales toward masculinity and put moral advantage in the white man's court. According to Billy Sunday, men's own volition and strength would bring them to Christ; the responsibility for that moral balance now tipped toward men.

Billy Sunday's success was attributed to his manly attributes. The revivalist's well-publicized history as a professional baseball player as well as his physical mannerisms and vernacular style marked a surge in masculinity that valued the competitive and successful qualities of men.[50] Sunday's willingness to "fight" with the devil and "wrestle" with sin also counteracted the more feminine appeal that had characterized much of the Third Awakening. In one evening sermon entitled "Carry a Punch for Religion," Sunday directly attacked this feminine version of the Gospel. He preached: "Of course, there are some church members that won't come to the meeting. They don't want to have the smell of brimstone and hell fire as it vomits from the inferno below. They want the deodorized, disinfected sermons of the tabloid sister, they want the sermons about the birds that sing in the woods and the flowers that bloom in the spring, tra-la."[51]

49. *New York Sun*, April 30, 1917, Scrapbook 13, Billy Sunday Papers; Martin, *Hero of the Heartland*, 86–92; Morone, *Hellfire Nation*, 304.

50. Clifford Putney, *Muscular Christianity: Manhood and Sports in Protestant America, 1880–1920*, 59–60; Filene, *Him/Her/Self*, 94–101; Martin, *Hero of the Heartland*, 81–94.

51. *Chicago Tribune*, March 22, 1918.

"Billy" Sunday in Chicago

By S. A. Woodruff

"Billy" Sunday

Homer A. Rodeheaver
Members of the Sunday Party

Mrs. William A. Sunday

Miss Alice Miriam Gamlin

Miss Grace Saxe
Members of the Sunday Party

Mrs. William Asher

Billy Sunday in Chicago. The makeup of the Sunday staff reflects the professionalization of revivalism and women's key roles. *Christian Worker's Magazine*, May 1918.

Sunday's masculine presence plus the revival's centralization marked a significant evolution within this Third Awakening period. Revivals that emphasized the evils of masculinity and the saving power of domesticity were replaced by Sunday's promotion of masculine virtues and man's ability to use these virtues to transform society.

The virtue of masculinity was further touted by the revival's alliance with the Prohibition movement. Shortly after arriving in Chicago, Billy Sunday mounted the anti-saloon rampart. Speaking in Evanston's Patten Gymnasium under the auspices of the Young Woman's Christian Temperance Union, Sunday reiterated his opposition to breweries and liquor consumption. "Booze is the one big devil I have fought all my life, and just now when he's groggy, it's a cinch I'm not going to quit hitting. . . . Horse racing, gambling, segregated vice are all gone, and now the grand-dad of all the crookedness in the world is going to take a knock-out." Certainly Billy Sunday's description of the "liquor crowd" managed to compact most urban evils into saloon space: "every black-legged gambler, every brewer of the state, every saloon keeper, every Madam of the red-light, every gunman, every good for nothing God forsaken hobo, riff-raff, plug-ugly rag-shap and bobtail of society that feeds and fattens and gormandizes on the virtues, the manhood, and womanhood of others." Under Billy Sunday's skilled rhetoric, Prohibition mobilized all sober, God-fearing women and men against society's immoral threat.[52]

Sunday's Prohibition stance also brought widespread denominational support to the revival. Defeating the saloon, along with its other vices, enabled Protestant churches to assert their moral voice in society. Dean Pond, the superintendent of the Episcopal City Mission Work, supported the revival because "there are 5,987 saloons in operation in our city limits today," along with "283 liquor-selling dance halls, 167 vicious poolrooms, and only 1,424 churches." The end result was "precisely 169,500 men, women, and children in some five penal institutions in the last three years." Pond argued, "The liquor business or the lust business seems to be the chief factor in the downfall of our people."[53] Standing alongside the Billy Sunday revival was indistinguishable from backing a "dry" Chicago. Like many Protestant churches, Chicago's Fourth Presbyterian not only combined its own Sunday service with the tabernacle meeting but also enlisted its congregants in the voter registration drive for the upcoming referendum. The church calendar reminded its members, "it is the duty of every one who is interested in the welfare of our city to be registered in view of the coming Dry campaign." Support was particularly strong in the suburbs. In Oak Park collections were taken up for the campaign, and a number of suburban churches organized groups of "dry" speakers to tour the city. Speakers from the Austin Christian Church, Willard Methodist Episcopal, Grace Episcopal, and Third Congregational churches participated in the speaker program. After this specific campaign, the recruited speakers continued to work for the Anti-Saloon League.[54]

52. Ibid., March 3, 13, 1918; *Union Signal,* March 14, 1918; Morone, *Hellfire Nation,* 305.

53. *Chicago Tribune,* March 14, 1918.

54. Calendar, March 3, 12, 1918, Fourth Presbyterian Church; *Chicago Tribune,* March 3, 1918.

Mayor "Big Bill" Thompson also tried to gain some political capital from the revival and from the upcoming anti-saloon vote. The Reverend J. P. Brushingham, speaking for the mayor at the tabernacle's inauguration, voiced Thompson's "sympathy" for the revival meetings and could not resist some politicking: "Mayor Thompson came over to the side of the churches when he enforced the Sunday closing laws. He signed the dry petition to give the people a chance to express themselves at the polls, and I want to say that if the dry cause is successful at the polls, Mayor Thompson will close the saloons seven days a week."[55]

On March 12, voter registration for the April ballot was held throughout the city. Buoyed by revival enthusiasm, eighteen thousand volunteers from the Dry Federation canvassed the city, enlisting nonregistered dry voters. At the tabernacle's next evening meeting, Sunday urged the Prohibition forces onward and linked Chicago "wets" to America's wartime enemy: "In my opinion, the whiskey gang is scared stiff. They're afraid to let the people vote on prohibition. But they're making their last stand. Thank God the world is to be rid of two damnations—Prussian militarism and the saloon." Sunday's vernacular verdicts against the liquor interests allied the Prohibition cause with the manly virtue of self-controlled abstinence, and at the same time identified the "liquor crowd" with an alien, threatening force. Chicago "wets," however, were not to be outdone. "Wets" fought back and challenged Sunday's sincerity; they argued that he made "veiled attacks among the labor unions." Their opposition prompted Sunday's vehement response: "it is being done by the filthy skunks of the liquor business," he declared, "and they'll find themselves holding the hot end of the poker—damn their dirty hides."[56] Sunday's opposition to liquor also took on a spiritual veneer; consumption and distribution of drink now warranted eternal punishment.

Despite the curses of Billy Sunday and Prohibition's best effort, on March 20 Chicago's Board of Election Commissioners ruled that the "dry" petition had fallen some seven thousand names short. This pronouncement, which threatened to sink the entire "dry" campaign, prompted a gathering of moral forces across the color line. Philip Yarrow, head of Chicago's Dry Federation, called for "the burial of all differences and to demand that all out forces for right get together. We would have even the Chinaman to help

55. *Chicago Tribune,* March 4, 1918.
56. Ibid., March 8, 12, 13, 1918.

Billy Sunday and Helen Thompson Sunday. The Sundays demonstrated a companionate marriage model. *Chicago Daily News,* Chicago Historical Museum.

us in this fight, for it is votes we need. On the question of cleaning up Chicago and driving the saloon from our beloved city, we welcome even the Roman Catholic and the Jew who will help us to drive this vampire out."[57]

57. Ibid., March 9, 1918. It is ironic that twenty thousand names were dropped from the petition because female voters failed to sign the "dry" petition with the same names as legally registered voters. The *Chicago Tribune* noted that "Mrs. John Smith" would not be counted as a legal signature when the woman was registered to vote as Mrs. Susie Smith. The strongest supporters for a "dry" Chicago were essentially kept away from the polls. *Broad Ax,* Chicago, March 23, 1918.

On March 23 Chicago ministers (black and white) met with the Dry Federation "to formulate plans for harmonious co-operation in the campaign to make Chicago dry." African American ministers responded in kind. One black pastor, the Reverend L. N. Daniels, said: "a great moral issue is at stake; that the race is drinking entirely too much for its good, and that it behooves us as leaders to get together and fight against this iniquitous traffic." The moral enthusiasm shared by blacks and whites against liquor, however, did little to put the "dry" petition on the ballot. Even accusations that the election commissioners were a "stuffed court" had no avail. The majority of Chicago voters paid little attention to the "dry" protests, and the Prohibition proposition did not move forward to the ballot. Even this setback did not deter the anti-saloon forces. Five days after the commission's ruling, the tabernacle filled with saloon opponents, both black and white, who came to hear William Jennings Bryan speak on behalf of the Dry Federation. Citing the failure of the anti-saloon petition, Bryan again attacked the "liquor crowd" and their corrupt tactics.[58]

Revivalism's anti-liquor fervor reveals that in terms of race, Prohibition was a double-edged sword. Drawn together by a common interest to raise the lower classes of both racial groups to a higher moral standard, Billy Sunday's anti-saloon goal united middle-class blacks and whites in its mission. In this sense, revivalism's moral mantel intended to overcome or obscure racial differences. But as we have seen, revivalism's call for abstinence was strongly identified with a domestic morality defined by female piety and virtuous manhood, and its respectability quotient was also inextricably tied to whiteness. In Billy Sunday's revival "respectability" continued to be white. Manhood may have taken control of its own passions, but man's power derived not only from his manliness but also from his whiteness.

True masculinity entailed not only taking control of one's own life, but also asserting one's manhood over those considered outside the realm of civilization.[59] While the middle-class appeal of revivalism's anti-liquor agenda united blacks and whites, Prohibition's moral justification still assumed and promoted white racial supremacy. Even though Sunday's anti-liquor ideal attracted middle-class blacks, the implicit message of Prohibition was

58. *Chicago Tribune,* March 23, 1918; *Union Signal,* March 28, 1918; John D. Buenker, "The Illinois Legislature and Prohibition, 1907–1919," 363–84.

59. Bederman, *Manliness and Civilization,* 84, 235. Bederman argues that in their popular usage the terms "civilization" and "the white man" were almost interchangeable.

that foreigners and blacks were inferior to whites. The 1918 model of the "in-control" male walked lockstep with the rationale for white male superiority and did little to challenge the color line. Revivalism's emotionally charged rhetoric against liquor critiqued the moral status of all persons who drank, but further tainted the character of blacks in general and raised the sexual threat of black men toward white women in particular. Prohibition arguments pounded one more nail in the coffin of black respectability and allowed whites to discriminate against lower-class blacks in the name of morality. Understanding this, one is not surprised to learn that the Ku Klux Klan was a willing supporter of the Anti-Saloon League.[60]

Women for Christ

Women held visible positions of leadership in the Billy Sunday organization. As in earlier revivals, the Sunday campaign drew in Chicago's own Protestant women to organize and implement the revival. Shortly after the revival started, the *Tribune* reported that "women seemed to predominate, women mostly of middle age and older." In the early stages of the revival a Women's Advisory Committee was formed, which included the religious and extension secretaries of the Y.W.C.A. and a representative from six of Chicago's leading denominations. In Chicago, Mrs. Thomas R. Lyons was the general chairman of the Women's Work, Mrs. C. E. Vickers headed the central division, and Mrs. George W. Dickson was in charge of the extension committee.[61] In addition to these Chicago women, the female "specialists" on Sunday's staff assumed highly visible positions. Along with Helen Thompson Sunday, the 1918 revival headlined three women who were long-term leaders in the Third Awakening: Frances Miller, Virginia Asher, and Grace Saxe. By 1918, these well-trained professionals had become full-time veterans of the revival circuit.

Virginia Asher joined the Billy Sunday staff shortly after her work with the Simultaneous Campaign. Although she remained married to Bill Asher, her evangelist husband, Virginia Asher established her own independent revival career, which left little if any time for home matters. The Ashers, in

60. Burns, *The Spirits of America*, 178; Morone, *Hellfire Nation*, 337–38; Kathleen M. Blee, *Women of the Klan: Racism and Gender in the 1920s*, 45, 104.
    61. *Chicago Tribune*, February 20, March 11, 1918.

fact, did not live together, which allowed Bill Asher to preach on his own and his wife to do likewise. When questioned about this incongruous marriage arrangement, particularly for domestically oriented fundamentalists, Virginia Asher explained: "Mr. Asher and myself have always worked together until I joined the Sunday party. His field is not so wide as that of Mr. Sunday and he felt that perhaps I could do more good in this work than with him. My husband and myself are on friendly terms, though we do live apart."[62] William Asher led smaller revivals throughout the Midwest while his wife became a revival persona. Virginia Asher headed the Sunday campaign's extensive work with businesswomen and created a nationwide network of Virginia Asher Business Woman's Bible Councils. The councils were initiated within the revival organization in specific cities but continued to meet after the revivals' end. In Chicago, the Business Woman's Councils, in conjunction with the YWCA, rented rooms in Chicago's business district. The rented rooms, which held four hundred women, were used twice a week for lunch, and were also open on Thursday nights. Through the Business Woman's Councils, Asher became a celebrity in her own right. She also regularly sang in tabernacle performances. Asher went from singing to prostitutes at the Everleigh House to performing featured duets with Homer Rodeheaver, Billy Sunday's music director. Eventually Virginia Asher took advantage of the emerging music industry and recorded a number of her revival songs, including the "Old Rugged Cross" and "Tell Me the Story of Jesus."[63]

Grace Saxe was the revival's director of Bible studies. Before working with the Billy Sunday campaigns, Saxe trained at the Moody Bible Institute and traveled with the revivalist R. A. Torrey teaching Bible study methods to women and men. Billy Sunday referred to Saxe as "the greatest Bible teacher in America." Strongly influenced by the work of Grace Saxe, Frances Miller also organized Bible studies after revival meetings, "instructing how to diagnose the sinner's heart and apply the specific Scripture remedy with chapter and verse." By 1918 Miller had worked with Billy Sunday for twelve years. In Chicago, in an updated and much more consolidated version of Moody's home visitation program, Grace Saxe organized and taught a home Bible

62. *Post Standard* (Syracuse, N.Y.), November 5, 1915, Scrapbook 6, Billy Sunday Papers.
63. Sanders, *The Council Torchbearer;* Thekla E. Caldwell, "Virginia Healey Asher," in Schultz and Hast, eds., *Women Building Chicago,* 48–50.

study program that was initiated during the Chicago revival. Virginia Asher was responsible for organizing the "extension work" for women who worked in industries away from the downtown, while Francis Miller organized downtown clerical workers and department-store clerks. In addition to Asher, Saxe, and Miller, Jean LaMont worked as the assistant director of Bible studies, Florence Kinney directed the student work, and Alice Miriam Gamlin organized the outreach to boys and girls.[64]

Over and above these professional female revivalists loomed the highly visible Helen Thompson Sunday, typically referred to as "Ma." Helen Sunday lived the contradiction inherent within revivalism's moral regime. She propagated woman's submissive and spiritualized role, while her praxis undermined and challenged that acquiescence. It was widely acknowledged that Helen Sunday was the business manager of the Sunday campaign. She was also the "common sense member of the marriage," the "boss" who not only orchestrated Billy Sunday's life but organized his revivals as well. According to William Ellis, a Sunday biographer, "She it is who holds her generous careless husband down to practicalities of life. . . . He makes no important decisions without consulting her, and she travels with him nearly all the time, attending his meetings and watching over his work and his personal well being like a mother." The media frequently noted Helen Sunday's organizational capabilities. "It is Ma who puts the final O.K. on engagements," one newspaper noted.[65]

Despite her exceptional capabilities as an administrator and her ability to work in the public arena, Helen Sunday presented herself within the domestic paradigm. Like her husband, Helen Thompson Sunday was also media-savvy and her role in the campaign provided a symbolic domestic balance to her husband. Her nickname "Ma" connoted homey and rural roots, even though Mrs. Sunday was the product of urban Chicago. Likewise, her dress and activities were orchestrated to evoke the domestic and maternal. Newspapers frequently noted her gingham dress or her knitting of caps and wristlets for the soldiers fighting on the Western Front. These representations were designed to symbolize woman's "true" domestic

64. "Billy Sunday Extra," *New York American,* 1917, Scrapbook 12; Billy Sunday Campaign Souvenir (Spokane, Washington), 1909, Revival Files, Billy Sunday Papers; *Chicago Tribune,* March 10, 1918.

65. Martin, *Hero of the Heartland,* 54; Ellis, *Billy Sunday, The Man and His Message,* 47; *YWCA Bulletin,* May 6, 1917, New York Campaign, Revival Files, Billy Sunday Papers.

inclination even though the Sundays were national celebrities. Despite her constant travels on the revival circuit, Helen Sunday was portrayed as the nurturer of spiritualized domesticity wherever she went. One New York newspaper noted: "Ma Sunday helps to maintain a religious atmosphere about her own hearthstone, be it the Indiana hearthstone or a temporary one set up far away."[66]

As a couple, Helen and Billy Sunday symbolized a thoroughly modern companionate marriage. Newspapers often photographed the two together and revival publicity also gave them an opportunity to provide marital advice, frequently headlined as "How to Be Happy, Married Rules of Ma and Pa Sunday." Billy Sunday represented on the male side of the equation what Margaret Marsh has described as "masculine domesticity," a gender construct that was facilitated by the growing economic security of many middle-class men as well as their realization of the importance of a supportive marriage relationship. Sunday advised husbands to treat their wives well: "If you want your wife to act like an angel, treat her like one—not like the devil," was his common admonition. Helen Sunday was also an integral part of the companionate model. She instructed wives to keep themselves physically attractive. "The girl who can look attractive in a hammock in the moonlight will get a man, but it is the girl who can look attractive across a breakfast table in the morning, who will keep him," she wrote. For Helen and Billy Sunday, however, the companionate ideal did not mean relational equality. While the powerful Helen Sunday continually displayed her acquiescence, her husband Billy epitomized the modern and thoroughly masculine male. In many ways, however, the revivalist's behavior was that of an adolescent, incapable of fending for himself or caring for even his basic needs apart from a devoted woman. Throughout the Chicago revival, Helen Sunday incessantly fended the press away from her husband. She also ensured that her husband was properly attired in warm clothes to prevent chilling, and even dictated when he should go to bed.[67] Under his wife's hand, the aggressive and highly volatile Billy Sunday became a docile

66. "Billy Sunday Extra," *New York American,* 1917, Billy Sunday Papers.

67. *Los Angeles Times,* September 9, 1917, Scrapbook 15, Billy Sunday Papers; Margaret Marsh, "Suburban Men and Masculine Domesticity, 1870–1915," 165–86; *Chicago Tribune,* March 14, 1918; May, *Great Expectations,* 64–66; Lois W. Banner, *American Beauty,* 202–25; Ma Sunday's column, October 15, 1917, Billy Sunday Papers. "Putting Billy to Bed" was a lengthy article in the *Tribune* that described the highly adolescent maneuverings of Sunday to avoid Ma's attempts to get him to sleep. *Chicago Tribune,* March 12, 1918.

Helen and Billy Sunday "at work" at a wringer washer. *Chicago Daily News*, Chicago Historical Museum.

and sheepish child, incapable of making even the most mundane decisions. Despite her acquiescent pose, Helen Sunday ruled her husband's life and held off the public world in order to protect him.

Helen Sunday's position in the revival, like that of the other female members of the Sunday staff, was an influential one, but it was power growing out of a symbolic effacement of her capabilities. Her publicized importance was less about her administrative or organizational skills than her ability to take care of, or at times cleverly manipulate, her husband. Her position, in effect, represented a denial of female capability and independence in the

Helen and Billy Sunday examine a well-stocked pantry. Such domestic portrayals balanced Mr. Sunday's virility.

name of taking care of Billy. Like Helen Sunday, other female evangelists such as Virginia Asher, Grace Saxe, Frances Miller mirrored the increased participation of women in public life. These were not sheltered women; rather, like Billy Sunday himself, they became evangelist-celebrities who organized, sang, lectured, and traveled. The possible contradictions raised by revivalist women participating in the public arena were subsumed and shrouded within revivalism's mandate to save souls. Like their earlier revival sisters, these women wrapped themselves in domestic piety while they pursued modern and highly public careers. Revivalism allowed its evangelists to reach a certain level of celebrity while at the same time it publicly scrutinized, and in most instances condemned, female autonomy.

By 1918, women's integration into the workplace, politics, and public society had so disrupted the domestic balance that revivalists could neither rhetorically nor ritually celebrate women as the spiritual center of family life. They began to focus instead upon woman's proclivity for evil and the need for male control. Whereas past revivals had touted the virtuous woman as a means of ameliorating male sin and facilitating man's salvation, the 1918 revival called females to task for their failure to uphold their spiritual mandates. Revival narratives increasingly questioned woman's virtue and her ability to influence her husband, family, and society in the right direction.

The Feminization of Sin

For the middle class, divorce and fertility decline signaled a woman's strong challenge to the domestic balance that was so integrally tied to revivalism's moral ideal. Middle-class concerns, exacerbated by more women in the workforce and their seemingly unfettered desire for sex, caused many to reference what they perceived as a "revolution in morals." Revivalism's moral regime increasingly tipped toward men, as women became more and more visible in the public sphere. In Chicago, the social anxieties expressed by the Vice Commission were quickly redirected toward what seemed to many, revivalists and reformers alike, to be an overall decline in public morality. Throughout the nation and in Chicago, middle-class reformers turned their attention away from the issue of segregated vice and instead looked toward the corruptive influence of popular amusements such as vaudeville and the nickelodeon.[68]

Refocusing this concern was partly rooted in the anti-prostitution campaign itself; reformers who had routed out vice saw public entertainment sites as places that harbored prostitutes and pimps. After shuttering the Levee, reformers began to focus on what they perceived as the equally ominous threat of popular culture to traditional gender and status roles. Cultural historian Lauren Rabinovitz argues that newer forms of entertainment, like the nickel theater, offered an "alternative culture" to immigrant and working-class women who had been excluded from the dominant forms

68. "The Amusement Question," *Northwestern Christian Advocate,* June 24, 1914, 804–5; "Cards, Theater and Dancing, Considered from the Viewpoint of the New Testament," *Christian Worker's Magazine,* May 1915, 548–53; "Morals of the Picture Show: A Discussion of This Popular and Growing Amusement from the Bible's Standpoint," *Christian Worker's Magazine,* October 1915, 88–90.

of public culture and was one of the ways that working-class immigrant women entered and reorganized urban space.[69] So while revivalist women like Virginia Asher and Frances Miller intervened in public culture through moral activism, their more secular sisters pursued other venues for entry. Just as revivals created an alternative, albeit a "moral," space, popular amusements created a place for women outside the home and church, a public arena where, in the absence of traditional gender boundaries, female sexuality was recognized and women were permitted to socialize with men. Vaudeville shows, the nickelodeon, "thrill" rides, or social dancing all offered public arenas of spectacle and sensual enticement.

Many in Chicago's middle class deemed these amusements as less than "respectable," and fundamentalists judged them downright sinful. Because these amusements took women away from domestic control and facilitated the creation of an "alternative culture," they were suspect. To revivalists, woman's apparent eagerness to leave domesticity, the source of her moral strength, and to knowingly venture into public spaces without even looking back raised troubling doubts about her moral authority. As revivalists questioned the onslaught of popular culture and its seemingly negative impact on woman's sexual purity, banking on a virtuous manhood seemed a much stronger bet.

Unlike earlier revivals' sympathetic outreach to the "innocent" working girl, the 1918 revival cast women as independent agents who, in their pursuit of public amusements, cast off domestic restraint and were out of control. The revival obsessed about the possible temptations for working women and intervened with an organizational machine designed to corral working girls, now referred to as "businesswomen." The Sunday campaign divided Chicago's working women into two groups; the Central Division, for women who worked in the downtown or Loop district, and the Extension Division, which included women employed in industries outside the central area.[70]

Throughout the ten-week revival, the Central Division held noon meetings in the Loop three days a week in the former A. G. Spalding and Brothers sporting-goods store whose use had been donated by Carson, Pirie, Scott and Company. Women attending these meetings purchased a ten-cent lunch on the first floor and then moved to the second floor for a "continuous

69. Rabinovitz, *For the Love of Pleasure*, 10, 117–18.
70. *Chicago Tribune*, March 19, 1918.

inspirational Bible talk," delivered by either Frances Miller or Virginia Asher.[71] Businesswomen from areas outside the Loop usually met at the Fourth Presbyterian Church, whose congregation and pastor, John Timothy Stone, were active revival supporters. After dinner at the church, business-women attended the evening revival meeting en masse.

As revivalists engaged with businesswomen, their earlier rhetoric shifted from sympathy for working women toward an attitude now tainted with suspicions about their immoral behavior. In a series of syndicated articles entitled *Ma Sunday Speaks,* Helen Sunday insistently raised questions about female morality. These narratives, which were published in various news-papers across the country, reflected the increasing distrust with which revivalists and their fundamentalist supporters came to view women. The topics of *Ma Sunday Speaks*—"Vanity," "The Girl Who Paid the Price of Folly," "The Woman Who Believed in Birth Control," "The Girl Who Went Joy Riding Too Often," "The Girl Who Was Dance Mad," "The Girl Who Gave Her Life to Dogs," or "The Girl Who Wanted to See Life," make clear that these articles are object lessons in a woman's potential for immoral choices.[72]

In one account, Helen Sunday delineates women's options. The article "Mazie's Wonderful Silk Stockings" tells the story of a young and innocent stenographer, Mazie, who purchases a pair of silk stockings and hides them from her mother. After dressing up, Mazie goes out on the street and "notices men admiring her legs." The young woman is then offered a ride in a chauffeured automobile. "For one wild moment Mazie hesitates. What a combination of luxuries—motor ride and first pair of silk stockings." The article includes some rather obvious references to the minefield of tempta-tions Mazie faces, temptations that revivalists viewed as siren songs aimed at women: too much economic independence (at least enough to buy lux-ury items like stockings), betrayal of maternal intimacy (hiding the stock-ings from her mother), an awareness of her own body (her legs), her potential sex appeal (the male gaze), the lure of technology (automobile), and a man's sexual advance (the offered ride). As Mazie takes a fatal step

71. Ibid., March 17, 1918; "Outline of the Plan of Work under the Leadership of Rev. William Sunday," presented by James E. Walker, September 13, 1916, Revival Files, Billy Sunday Papers.
72. Ma Sunday's column, September 28, 1917; February 27, 1918; *Women of America,* Billy Sunday Papers.

toward the automobile, however, she sees a run in her silk hosiery and quickly turns from the car. "Just as the stitch had given way in her cheap stockings and the ruinous 'run' had started," Helen Sunday concludes, "she knew now with an illuminating clearness that an equally ruinous 'run' would have started in her life had she heeded the voice of the tempter and accepted the automobile invitation. Something told her she had been saved just on the brink." The message of Mazie's story was that women were poised at the edge of the slippery slope of immorality. "Mazie" may have made the right decision, but other "Mazies" in the workforce needed to be channeled toward moral ends and inspired toward domestic virtue.[73]

Revivalism's historic alliance with the Social Purity, now Social Hygiene, movement explains part of the shift in revivalist rhetoric. Initially, Social Purity sympathized with society's "fallen sister" and deplored the illicit activities of bad men. By 1918, however, revivalist concerns mirrored the Social Hygiene movement's response to World War I. In particular, the Hygiene movement dedicated itself not to protecting women, but to shielding America's fighting men from the danger of sexually transmitted diseases.

Initially, World War I had been a highly unpopular war with the American people. Once the country entered the conflagration, however, it was imperative to convince the American people that this was a war worth fighting. In order to sway public opinion and to fill recruitment rosters, the government and draft boards couched their appeals in the rhetoric of a patriotic masculinity dedicated to the national interest. According to recruiters, when a man enlisted in the American Expeditionary Force he not only proved his own masculinity but also redeemed manhood from the effeminizing effects of modern culture. The male quandary of "how to be a man" could be indisputably resolved through his courageous and honorable wartime commitment. In a Social Hygiene pamphlet entitled "Live Straight if You Would Shoot Straight," Josephus Daniels, U.S. secretary of the Navy, summarized the war's purifying potential for the state, the home, and the soldier:

> We stand for a democracy which, while recognizing man's inherent right to self-government, insists that the right carries with it obligations to the State, most sacred in character. These obligations require

---

73. Ma Sunday Speaks, Atlanta, October 27, 1917, Scrapbook 16, Billy Sunday Papers; Meyerowitz, *Women Adrift,* 123–26.

the individual to curb his passions and exercise self-restraint in order that the institution of the family which is the fountain-head of the State, and from which spring all our noblest aspirations, shall remain pure and undefiled. . . . . We must cut out the cancer of disease if we would live.[74]

In the 1918 revival, loyalty to the war became an essential part of Billy Sunday's moral regime. The war's cause promised both a military goal and a moral purpose for all men; once and for all men could purge manhood of its evil character and prove that they were able to sacrifice for a higher good. The war affirmed that man was moral after all.

Wartime rhetoric also portrayed male sexual control as a patriotic responsibility, which "real men" embraced for the sake of national greatness. Following her husband's lead, Helen Sunday touted the war's moralizing potential for men. In an article entitled "Camp Morality," Mrs. Sunday responded to a hypothetical question about red-light camps that were sprouting up around military bases both at home and in Europe. "As a mother," she wrote, "I am almost glad in some ways for this crisis. If my son goes to the front, I know, if he is privileged to return to me, he will come back a better man, with higher, more sympathetic, and more enduring ideals." She continued: "This talk of lax moral conditions in our camps is worse than absurd. It is almost treason in its most insidious and damaging form. Our soldiers are being given something in their lives that many of them have never had before—the fire and zeal of a big purpose."[75]

But the war did not hold such lofty potential for women. Women could roll bandages or knit for soldiers at the front, but the independence offered to women by the war, both in the workplace and in the broader society, aroused suspicion.[76] Initial misgivings about women, however, gave way to outright fear when venereal disease spread rapidly among the American forces. The alarm generated by this health threat caused the Social Hygiene movement to recommit its effort, along with that of the American military, to stop the spread of the dreaded disease. Social Purity's earlier expressions

74. Josephus Daniels, "Live Straight if You Would Shoot Straight," pamphlet, no date, American Social Hygiene Association Papers, Box 131, Folder 5.

75. "Camp Morality," Ma Sunday's column, December 14, 1917, Billy Sunday Papers; Peter Filene, "In Time of War," 321–35.

76. "The Passing of the Butterfly," Ma Sunday's column, March 29, 1918, Billy Sunday Papers.

of anguish regarding the fate of young innocent prostitutes now turned to strident calls for control of "bad girls." Fear of infection and concern for stopping its spread quickly overran the movement's moral arguments. The result was increasingly repressive actions and legislation regarding prostitutes. Fear also motivated Social Hygiene's new cooperation with the American government, which rounded up prostitutes, submitted them to invasive, often painful pelvic examinations, and sometimes imprisoned them. The government's "American Plan," which most Purists, now Social Hygienists, strongly supported, prohibited prostitution in the vicinity of military camps and suspended the civil rights of any woman found infected with venereal disease. In its 1918 report, the Committee of Fifteen, Chicago's Social Hygiene organization, supported this redirection from sympathy to overregulation. "We are gratified that the Committee has been able to render efficient service toward protecting soldiers and sailors from the contamination of immoral women," the committee's president, H. P. Crowell, wrote.[77] Social Hygiene advocates publicized the threat of women as potential disease carriers who could disrupt and indeed infect the moralizing mission of the men of the American Expeditionary Force.

The Social Hygiene movement and the Billy Sunday revival shared both personnel and moral perspective and together became increasingly strident in their call for female control. The revival's solicitation of businesswomen was characterized by an adamant message of sexual restraint. In an earlier Baltimore revival one headline blared: "MISS MILLER WARNS 6000 GIRLS AGAINST TEMPTATIONS." Miller's talk consisted of several admonitions: "Don't pay the price you have to pay for joy rides and clothes and good times. Don't let your natural and your innocent love of life and pleasure lead you into the awful mistake of believing that you can escape paying the price. If you don't pay it, some other woman will." Similarly, in Chicago, Virginia Asher spoke to businesswomen about the "error of sin, of ways to avoid its insidious advances and penalties suffered by those who had failed to depart from sinful ways."[78] Like Helen Sunday's narratives, these female revivalists focused on the dangers of women who submitted to the immoral temptations of public life.

77. "Milestones in the March against Commercialized Prostitution, 1886–1949," pamphlet, Box 1, Folder 1, American Social Hygiene Association Papers; Rosen, *The Lost Sisterhood*, 33–37; Pivar, "Cleansing the Nation," 29–40; Annual Report of the Committee of Fifteen for the Year ended April 20, 1918.

78. Baltimore, 1916; *Syracuse Post Standard*, 1915, Scrapbook 6, Billy Sunday Papers.

Billy Sunday took a similar posture on the purity issue. In a *Tribune* column entitled "What Billy Sunday Thinks and Says of Some Modern Daughters of Eve," the revivalist outlined his position to Chicago businesswomen: "The girl who insists on spooning with every marriageable young man in the community ought to be backed into a woodshed and a number 11 shoe applied across both hiplets." Revivalists believed that society needed its domestic balance in order to maintain godliness: "I'd rather have one God-fearing, bread-making, floor-sweeping, sock-darning daughter of Israel than two trainloads of these gum chewing, manicured, painted, camouflaged, frizzle-headed little sissies," the revivalist exclaimed.[79] Even though in practice the Sunday revival relied extensively upon female leadership in the public arena, the rhetoric of the 1918 revival reiterated fundamentalist fears that women had abandoned their domestic assignment and that as a result society was in a moral free fall. Revival rhetoric and narratives enforced this message insistently. Both Helen and Billy Sunday's skillful use of the media meant that damning words were continually propagated and reiterated for fundamentalist followers and for the broader culture. Revivalists positioned fundamentalism's gendered morality like a sword that separated the righteous from the sinner, giving spiritual credibility to men while chastising woman's immorality.

By 1918, many of the attitudes and activities that revivalists had once decried as the dissolute signs of working-class culture were now evident in the middle class. This reality caused revivalists to broaden their critique beyond the immorality of "bad girls" to include any woman who did not toe the domestic line. Revivalists criticized upper-class "women of leisure" for their seeming maternal neglect just as much as they critiqued working-class participation in popular amusements. All were categorized as detrimental to woman's moral and familial status. Sunday's frequently delivered sermon, *The Home,* included a lengthy tirade on the "curse of idle mothers . . . who just board around. They never darn a sock, they never patch a pair of pants, they never stitch a handkerchief. They just drag themselves down to their meals." Revival rhetoric focused on cocktail parties, card parties, downtown shopping, and other "frivolous" leisure pastimes, portraying each woman as defying her God-intended purpose and heading down the road of sin. "There seems to be the feeling today in the 'higher circles' that

79. *Chicago Tribune,* March 11, 1918.

Billy Sunday shaking hands with Mrs. George Pullman. The revivalist hobnobbed with Chicago elites, yet criticized them as well. *Chicago Daily News,* Chicago Historical Museum.

it is extremely old-fashioned to raise a family." "This condition," declared the revivalist, "was a menace to our national life."[80]

Revivalists delivered this message to Chicago elites via weekly meetings organized by the Sunday revival in the homes of prominent Chicagoans. Media coverage of these admonishments was placed on the "Society and Entertainment" page of the newspaper, thus enabling middle-class readers to take in Billy Sunday's critique of "high society" alongside the descriptions of Chicago social events. At several meetings Sunday chastised those who thought, "Their wealth and social position would open the gates of heaven," and reiterated fundamentalist fears concerning the high rate of divorce.[81] Divorce was a particularly pertinent topic because Billy Sunday's

80. Ibid., March 15, 1918; Buffalo campaign, March 9, 1917, Scrapbook 11, Billy Sunday Papers.
81. *Chicago Tribune,* March 29, 1918.

tirades paralleled headlines that heralded a significant increase in Cook County divorces: "Divorce Rate on Climb to Record; 500 for a Month." The percentage of divorces in Cook County, already the highest in the country, had now risen to 20 percent. Analysts, who blamed the increase on the availability of divorce in Cook County as opposed to other counties in the state, used the statistics to call for a universal divorce law. For Billy Sunday, the numbers provided fertile ground for espousing his domestic rhetoric. In one sermon entitled "I Believe in Hell-Hell-Hell," the revivalist equated overall social decline with the availability of divorce. "We seem to be living in a new era politically, physically, socially, economically, educationally, and religiously. There never has been a time when people seemed to be more self-centered, self-complacent, than in your day and mine. I read a book some time ago where the author advocated that marriage should not be a life contract but on the installment plan—like we buy furniture."[82]

Motherhood also came under the revival's scrutiny and was found wanting. Maternal neglect, Sunday argued, led to "children who are orphans. In India they throw their children to crocodiles in the filthy Ganges. Today we are tossing them into the incarcerator of indifference, of apathy." He reiterated, "Who knows but that Judas became a godless, good-for-nothing wretch because he had a godless, good-for-nothing mother? Do you know?"[83] Helen Sunday also criticized mothers for failing to fulfill their maternal responsibilities. In one narrative, "The Girl Who Was Sold for a Bargain," Mrs. Sunday describes a mother who flirts and fails to teach her daughter proper reserve. The mother's failure grows a daughter that "has the instinct to play with fire. She has never learned how to blush and a remark which ought to send her crying to her mother only makes her laugh." The dire consequence of this mother's failure ends with her daughter having an illicit tryst and dying at the age of eighteen. "The disease which had dragged her down to her grave," Mrs. Sunday concludes, "was a leprosy, caught from her sin, that had made her once beautiful face a mass of evil sores. Such was the price this mother paid—for bargains!"[84]

Billy Sunday's critique of women's unprofitable use of time, divorce, and declining fertility enabled middle-class listeners and readers to judge nou-

82. Ibid., March 6, 18, 1918.

83. Ibid., March 15, 1918; "The Vanishing Mother," *Northwestern Christian Advocate,* June 29, 1914, 940; *Denver Times,* September 25, 1914, Revival Files, Billy Sunday Papers.

84. Ma Sunday, *Women of America,* Billy Sunday Papers; William Parker, "True Womanhood," *Christian Worker's Magazine,* November 1915, 184–85.

veau riche decadence. Female activities that assumed the guise of "culture" were disdained: "The world needs girls who can wash dishes as well as play the piano; girls who can cut dresses as well as they can tango; girls who would rather have workingmen for husbands than whiskey-soaked scions for fortunes; mothers who love babies more than ballrooms," Billy Sunday said.[85] Such foolish women undermined maternity and domesticity and modeled dangerously independent lives to lower-class women; elite women were admonished to forsake leisure and accept their God-given maternal responsibilities.

Inherent within revival narratives are not only accusations against bad mothers, but generational tensions as well. If mothers had seemingly failed in their nurturing responsibility, daughters were also called to task for their unwillingness to follow parental supervision. Accounts, particularly those penned by Helen Sunday, frequently begin with a mother-daughter interaction in which daughters fail to take the advice of their mothers in regard to men, fashion, or public amusements. In an act of rebellion against her mother, the daughter reads "real life magazines," or "associates with the type of persons who call themselves broadminded." In the end, however, the daughter's failure to heed maternal advice leads to tragedy, most likely injury and death. Such narratives overtly symbolize the widening gulf between mothers and daughters in urban society as the more independent daughters clashed with the more home-centered experiences of their mothers. Such divisions were particularly acute for fundamentalist daughters who, like their more secular counterparts, turned away from domesticity. This new direction for daughters was particularly difficult for fundamentalist families because, from their perspective, turning from motherhood implied turning from God.

Revivalist concern for mother-daughter divisions also reflected the generational divisions that resulted from parents who could not prevent their children from being lured away from home by the enticements of popular culture. The *Christian Worker's Magazine,* for example, published "Morals of the Picture Show—A Discussion of This Popular and Growing Amusement from the Bible Standpoint," which revealed fundamentalism's troubling insecurity over its own children seeking out popular culture. The writer, a Texas pastor, recounts a small boy who returns home from his first picture show and enthusiastically tells his mother that if she would go to one show

85. Buffalo campaign, 1917, Scrapbook 11, Billy Sunday Papers.

Masses thronged the Billy Sunday revival in Chicago. *Chicago Daily News,* Chicago Historical Museum.

she would never want to go to another prayer meeting.[86] The pastor used the story to justify why children should never be permitted to attend movies. Urban fundamentalists who supported the modern, consumer-oriented elements of revivalism found themselves in a world in which the consumption of popular culture encroached on their domestic sphere, challenged its morality, and drew their children to its attractions.

Liminal Space of the Tabernacle/Segregated Space of Chicago

At the center of the Billy Sunday revival stood the tabernacle, a physical testament to the "success" of Third Awakening revivalism. The tabernacle was more than simply a showcase for religious indoctrination or ideology; by 1918, it had become a highly modern and centralized business. The tabernacle also functioned as an interactive liminal space for a broad range of

86. "Morals of the Picture Show," *Christian Worker's Magazine,* October 1915, 88–90.

social groups, many of whose interests went beyond the narrow parameters of the stated religious mission. By March 18, the crowds at Sunday's tabernacle were so large that all comers could not be accommodated; ushers were forced to turn some individuals away. The *Tribune* reported that "Sunday who had hoped and prayed from the beginning that the Chicago campaign would be the climax of his career, was delighted." The revivalist himself praised the city's response: "Chicago certainly is putting it over—sure putting it over," Sunday said. In the final count, Billy Sunday's 1918 Chicago revival attracted 49,165 converted trail-hitters, placing the city third, behind New York and Boston, in the number of revival converts.[87] The numbers actually attending and participating went far beyond this figure. For this reason, it is important to see the revivals as social activities that went well beyond the official intentions of Sunday and his workers. Others clearly had an investment in the crusades, and the social and racial politics of Chicago at the time provide a particularly important context in which to understand these other interests. The increasingly segregated and contested social spaces of Chicago that boiled over into violent acts of class and racial exclusion provide one obvious contrast to the benign, consensus-seeking threshold for collective negotiation that the revivalists were espousing.

Certainly the tabernacle itself contributed to revivalism's appeal as a spectacle. As one approached the building, the sight of thousands of individuals streaming through its many entrances would have had to impress if not inspire all onlookers. Similarly, the sound of revival participants joined in song, Billy Sunday's athletic performances, and even the anticipation of "hitting the trail" kept tabernacle attendees on the edge of their seats. Many perhaps lined up specifically to see the tabernacle spectacle, seeking out Sunday's revival as an acceptable form of urban entertainment, the intersection of religion and popular culture, of "piety" and "pleasure," which in the process brought greater democracy to American Protestantism. Others, particularly women, may have sought out the revival for the revivalist himself; Sunday's masculine appearance and sex appeal contributed to an environment of spectacle, celebrity, and consumption, turning faith into a product that could be pitched and then bought or sold—a market that put religious faith up for consumption.[88]

87. *Chicago Tribune*, March 18, 1918; McLoughlin, *Billy Sunday*, 103. This number of "trail-hitters" is not an official count. The Billy Sunday organization did not release statistics.
88. Kathryn Oberdeck, *The Evangelist and the Impresario;* Margaret Bendroth, "Why Women Loved Billy Sunday," 253.

Despite its centralized, corporate design, the Billy Sunday revival was not a monolithic affair. People arrived at the tabernacle with vastly different agendas, even as the press and political institutions generated their own varied and vested cultural interpretations. According to Turner, liminal spaces like the tabernacle give agency to the human participants that ritualistically interact within them. Sunday's organizers were also social choreographers who acknowledged the agency of participants even as they directed the diverse social groups attending toward common values and community. In this sense, the tabernacle's liminal space and the collective rituals that occurred within it can be seen as attempts to negotiate and resolve Chicago's intractable problems and provide a new vision for the future. Whether or not collective ceremonial rituals actually resolve social conflict is beside the point. The fact that revival participants were also citizens of an emerging and unstable new social order in the city meant that the neighborhood residents who participated in them necessarily brought their own anxieties and social preoccupations to the bracketed narratives and rituals in which they participated. In the midst of a city that was divided ethnically, racially, and status-wise, Billy Sunday said, "Chicago represents everything good and bad in the history, the traditions, and the ambitions of this vast inland empire. . . . Drive the devil out of Chicago and we drive sin out of the Midwest." The nature of tabernacle space and ritual was to fill the urban vacuum with a normative "right" based on the values of domesticity. And here lies a most intriguing contradiction in the Third Awakening enterprise. Sunday's ultimate goal of separating the wheat from the chaff (a grand segregating impulse) depended on vast and effective community-building and consensus-forming rituals (a local integrating tactic). But both of these activities would necessarily evoke in participants the dissensus-forming patterns of exclusion that increasingly defined the city in the years 1917 and 1918 (institutional divisions and strategic acts of segregation). Such activities provided the social fabric and collective experience from which revivals were inseparable.

This conflicted package of social exclusion/rhetorical consensus played out in new articulations of gender, ethnicity, and class distinctions, and can be viewed within a new cultural geography that surrounded the revival centers. Understanding the individual to be at the center of the faith, and domestic balance to be the last bastion of moral order, revivalists sought to bring an overdetermined domestic sanctuary to bear on the urban population. Ironically, however, domesticating urban space entailed a massive, modern interaction with a large and unstable social space. By 1918 the tabernacle became more "respectable," more masculine, and more modern. In short, to propagate its moral message, revivalism became more like the culture it sought to redeem.

Unfortunately, revivalism's adaptation to culture also meant that it perpetuated the very separations that divided the urban community. The tabernacle, for example, was built on the lakefront at the end of Chicago Avenue. Part of the tabernacle's modern appeal was its easy access from any of the Chicago streetcars via the Northwestern Elevated station. Yet, revival "modernity" allowed Chicago suburbanites to now reenter the city without actually encountering the neighborhoods through which they passed. The tabernacle may have provided an opportunity for the working man and high society to rub elbows, but the constant affirmation of middle-class values and the castigation of both the lower and higher end of the social spectrum furthered class distinctions.

Within this reorganization of space, the moral regime offered by revival portrayed the family as sanctifying the industrial order. This moral equation justified women's participation within revivalism and created a feminized rhetoric that placed women at the center of the moral order. Ultimately, however, female independence implicitly challenged women's moral assignment and men's traditional dominance. While earlier revivals had portrayed urban sin as uniquely male and in need of the moralizing influence of women, the Billy Sunday revival spiritualized and urged its followers to emulate male qualities. "I think," Sunday said, "to be a man is greater than to be an angel. You sing, 'I want to be an angel and with the angels stand,' but I'll never be an angel if I haven't manhood enough to be a man."[89] This shift to masculinity took virtues that, under the teaching of Dwight L. Moody and J. Wilbur Chapman, had belonged uniquely to women and now ascribed them to men. The insistence on this domestic accord, now in the hands of men, worked to erase moral ambiguity to create a righteous cause, and to resolve conflict. Like its predecessors, the 1918 revival cultivated the idea that class, ethnicity, race, and even generational differences could be overcome by individual personal morality. Their desire to create moral people and thus a moral society motivated revivalism's engagement in social and political activism as they worked to reform urban America.

---

89. *South Bend Tribune,* June 16, 1913, Press Clippings, Billy Sunday Papers.

In rather dramatic ways, the moral geography of Billy Sunday's tabernacle was very much mapped onto the social geography of Chicago. Sunday's increasingly strident enforcement of this now masculinized morality, in addition to the highly centralized and hierarchical nature of the revival, helped widen the city's racial, ethnic, socioeconomic, ecumenical, generational, and gender gaps. Instead of simply bringing Chicago together into moral harmony through consensus-forming rituals, the revivalist also simultaneously cultivated a de facto dissonance that allowed the sins of the city—other than those of the heart—to continue unabated.

"Thank You, Lord, for Our Testosterone"
THE END (TIMES)

World War I marked a turning point, if not the end, of the Third Awakening. Despite the media blitz that surrounded Billy Sunday's 1918 campaign and his popularity in Chicago, revivalism as a whole became far less extravagant and moved to much smaller venues. Several factors contributed to the decline in enthusiasm. First, largely in response to Billy Sunday's reputation as an evangelist and as a modern-day celebrity, hundreds of aspiring evangelists had flooded the revival circuit. By 1918 the field of revival was filled with preachers who mimicked Sunday's revival style and hoped to imitate his success as well. This abundance of evangelists resulted in a deluge of revivals across the country. Revival historian William McLoughlin conservatively estimates that between 1912 and 1918, as many as thirty-five thousand revivals were organized across the country. These revivals put a heavy financial burden on churches. McLoughlin again estimates that, above their own denominational budgets, Protestant churches were spending as much as $20 million a year in support of professional evangelism.[1]

The barrage of revivals organized in the second decade of the century precipitated a type of "revival fatigue"; many people, churches, and communities grew weary not only of the cost involved but also of what they saw as the increasingly outlandish antics of revivalists. Even the Moody Bible Institute's *Christian Worker's Magazine,* a mouthpiece for revivalism, expressed concern about the propriety of Billy Sunday's revivals. Revival weariness was also

---

1. McLoughlin, *Billy Sunday,* 260–61.

coupled with a growing sense that as spectacular as they were, revivals could not compete with other forms of entertainment and popular culture like vaudeville, radio, and movies and would be outdone by commercialized mass entertainment by the end of the revival era.[2] As a result of the war, Americans were poised economically, technologically, and morally to pursue all avenues of commercialized leisure. The entertainment industry's burgeoning appeal was in some ways based upon and in other ways antithetical to revivalism's collective rituals and viewing spectacle. Third Awakening revivals required personal, public disclosures through interactive rituals. The new commercialized leisure forms that eclipsed revivals, however, required no such acts of voluntary, public disclosure. Film, nickelodeons, and popular theater spread in part because they offered and allowed leisure consumption in the dark or in spaces involving anonymity.[3]

While early Third Awakening revivalists attempted to spiritualize the new urban space, film and popular theater eventually succeeded in commercializing the same public sphere. Both revivals and the emerging entertainment of classical Hollywood were based on conventions of narrative storytelling, dramatized moral conflict, and public ritual. Nickelodeons and vaudeville, however, created narratives and performances that demanded far less agency, accountability, or responsibility on the part of participants. In these ways, the aesthetic forms of Third Awakening revivals can be viewed as "proto-theatrical" and "proto-cinematic" cultural activities.[4] Although they predated and in some ways prefigured the movies, their melodramatic narratives and religious themes of revival proved far less exploitable by the new Fordist entertainment industries that emerged out of the early nickelodeon and movie-going practices. In this growing secular climate, revivalists fell behind in popularity, respectability, and relevance, arguably because they demanded so much on the part of their audiences. Ironically, the religious activity of revivalism, which dramatically highlighted actual human

---

2. Ibid., 260.

3. George Lipsitz, *Time Passages: Collective Memory and American Popular Culture.*

4. Anne Friedberg and Lauren Rabinovitz have demonstrated that the defining roots of cinema are in pre- and proto-cinematic forms. They show how amusement park rides, trains, and optical mechanical forms of entertainment predated and prefigured the cinema that would soon dominate popular cultural activity in American cities in the twentieth century. Friedberg, *Window-Shopping: Cinema and the Postmodern;* Rabinovitz, *For the Love of Pleasure.*

relations in the urban centers, provided far less escapism than did the new theatrical experiences of Hollywood.[5]

Revival activity also declined as a result of a new era of separatism fostered by fundamentalists who decidedly detached themselves, their families, and their organizations from American culture and from any highly organized or aggressive attempts to reform it. The Third Awakening's dedicated alliance with political forces to create moral law and government began to fade in the 1920s and Third Awakening fervor that once was geared toward effecting municipal, state, and national reform weakened. For many fundamentalists, revivalism's reputation perhaps became too attuned to modern culture and too closely related to those popular attractions that they subsequently disdained. Fundamentalism's retreat and separation from the Protestant mainstream in the 1920s moved some cultural pundits to declare its "defeat." The Scopes Trial in 1925, in particular, with its humiliating outcome for the faith's defender, William Jennings Bryan, seemed to put to rest once and for all what many labeled as the "old-time religion."[6]

Billy Sunday continued to preach into the 1930s, but his importance as a large-scale attraction significantly declined in terms of not only the size of his venue but also the number of individuals on his staff and in his revival audiences. After the revivalist died in 1935, Virginia Asher, who had worked with the Billy Sunday organization for seventeen years, continued to organize and work with her Virginia Asher Business Woman's Bible Councils.[7] It is not clear how long the council continued in Chicago, but several of the organizations continued to meet after Asher's death in 1937. In St. Louis, for example, the council met until well into the 1950s. Through her organization, Virginia Asher continued to promote revivalism's gendered Gospel and to "mother them [working women] with divine love." Asher also developed her own collective rituals to impress council members with the importance of their Christian commitment.

---

5. Historians since E. P. Thompson have regularly explained religion as a form of escapism that served the emerging needs of industrial capitalism. This scheme does not convincingly explain the actual social practices of Third Awakening revivalists. Historians are just beginning to reconsider the lived, embodied, and material conditions of religious practice for this era rather than writing it off as the linchpin of ideological subjugation.

6. Balmer and Winner, *Protestantism in America*, 220–21.

7. Dorsett, *Billy Sunday*, 124–43.

The most impressive of these rituals was the "Galilean service," which was enacted on the shores of Winona Lake, a gathering place for fundamentalists as well as home to revival leaders like Helen and Billy Sunday and Virginia and William Asher. At the lake, Asher organized a Galilean service, which was held at twilight. This ritual featured Virginia Asher coming across the lake singing "Jesus, Savior, Pilot Me." "Then," as Asher's biographer describes, "in the glow of the setting sun, Mrs. Asher rises from her seat in the boat, reads of Jesus by the seaside and speaks briefly of the Man of Galilee. There is a prayer, and the boat moves away into the growing twilight." While this rather solemn ritual could hardly compete with tabernacle fervor, it does show that in spite of fundamentalism's shift toward masculinity, fundamentalist women continued to organize in associations and to find meaning within the parameters and rituals of their sphere.[8] Such organizations also ensured that the gendering of fundamentalism continued well after Sunday's death.

It is, however, a misrepresentation to portray fundamentalists as "going away." Even as the popularity of revivalism faded, fundamentalists retrenched in order to sustain their biblical beliefs and conservative social agenda. Organizations like the Business Woman's Bible Councils as well as Bible schools and camps continued to promote many of the same rituals and ideals that had energized the Third Awakening.[9] As a result, fundamentalism remained very much alive, particularly in terms of its moral regime that had been the Third Awakening's focal point. The core of this moral system continued to center on belief and behavior, an individual's decision both to choose salvation and to choose right living that spurred an almost adamant focus upon the individual and individual "sin."

On one level, it would appear that the efforts of Third Awakening revivalists to redeem the city paid off in terms of promoting Protestant hegemony in the city and the nation. On the whole, Protestantism fared well during the era of the Third Awakening. Between 1890 and 1916, the percentage of church members in Chicago grew from 35 percent to 43 percent, an increase that was mirrored in other urban centers as well.[10] Concrete changes that

8. Sanders, *The Council Torchbearer,* 15–18; Bendroth, *Fundamentalism and Gender,* 85.

9. Brereton, *God's Army,* 131.

10. Jon Butler, "Protestant Success in the New American City, 1870–1920: The Anxious Secrets of Rev. Walter Laidlaw," in Harry S. Stout and D. G. Hart, eds., *New Directions in American Religious History,* 313.

had been part of the revivalist agenda were also enacted in public policy and law. As early as June 1910, President William Howard Taft signed the Mann Act into law. This legislation outlawed transporting any woman or girl across state lines for the purposes of prostitution or any other immoral practice. In direct response to the moral indignation aroused by the white slave trade, Congress and the president put the force of federal law against vice. And then in 1919 the Eighteenth Amendment outlawing the manufacture, sale, or transportation of liquor within the United States was ratified. Within the era encompassed by the Third Awakening, Congress passed the Mann Act, legislated the Volstead Act to implement Prohibition, and created the FBI to enforce both pieces of legislation.[11] The legal record at least suggests that the moral mandate so insistently touted throughout the Third Awakening had triumphed, or at least gained widespread approval among those in government. In effect, revivalists had taken the complexity of urban, industrial America, reduced it to individual sin, and mobilized the government in support of moral aims.

The accomplishments of the Social Purity and temperance movements, both allies of the Third Awakening, produced a mixed political legacy. Demonizing brothels and saloons and legislating their demise essentially pushed these institutions underground where they continued to prosper. In Chicago, people now drank liquor in their own homes or in a growing number of illegal speakeasies; prostitutes moved into downtown hotels or flats. Criminalizing liquor and prostitution caused these "sins" to align with even more illicit elements of society. By the 1920s, this realignment was perhaps best represented by contrasting aldermen such as "Hinky Dink" Kenna and "Bathhouse John" Coughlin with the likes of a different type of Chicagoan—Al Capone. Kenna and Coughlin were corrupt and greedy ward bosses, but they were not professional criminals. Capone, on the other hand, developed a Chicago syndicate estimated to have grossed $100 million in 1927 alone and, with the help of guns and cars, murdered more than eight hundred individuals. Enforcing both the Mann and the Volstead Acts also led to more invasive government: "Under cover of moral regulation, federal authority barged into the everyday lives and habits of American people." Somewhat ironically, the Prohibition amendment that was designed to protect home and family from the evils of the public sphere was enforced by expanding the power of the public sector: "federal agencies

11. Morone, *Hellfire Nation*, 265–71, 308–17.

developed new skills, the courts explored new doctrines, and the states organized new kinds of enforcement policies."[12]

Revivalism's primary focus on prostitution and liquor also had the perhaps unintended effect of diverting attention away from other "sins" of the city. Despite the willingness of the Billy Sunday revival to cross color lines for the sake of Prohibition, the "moral cleansing" that revivalists believed would erase other social divisions in actuality did little to alleviate Chicago racism or racial discord. Shortly after the end of the 1918 revival, the *Chicago Defender* reprinted an article that had been written by a black pastor after Sunday's revival in Washington, D.C.: "Of one thing we may be assured, whatever changes his [Sunday's] presence in our midst may have wrought, the devil of race prejudice, rotten, stinking, hell born race prejudice will be just as strongly entrenched in the white churches and in the community as it was before he came."[13]

In Chicago the large influx of African Americans undoubtedly exacerbated the deep racial tensions within the city. In 1917 the race riot in East St. Louis further escalated fears of blacks and whites that such hostilities would come to Chicago's neighborhoods as well. By early spring 1918, the period of the Sunday revival, armed white gangs were organizing throughout the city purportedly to "protect" their homes by attacking black workers and firebombing black homes.[14] The worsening of race relations was mirrored in other cities that had also experienced a Billy Sunday revival. In November and December of 1917 Billy Sunday organized a large revival in Atlanta. In this earlier southern event Sunday also crossed the city's color line by preaching a special sermon to a black-only crowd and holding simultaneous revivals in black churches. According to Atlanta newspaper accounts, the revival's black-only tabernacle night promised the attendance of some fifteen thousand African Americans, "the largest number of colored people in attendance that have ever been seen under one roof anywhere in the country." The revivalist, according to reporters, "made a hit with the colored people." Sunday sermonized that "the race had made marvelous progress," but he also warned his black listeners to "think more seriously on morality and Christian lives." The revivalist also added that he thought blacks would be wise "to consider the southern people as friends who would

12. Ibid., 327, 330.
13. *Chicago Defender,* March 23, 1918.
14. William M. Tuttle, Jr., *Race Riot: Chicago in the Red Summer of 1919,* 11–14.

not forsake them." Several days later the Atlanta revival featured a five-hundred-person black choir singing to a crowd of twelve thousand whites. Such events caused many to remark about the obvious evidence of racial harmony in the city.[15]

Like the Chicago revival's willingness to join black and white forces for the Prohibition cause, Billy Sunday's Atlanta campaign sought to efface the South's racial divide with a moral regime of right belief that would produce right living. Within several months of the Atlanta campaign, however, revivalism's moral veneer seems to have worn thin. In April 1918 the Broad Ax emblazoned a desperate appeal from the "leading colored citizens of Atlanta, Georgia" in its headline. The plea was directed to the U.S. president, members of his cabinet, members of Congress, as well as to governors and legislators imploring the government to suppress mob violence and to make lynching a federal offense. What prompted this appeal from Atlanta's black leadership was the "conditions and sentiment here [in Atlanta] are unsettled in regard to the lynchings as the result of mob violence so prevalent in this vicinity." They pleaded, "Do not these undemocratic conditions, these inhumanities, these brutalities and savageries provoke the Rulers of the nation to speak out of the sphinx like silence and utter a voice of hope, a word of promise for the black man?" Then, just a little more than a year after Sunday's Chicago revival, in July 1919, Chicago was convulsed by one of the worst race riots in America's history, one that left both blacks and whites dead and hundreds wounded and homeless.[16]

Certainly the Billy Sunday revival had no direct influence on this riot, and in one way the revival may be seen as an attempt to bridge the racial chasm. However, in its quest for individual morality, the Sunday revival, like its predecessors, had insistently normalized and spiritualized white middle-class norms of sexual and racial purity to the exclusion of others. With this implicitly racialized Gospel, the Billy Sunday revival rallied thousands to his domestic cause in pursuit of a better manhood and womanhood. Within this gendered Gospel, however, was an implicit portrayal of blacks and foreigners as socially inferior and sexually dangerous. This positioning did not go unnoticed. The Defender's critique of the Sunday revival continued: "Members of white churches have the right now to feel, or to assume that there can't be anything wrong about race prejudice, nothing inconsistent

15. Billy Sunday Papers, Scrapbook 17.
16. *Broad Ax,* April 27, 1918; *Chicago Defender,* April 27, 1918; Tuttle, *Race Riot,* 242.

between it and Christianity, or this man, who claims to speak for God, to be on the most intimate terms with Jesus Christ, would certainly have included it among the sins that were denounced by him."[17]

By focusing only on individual sins that were made to appear intrinsic to certain groups, revivalism avoided or obscured larger evils. The Billy Sunday revival not only raised man's moral stature but also further aligned the now masculine order with whiteness as the standardized value construct and norm. As men became the conduits of moral purity, and as revival rhetoric insistently touted man's respectability and moral uprightness, the message continued to implicitly underscore the moral supremacy of the whites who preached these values. So while revivalism's domestic balance had shifted from female purity to male righteousness, and while revivalists asserted the virtue of man over woman, both perpetuated a standard of whiteness and its inherent racism; a racism that is seldom referred to or recognized as such, since "white" is the unnamed racial norm that makes every other color apart from white synonymous with "raced."[18] Whether masculine or feminine, the gendered assertions of revivalism elevated white morality and respectability to an unnamed and unquestioned cultural center. In effect, this habit placed ethnics and African Americans on the cultural peripheries. Unfortunately this also placed them in the same margins where revivalists had so dramatically placed depravity and "sin" in their narratives and rituals.

Culture "Wars"

Since the election of Ronald Reagan in 1980, evangelicals (who reentered the public arena as a demographic category in the 1950s) have been engaged in what they deem a "culture war."[19] In 1991, more than a decade into the conflict, sociologist James Davison Hunter defined this conflict as "political and social hostility rooted in different systems of moral understanding. The end to which these hostilities tend is the domination of one cultural and moral ethos over all others."[20] In the years since the publica-

17. *Chicago Defender,* March 23, 1918.
18. Omi and Winant, *Racial Formation in the United States,* 55–76; Richard Dyer, *White,* 8–30.
19. Balmer and Winner, *Protestantism in America,* 63–67.
20. James Davison Hunter, *Culture Wars: The Struggle to Define America,* 42.

tion of Davison's work, evangelical efforts to enforce their moral regime have intensified and, in a somewhat comfortable alliance with the Republican Party, coalesced into a political movement dedicated to imposing its moral, social, and racial authority upon the nation and, some would say, on the world. By 2005, 82 percent of Republican Party respondents identified themselves as "white Christians."[21]

The 2000 and 2004 election of a self-proclaimed evangelical Protestant, George W. Bush, into office has put evangelicalism's political clout and social influence at a high point in public consciousness. His election, many would argue, was the result of his overt promotion of evangelical values and a moral call to arms. Clearly many evangelicals themselves saw the Bush victory as a vindication of their moral regime, and their rhetoric resounds with Third Awakening fervor: "The voters have delivered a moral mandate," said D. James Kennedy, president of Coral Ridge Ministries in Fort Lauderdale, Florida. "Now that values voters have delivered for George Bush, he must deliver for their values."[22]

Despite the century that separates the Third Awakening from the activism of the current evangelical Right, the two are linked in terms of moral perspective and a willingness to impose that morality through reform activism. Many current evangelicals look to Third Awakening revivalists as "saviors" of the faith, practical, plain-speaking men who stood their ground against the forces of biblical liberalism and social secularism. The Third Awakening's widely publicized admonishments against modern culture, with little recognition of the revivalists' adaptations to it, reinforce an "outsider" cultural stance with which many twenty-first-century evangelicals claim to identify. This defensive posture enhances evangelicalism's moral critique of society and strengthens an "us versus them" perspective.[23]

Both the current religious Right and the Third Awakening are ecumenical in their makeup. The moral activism of the Third Awakening was supported by a bloc of largely urban Protestants, while today's religious Right includes an even broader and more assorted coalition of Protestant

21. This statistic, overwhelmingly conflating Republicanism with conservative Christianity, was reported as part of a CNN/USA Today poll, broadcast on The Lou Dobbs Report, CNN, June 8, 2005.

22. Quoted in Michael Skube, "We're Saved. You're Lost. Now What?" Los Angeles Times, November 7, 2004.

23. James Davison Hunter, American Evangelicalism: Conservative Religion and the Quandary of Religion.

evangelical denominations, independent Bible churches, Pentecostals, as well as conservative Catholics and Jews.[24] New Right activism is also shored up by parachurch organizations that are eclectic in terms of religious belief, but distinctly focused in terms of moral intent. Vague in their theological pronouncements, such organizations profoundly shape the social agenda and rhetoric of this conservative bloc. Focus on the Family, Concerned Women for America, and the Family Research Council strongly parallel the Third Awakening's alliance with moral lobbies like the WCTU, the Anti-Saloon League, and the Social Purity movement. These organizations of the Third Awakening deeply influenced revivalism's understanding of salvation and defined the moral order based on the behavioral norms determined by these groups.[25] The Third Awakening's inordinate focus on the "sins" of liquor and vice was largely the result of the social and political influence of these movements. The same organizational influence is present in the current New Right. Parachurch groups carefully craft a conservative social agenda that correlates with, or many times supersedes, denominational affiliation or doctrine.

A New Moral Geography

Other similarities mark these two historical movements, particularly in terms of their attitudes toward the city, domesticity, and gender. The latter two themes, domesticity and gender, are among the most-known areas of discord within the current "culture wars." Yet ideas about space, and particularly a new moral geography of the twenty-first century, are also quite relevant. Like revivalists in the Third Awakening, the conservative evangelical Right builds consensus within their subculture by cultivating a sense of being overwhelmed or embattled by evil on the peripheries. Evangelicals see popular culture as "invading" and threatening a center that they term "family values."

Part of this attitudinal estrangement and "othering" of deleterious forces may be traced to the culturally separatist "outsider" position assumed by fundamentalists in the 1920s and 1930s. Another equally significant part of

---

24. Hunter, *Culture Wars,* 97–102.

25. Erwin W. Lutzer, *The Truth About Same-Sex Marriage: 6 Things You Need to Know About What's Really At Stake,* 101.

this attitude and symbolic segregation may be attributed to the deep-seated suspicions embedded within the Third Awakening's understanding and portrayal of the city. Because of its highly public nature, the twentieth century's "new" American city was seen to be a place of great peril, filled with immorality and sin, a place to be confronted and conquered. Revivalism's insistent and public pronouncements against the city at the beginning of the twentieth century have ramifications for the tenor of the contemporary conflict as well. Like their Third Awakening predecessors, current evangelicals see themselves battling against what they perceive as the immorality of public culture, much of which continues to be in cities that still loom as places of darkness and peril in evangelical rhetoric.[26] For evangelicals, urban "multiculturalism" (one of Ronald Reagan's most effective targets), in addition to the proliferation of alternative lifestyles (single-parent families, gay partnerships, combined households), continues to threaten morality and provoke social disorder, and, as a result, elicit suspicion.

Suburban or exurban areas, on the other hand, whose well-ordered and hegemonic patterns maintain both social and racial boundaries across the country, have replaced the idyllic and untainted rural areas that Third Awakening revivalists and elites once touted as an antidote to the "sins" of the city. The geographical and cultural position of evangelicalism simultaneously shifted to the peripheries of cities even as it migrated westward. Various churches and institutions in the Chicago area (Moody Bible Church, Moody Bible Institute, Wheaton College, Willow Creek Community Church) continue as evangelical powerhouses, but much of evangelical clout has shifted to the West, particularly to Orange County, California (Saddleback Church) or to Colorado Springs, Colorado (now referred to as the "evangelical Vatican").[27]

Within this new geographic and moral landscape, evangelicals have replaced the traditional urban threat as its target of evangelical activism. In its place, the current Right has set its rhetorical and policy sights on something far less spatial: the "liberal agenda" of "big government" and "media

26. *Los Angeles Times,* November 4, 2004. "Like the red-blue geography, the breakdown of the balloting was also similar to four years ago. Bush carried the vote among men, whites, rural residents, and the more religious, while Kerry won the vote among minorities, city dwellers, and the more secular, exit polls found." The results of the 2004 election showed the connection between more religious voters and their suspicions toward the city.

27. Jeff Sharlet, "Inside America's Most Powerful Megachurch," *Harper's Magazine,* May 2005, 41–54.

elites." At Values Voters Summit in September 2006, with several GOP hopefuls making appearances, attendees participated in sessions devoted to "attacking Hollywood liberalism."[28] In effect, revivalism's antagonism toward the city (a moral geography) has metamorphosed into an antagonism toward something far more abstract and amorphous: the specter of a monolithic media or governmental control. Third Awakening revivalists locked on to their targets by adopting modern tools of communication and advertising and physically intervened in the city. The current right again wages a war of rhetoric and public relations, but this time the war is against a faceless bureaucratic enemy that is everywhere, and nowhere.[29] As a result, the points of engagement are wide-ranging and complex, extending from abortion to marriage to judicial appointees. Whatever the issue, however, evangelicals accuse the American government of "meddling" in economics and society, and of deliberately suppressing morality and the nation's true potential for righteousness.

In this climate the moral geography of the sinful city has been disassembled and remapped by radical changes in the nature of popular culture itself. An emerging culture of commercialized leisure being normalized through nickelodeons, vaudeville, and the stage was only in its formative stages in Chicago at the turn of the century. By the 1990s, Hollywood, entertainment culture, television, and new media activities reached into every neighborhood in the nation, becoming a defining and ubiquitous—but always suspect—part of America. In essence, "sin" is no longer specifically located in urban saloons, brothels, gambling dens, or political cronyism. Sin now potentially travels toward every home through the Internet, television, and video games, as part of a general culture of consumerism. This entertainment and recreational consumerism is now largely sanctioned by economic conservatives, but not by their political bedfellows, religious conservatives. In this conflicted alliance, conservative evangelicals blame media liberals ("elites") for their "distorted" liberal bias and their promotion of a reprehensible immorality, which threatens to unseat the parental authority so important to maintaining "family values."

In the new moral geography, therefore, evangelicals are more likely (at least in rhetoric) to resist the specter of defilement by and from media enter-

---

28. *Los Angeles Times,* September 23, 2006.

29. Evangelicalism's insistent positioning of the government as the enemy is quite ironic given that the GOP holds significant sway in all three branches of the federal government.

tainment and big government through home schooling rather than through large public revivals deep within the sinful urban interior.[30] Paradoxically, the same conservatives who demonize Hollywood and the liberal elites that produce popular culture are far from separatist when it comes to participating in popular entertainment and the consumer culture that fuels it. As a result, despite some fundamental similarities between Third Awakening revivals and the current religious Right, one cannot help but note some glaring differences.

Specifically, the nature and use of social ritual as a mobilizing strategy has changed in both scale and scope. Failing to achieve the broad appeal of a Dwight L. Moody or Billy Sunday, evangelicals have developed "niche evangelism" that keeps the public face of evangelism while appealing to specific constituencies. Some "niche" outreaches include evangelistic meetings offering break-dancing contests, Velcro walls, and wrestling in inflatable sumo costumes.[31] Others appeal directly to larger groups, as in the "God Men" movement. One journalist noted, "In daybreak fraternity meetings and weekend paintball wars, in wilderness retreats and X-rated chats about lust, thousands of Christian men are reaching for more forceful, more rugged expressions of their faith." "It's the wussification of America that's getting us," shouts one of the movement's leaders, and moments later adds, a bit more reverently, "Thank you, Lord, for our testosterone."[32] Yes, Billy Graham or Greg Laurie still pack thousands into stadiums for public revivals, but the most vigorous rituals deployed to negotiate cultural and moral difference are no longer large collective physical interactions in a public sphere.[33] Rather, the religious Right places much more emphasis on personal devotion and family rituals intended as prophylactic measures against evil (small-group Bible studies, home schooling, women's prayer meetings, or men's retreats).

At the same time, sinful images and messages from the urban core now travel out to the evangelical suburban family in the form of Internet pornography (widely demonized in pulpits today but accessed by many

30. According to the documentary film *Jesus Camp,* 75 percent of home-schooled students are evangelicals. *Los Angeles Times,* September 29, 2006.

31. "Niche evangelism" was coined by Randall Balmer. "Christian Events to Take Center Stage," *Los Angeles Times,* July 15, 2005.

32. *Los Angeles Times,* December 7, 2006.

33. "Graham Defies Age, Ailments to Open Crusade," *Los Angeles Times,* November 19, 2004.

congregants), or in the form of a free-floating black, hip-hop culture (that white exurban boys adopt pervasively even as they jettison rap's defining socioracial critique for a spiritual agenda). Armed with insights from Christian broadcasting, conservative evangelicals now are just as likely to bunker themselves within their homes to fend off evil as to embark on crusades to intervene and redeem or reform sinners in the city. Given the theological continuities and similarities between the Third Awakening and the current religious Right, alongside the extreme cultural differences between the two historical eras, one wonders how effective gifted and successful organizers like Virginia Asher or Billy Sunday would navigate the disorienting world of a new, inverted moral geography that has been mapped around American domesticity in the twenty-first century.

This new twenty-first-century moral geography has significant ramifications for evangelicalism's domestic ideal, which now, more than ever, poses as a bulwark against the assaults of public culture. At the very heart of the "culture wars" is evangelicals' adamant belief that an appropriately checked individualism is the supreme virtue in all areas of endeavor. Given this focus, it is no coincidence that the primary battle lines in the "culture wars" are drawn around domesticity. Harkening back to the nineteenth century and to its Third Awakening voice, evangelicals believe that the potential excesses of individual independence and initiative must be constrained by the morality of the home and family. This tension that balances the spheres of self-interest and family is at the core of evangelicalism's harmonious society. The Christian Right's support of the unreined and unregulated individual in areas of religious belief, social policy, and economics must simultaneously raise the importance of limits imposed on individualism by the nuclear family in the social equation.[34] If one prioritizes individuality above all else, and if one views competition and free markets as the solution to all economic and social issues, then one has to assume or hope that individuality will be controlled by moral conscience. The origin of these moral virtues, according to evangelicals, must be the family. Their prescribed form of marriage and domesticity, which also serves both practically and symbolically, as a mechanism of sexual control for both women and men, must be upheld.[35]

Like its revivalist predecessors, the current Right also invokes protection of the domestic sphere as its primary justification for political engagement.

34. Hunter, *Culture Wars,* 180–82.
35. Sally K. Gallagher, *Evangelical Identity and Gendered Family Life,* 156–59.

By staking out the moral high ground in defense of home and family, the Christian Right stridently legitimizes its social and political activism with religious piety. Like the Third Awakening's aggressive efforts to outlaw prostitution and the saloon, the contemporary Right articulates what they see as affronts to the home in religious terms. To suppress vice and effect Prohibition, the revivalists portrayed the home as a moral sanctuary under assault. Third Awakening domesticity gave reason for not only widespread public ritualized interventions (temperance marches, songs, prayers) but also political activism. Petitions, referendums, and electioneering were the by-products of Third Awakening moral fervor. Today, the rituals of the new Right are enacted in the political arena via phone banks, fund-raisers, or rallies. Issues of domesticity, essentially seen as the moral purview of women, have increasingly shifted into the more overtly male sphere of public politics. In 1893 revivalists "solved" the city's political problems with moral means; at the beginning of the twenty-first century, evangelicals seek to "solve" moral problems by sociopolitical means.

The issue of same-sex marriage illustrates this trajectory. Along with anti-abortion activism, moral opposition to gay marriage has galvanized churches and parachurch groups on the evangelical Right to take political action. In his book *Marriage Under Fire*, Dr. James Dobson, founder of Focus on the Family and a central spokesperson for the evangelical Right, raises the moral rhetoric against same-sex marriages as an assault on traditional Judeo-Christian values and as a threat to the divinely ordained nuclear family. Dobson portrays gay marriage as the product of a sixty-year "master plan" orchestrated by activist homosexuals whose primary agenda is "the utter destruction of the family." Activist jurists and the media, as characterized by Dobson, have then carried out this "hurtling toward Gomorrah." "Marriage is defined by the God of nature and a wise society will protect marriage as it has always been understood. . . . Man and woman were made for each other, and the state has a compelling interest in supporting this undeniable and ancient truth." Dobson concludes: "There is only one answer: Congress and the state legislatures must pass a Federal Marriage Amendment to define this historic institution exclusively as being between one man and one woman."[36] For Dobson, along with other

36. Dr. James Dobson, *Marriage Under Fire: Why We Must Win This Battle*, 17, 79, 97–98.

conservative spokespersons, the solution for this moral "crisis" rests with the passage of a federal amendment that would forever ban any legal recognition of gay marriage.

On March 11, 2004, in a speech before the National Association of Evangelicals, President George W. Bush affirmed his religious and political support for the same-sex marriage ban: "I will defend the sanctity of marriage against activist courts and against local officials who want to redefine marriage. The union of a man and woman is the most enduring human institution, honored and encouraged in cultures and by every religious faith. Ages of experience have taught humanity that the commitment of a husband and wife to love and serve one another promotes the welfare of children and the stability of society."[37] In the 2004 state contests evangelicals claimed that their "moral vote" resoundingly approved bans on gay marriage in eleven states, and in the process of voting against this referendum helped reelect Bush.[38] Tony Perkins, head of the Family Research Council, termed gay marriage "the hood ornament on the family values wagon." "Clearly, the supporters of traditional marriage helped President Bush down the aisle to a second term," he said.[39] Not satisfied with statewide referendums, however, the evangelical lobby continues to push for passage of the constitutional amendment that would define marriage as a union exclusively between a female and male.

While attempting to shore up this position with religious proofs, Dobson also articulates a central dilemma that characterizes the legislating of morality, and a dilemma that was revealed through Third Awakening activism. The passage and enforcement of moral legislation such as an anti-gay marriage amendment entails a greater expansion of governmental authority. Current social and economic conservatives insistently call for smaller government and criticize bureaucratic intervention into individuals' lives, yet the same religious Right simultaneously demands legislative intrusion in support of their moral ideals. The Right's moral mandate demands a return of authority to individuals and the family while at the same time it seeks to legislate evangelicalism's moral regime into the lives

37. Quoted in David D. Kirkpatrick, "Bush Assures Evangelicals of His Commitment to Amendment on Marriage," *www.nytimes.com/2004/03/12.*

38. *Los Angeles Times,* November 6, 2004.

39. Mark Crispin Miller, "None Dare Call It Stolen: Ohio, the Election, and America's Servile Press," *Harper's Magazine,* August 2005, 39–40; *Los Angeles Times*, November 4, 2004.

of all Americans. In spite of this contradiction, the religious Right forges onward, seemingly content to use federal law to impose their beliefs with little or no regard for its unforgiving implications.

The Politics of Domesticity in the Twenty-First Century

In this era of individualism, domesticity is the incubator of "family values" and, as a result, woman's role in this sphere has taken on a new urgency. As in the Third Awakening, both women and men are to lead pure lives, but it is women and domesticity that provide the moral counterbalance for the evils of public life. The exemplar of moral values, evangelicalism's ideally "submissive" woman upholding the moral fiber of the middle-class family, is at the movement's heart. As a result, one of the primary markers of contemporary conservative evangelicalism is female submission to male authority. Sociologist Sally K. Gallagher's study on gender and current evangelicalism has documented that many current evangelicals hold firmly to a divine delineation between women's and men's roles and believe that woman's submission to men is mandated by Scripture. Gallagher's extensive interviews with evangelicals of both sexes show that the day-to-day work and family relations of evangelicals are quite similar to those of secular society; evangelicals practice what she terms "pragmatic egalitarianism." Yet despite this seemingly modern and equal praxis, in principle, female submission to male superiority continues to be central to one's identity as an evangelical. Gallagher continues: "Conservative evangelicals have the established institutions, networks, and rhetoric. The story of husband's headship and authority is articulated in hundreds of books, through thousands of radio broadcasts, and in millions of pulpits and Sunday school classes every week all over the country."[40]

An honest discussion of sexual equality (in marriage and family relationships, female leadership in the church, or ordination) raises the specter of "secular feminism" among evangelicals. As a result, current evangelicals somewhat hypocritically presuppose that domesticity, with its appropriate male head and submissive wife, continues to be the antidote to social problems. Wives and mothers as moral repositories, living out their appropriate domestic assignment, can balance a host of more public sins. Armed with

40. Gallagher, *Evangelical Identity,* 179.

this perspective, the contemporary religious Right now protests and counters the ostensibly long arm of the federal government and the "liberal media" by placing a renewed emphasis on motherhood and the middle-class home, and by touting the "sanctity of marriage" as the primary way to maintain morality and social order.

The Christian Right's domestic agenda and its emergence as a political force have also been contingent on legitimating specific norms related to economic status. The Right's acute (critics would say inordinate) focus on individual behavior and obsessions about the "decline" or health of the family shifts the focus of public attention toward concerns of the middle class (marital harmony, child-rearing, personal fulfillment and fitness) and away from broader (less personal) systemic issues that bedevil society.[41] In the wake of its domestic emphasis, the religious Right willingly negates issues that impact the daily lives of millions of women. Public policies that could potentially address issues of low wages, unplanned pregnancies, household labor, child care, and family abuse are issues that, from the perspective of many evangelical women and men, smack of "feminism" and are subsequently obscured within modern evangelicalism's domestic rhetoric. Just as domestic acquiescence covers a host of injustices against women, any need or call for the amelioration of society's economic and racial inequalities is subsumed within rhetorical appeals for individual transformation and moral reform.

Evangelicals continue to appeal to personal morality in order to cover a host of socioeconomic and racial differences, assuming that its moral regime will erase profound cultural and class differences. Like Third Awakening revivalists who crossed the color line for the sake of Prohibition, current evangelical groups such as the Traditional Values Coalition work hand-in-hand with the GOP to establish alliances with black pastors and their congregations in order to promote social conservatism and, in particular, block legislative approval of same-sex marriage. The 2005 "wooing" of black clergy by white evangelicals included such tactics as the unveiling of a six-point plan entitled "Black Contract with America on Moral Values" (is the implication here that America is white?) as well as the screening of a video, *Gay Rights, Special Rights*. The video includes an interview with Senator Trent Lott, who blasts gay marriage as "a moral degradation of our great country." A Mississippi Republican, Senator Lott clearly identifies himself

41. Bill McKibben, "The Christian Paradox—How a Faithful Nation Gets Jesus Wrong," *Harper's Magazine*, August 2005, 31–37.

with this "moral" Right against gays and lesbians. The actual intent of Lott's righteous stance, particularly in terms of African Americans, is questionable. This is particularly true in light of Lott's 2002 eulogy of Strom Thurmond, an avowed segregationist who Lott suggested would have made a good U.S. president.[42] Lott's statement, a slap to all civil rights activists, including African Americans, was, from an evangelical perspective, irrelevant to the "higher" cause of domestic preservation and defeating gay marriage.

And what about "sin"? Even though separated by close to a century, both the Third Awakening and the religious Right further their cause by not only disagreeing with their moral adversaries but also demonizing those who appear to be outside evangelicalism's domestic ideal. Early in the Third Awakening, the culprits were perceived to be evil men whose sins threatened the sanctity of home and family. Later, however, sin was defined as more of a feminine offense. The subsequent feminization of sin, which occurred at the beginning of the twentieth century, persists in the current "culture wars" portrayal of feminists and gays. The religious Right demonizes feminists, who symbolize a betrayal of biblically mandated and naturally determined gender roles. They malign feminists, even in what many would recognize as the "post-feminist" era, for their demands for female autonomy and equality with men as well as their celebration of female relationships, physicality, and sexuality. Perhaps most threatening to evangelicals, however, is that since the 1970s feminists have explicitly critiqued domesticity—marriage, motherhood, and child-rearing—as cultural constructions that are, in many instances, not empowering to women. Despite the benefits achieved by feminism, particularly for middle-class women, in terms of more career opportunities and higher pay, the feminist threat to the moral world of the religious Right still looms large.

Evangelicals also see homosexuality (men who "behave like women," or women who "act like men") as a subversive threat to the domestic ideal. Just as feminists are condemned for stepping outside evangelical gender ideals, gays are castigated for their "deviant" sexual orientation that again menaces the values of home and family. As in the past, evangelical domestic ideals are deployed both implicitly and overtly to critique those outside the fold. Unlike the past, however, today's public critique is likely to appear on a twenty-four-hour cable news channel or on talk radio. Unfortunately,

---

42. *Los Angeles Times,* February 1, 2, 2005.

those outside of the spiritual fold are also frequently outside of the racial, ethnic, and economic-class fold of evangelicals as well.

In short, the domestic legacy promoted, publicized, and ritualized by the Third Awakening is very much alive today. In its willingness to engage in sociopolitical activism to carry out goals, to focus on the individual and his or her need for family as a balance against excesses, to counter "feminism" via an ethos tied to women's submission to a male hierarchy, and to promote and articulate spirituality in middle-class economic and cultural terms, the current religious Right has updated the highly choreographed social rituals of the Third Awakening in order to intervene and heal a society they view as suffering a spiritual and cultural decline.

WORKS CITED

Abell, Aaron Ignatius. *The Urban Impact on American Protestantism, 1865–1900.* London: Archon, 1962.

Abbott, Lyman. "Mr. Moody's First Parish." *Illustrated Christian Weekly,* February 19, 1876. Lyman Abbott File, Moody Bible Institute.

————. *Silhouettes of My Contemporaries.* Garden City, N.J.: Doubleday, Page and Co., 1921.

Abbott, Lyman, File. Moody Bible Institute, Chicago.

Abstract of the Eleventh Census of the United States—1890. Washington, D.C.: Government Printing Office, 1894. Reprt., New York: Arno Press, 1976.

Abstract of the Thirteenth Census of the United States—1910. Washington, D.C.: Government Printing Office, 1913. Reprt., New York: Arno Press, 1976.

Adams, David K., and Cornelius A. van Minnen, eds. *Religious and Secular Reform in American Ideas, Beliefs, and Social Change.* Edinburgh: Edinburgh University Press, 1999.

Addams, Jane. *A New Conscience and an Ancient Evil.* New York: Macmillan Co., 1912.

————. *Twenty Years at Hull House.* New York: Macmillan Publishing Co., 1938.

Addams, Jane, Papers. University of Illinois at Chicago Manuscript Collection, Chicago.

Ahlstrom, Sydney E. *A Religious History of the American People.* New Haven, Conn.: Yale University Press, 1972.

————. "The Scottish Philosophy and American Theology." *Church History* 24 (1955): 257–73.

Allswang, John M. *A House for All Peoples: Ethnic Politics in Chicago, 1890–1936.* Lexington: University Press of Kentucky, 1971.

————. "The Political Behavior of Chicago's Ethnic Groups, 1918–1932." Ph.D. diss., University of Pittsburgh, 1967.

American Tract Society. *Alphabetical Index of the General Series of Tracts.* New York: American Tract Society, 1893.

Andrews, Wayne. *Battle for Chicago.* New York: Harcourt, Brace, and Co., 1946.

Annual Reports of the Committee of Fifteen. Pamphlets. Chicago Historical Society, Chicago.

Asbury, Herbert. *Gem of the Prairie: An Informal History of the Chicago Underworld.* DeKalb: Northern Illinois University Press, 1986. Reprt., New York: Alfred A. Knopf, 1940.

Balmer, Randall, and Lauren F. Winner. *Protestantism in America.* New York: Columbia University Press, 2002.

Banner, Lois W. *American Beauty.* Chicago: University of Chicago Press, 1983.

Barker-Benfield, C. J. "The Spermatic Economy: A Nineteenth-Century View of Sex." In Michael Gordon, ed., *The American Family in Social-Historical Perspective* (New York: St. Martin's Press, 1973), 336–72.

Barnes, Clifford, Obituary. *Chicago Daily News,* September 19, 1944. Clipping File, Chicago Historical Society.

Baylen, Joseph O. "A Victorian's Crusade in Chicago, 1893–1894." *Journal of American History* 51 (December 1964): 418–34.

Bederman, Gail. *Manliness and Civilization: A Cultural History of Gender and Race in the United States, 1880–1917.* Chicago: University of Chicago Press, 1995.

————. "'The Women Have Had Charge of the Church Work Long Enough': The Men and Religion Forward Movement of 1911–1912 and the Masculinization of Middle-class Protestantism." *American Quarterly* 41 (September 1989): 432–65.

Bell, Catherine. *Ritual Theory, Ritual Practice.* New York: Oxford University Press, 1992.

Bell, Ernest. *War on the White Slave Trade: A Book Designed to Awaken the Sleeping and Protect the Innocent.* Chicago: Charles C. Thompson Co., 1909.

Bendroth, Margaret Lamberts. *Fundamentalism and Gender.* New Haven, Conn.: Yale University Press, 1993.

————. *Growing Up Protestant: Parents, Children, and Mainline Churches.* New Brunswick, N.J.: Rutgers University Press, 2002.

————, and Virgina Lieson Brereton, eds. *Women and Twentieth-Century Protestantism.* Urbana: University of Illinois Press, 2002.

Benson, Susan Porter. *Counter Cultures: Saleswomen, Managers, and Customers in American Department Stores, 1890–1940.* Urbana: University of Illinois Press, 1988.

Bethel Record. Northeast Minnesota Historical Center. University of Minnesota–Duluth.

Bethune, Mary McLeod, File. Moody Bible Institute, Chicago.

Biographical Dictionary and Portrait Gallery of Representative Men of Chicago and the World's Columbian Exposition. Chicago: American Biographical Publishing Co., 1892.

Biographical Sketches of the Leading Men of Chicago. Chicago: Wilson and Clair, 1868.

Blee, Kathleeen M. *Women of the Klan: Racism and Gender in the 1920s.* Berkeley: University of California Press, 1991.

Blocker, Jack S., Jr. "Separate Paths: Suffragists and the Women's Temperance Crusade." *Signs* 10, no. 3 (1985): 460–76.

Blumin, Stuart. *The Emergence of the Middle Class: Social Experience in the American City, 1760–1900.* Cambridge: Cambridge University Press, 1989.

Bordin, Ruth. *Frances Willard, A Biography.* Chapel Hill: University of North Carolina Press, 1986.

————. *Woman and Temperance: The Quest for Power and Liberty.* New Brunswick, N.J.: Rutgers University Press, 1990.

Bosch, Allan Whitworth. "The Salvation Army in Chicago, 1885–1914." Ph.D. diss., University of Chicago, 1965.

Boyer, Paul. *Urban Masses and Moral Order in America, 1820–1920.* Cambridge, Mass.: Harvard University Press, 1987.

Boylan, Anne M. "Evangelical Womanhood in the Nineteenth Century: The Role of Women in Sunday Schools." *Feminist Studies* 4 (October 1978): 62–80.

Bradford, Gamaliel. *D. L. Moody: A Worker in Souls.* New York: Fleming H. Revell, 1927.

Brauer, Jerald. *Protestantism in America.* Philadelphia: Westminster Press, 1965.

Brereton, Virginia Lieson. *Training God's Army: The American Bible School, 1880–1940.* Bloomington: Indiana University Press, 1990.

Broad Ax, The. 1918.

Brown, Elijah P. *The Real Billy Sunday.* New York: Fleming H. Revell, 1914.

Brumberg, Joan Jacobs. *Mission for Life.* New York: Free Press, 1980.

————. "Zenanas and Girlless Villages: The Ethnology of American Evangelical Women, 1870–1910." *Journal of American History* 69 (September 1982): 347–71.

Bruns, Roger A. *Preacher Billy Sunday and Big-Time American Evangelism.* Urbana: University of Illinois Press, 1992.

Buechler, Steven M. *The Transformation of the Woman Suffrage Movement: The Case of Illinois 1850–1920.* New Brunswick, N.J.: Rutgers University Press, 1986.

Buenker, John D. "Chicago Ethnics and the Politics of Accomodation." *Chicago History* 3 (Fall 1974): 92–100.

————. "The Dynamics of Chicago Ethnic Politics, 1900–1930." *Journal of the Illinois State Historical Society* 68 (April 1974): 175–99.

————. "The Illinois Legislature and Prohibition, 1907–1919." *Journal of the Illinois State Historical Society* 62 (1969): 363–84.

Burg, David F. *Chicago's White City of 1893.* Lexington: University Press of Kentucky, 1976.

Burgess, Charles O. *Nettie Fowler McCormick, Profile of an American Philanthropist.* Madison: Department of History, University of Wisconsin, 1962.

Burns, Eric. *The Spirits of America: A Social History of Alcohol.* Philadelphia: Temple University Press, 2004.

Butler, Jon. "Enthusiasm Described and Decried: The Great Awakening as Interpretative Fiction." *Journal of American History* 69 (September 1982): 305–25.

Carnes, Mark. *Secret Ritual and Manhood in Victorian America.* New Haven, Conn.: Yale University Press, 1989.

————, and Clyde Griffen, eds. *Meanings for Manhood: Constructions of Masculinity in Victorian America.* Chicago: University of Chicago Press, 1990.

Carter, Paul A. *The Spiritual Crisis of the Gilded Age.* DeKalb: Northern Illinois University Press, 1971.

Cawelti, John G. *Apostles of the Self-Made Man.* Chicago: University of Chicago Press, 1965.

Centennial List of Mayors, City Clerks, City Attorneys, City Treasurers, and Aldermen Elected by the People of Chicago, March 4, 1837–March 4, 1937. Chicago: City of Chicago Municipal Reference Library, 1937.

Central Records. Moody Bible Institute, Chicago.

Chapin, Clara C., ed. *Thumb Nail Sketches of White Ribbon Women.* Chicago: Women's Christian Temperance Publishing Association, 1895.

Chapman, J. Wilbur, Papers. Billy Graham Center Archive, Wheaton, Ill.

Chatfield-Taylor, H. C. *Chicago.* Cambridge, Mass.: Riverside Press, 1917.

Chicago American. 1910.

Chicago Daily News. 1893, 1910.

Chicago Defender. 1917–1918.

Chicago Evening Post. 1893, 1910.

Chicago Examiner. 1910.

Chicago Herald. 1893.

Chicago *Illinois Idea.* 1915.

Chicago *Inter-Ocean.* 1893, 1910.

Chicago Record-Herald. 1910.

Chicago Tract Society. Annual Report. 1899.

Chicago Tribune. 1893, 1910, 1918.

Christ, Carol. "Victorian Masculinity and the Angel of the House." In Martha Vicinus, ed., *A Widening Sphere* (Bloomington: Indiana University Press, 1977), 146–62.

Christian Worker's Magazine. 1913–1918.

Christiano, Kevin J. *Religious Diversity and Social Change in American Cities, 1890–1906.* Cambridge: Cambridge University Press, 1987.

City Club Bulletin. Vol. 4, nos. 1–25 (January 1911–December 1911). Chicago: City Club of Chicago, 1911.

Clark, Norman H. *Deliver Us from Evil: An Interpretation of American Prohibition.* New York: W. W. Norton and Co., 1976.

Clayton, John. "The Scourge of Sinners: Arthur Burrage Farwell." *Chicago History* 3 (Fall 1974): 68–77.

Cominos, Peter T. "Late-Victorian Sexual Respectibility and the Social System." *International Review of Social History* 8 (1963): 18–48, 217–50.

Cott, Nancy. *The Grounding of American Feminism.* New Haven, Conn.: Yale University Press, 1987.

Couldry, Nick. *Media Rituals: A Critical Approach.* London: Routledge, 2003.

Cronon, William. *Nature's Metropolis: Chicago and the Great West.* New York: W. W. Norton and Co., 1991.

Cross, Robert D. *The Church and the City 1865–1910.* New York: Bobbs-Merrill Co., 1967.

Crowell, Henry P. *Annual Report of the Committee of Fifteen for Year Ended April 20, 1918.* Pamphlet, 1918.

Curtis, Susan. *A Consuming Faith: The Social Gospel and Modern American Culture.* Baltimore: Johns Hopkins University Press, 1991.

Daily News Almanac and Register. Chicago: *Daily News,* 1983.

Daniels, Josephus. "Live Straight if You Would Shoot Straight." Pamphlet, American Social Hygiene Association Papers, n.d.

Davis, George T. B. *Torrey and Alexander: The Story of a World-Wide Revival.* New York: Fleming H. Revell, 1905.

Day, Richard Ellsworth. *Bush Aglow: The Life Story of Dwight Lyman Moody the Commoner of Northfield.* Philadelphia: Judson Press, 1936.

DeBerg, Betty A. *Ungodly Women: Gender and the First Wave of American Fundamentalism.* Minneapolis: Fortress Press, 1990.

Dedmon, Emmet. *Great Enterprises: 100 Years of the YMCA of Metropolitan Chicago.* Chicago: Rand McNally, 1957.

Degler, Carl. *At Odds: Women and Family in America from the Revolution to the Present.* New York: Oxford University Press, 1980.

———. "What Ought to Be and What Was: Woman's Sexuality in the Nineteenth Century." *American Historical Review* (Winter 1974): 1467–90.

Deichman Edwards, Wendy J., and Carolyn Deswarte Gifford, eds. *Gender and the Social Gospel.* Urbana: University of Illinois Press, 2003.

Deutsch, Sarah. *Women and the City: Gender, Space, and Power in Boston, 1870–1940.* New York: Oxford University Press, 2000.

Diffee, Christopher. "Sex and the City: The White Slavery Scare and Social Governance in the Progressive Era." *American Quarterly* 57, no. 2 (June 2005): 411–37.

Dorsett, Lyle W. *Billy Sunday and the Redemption of Urban America.* Grand Rapids, Mich.: William B. Eerdmans Publishing Company, 1991.

———. *A Passion for Souls: The Life of D. L. Moody.* Chicago: Moody Press, 1997.

Douglas, Ann. *The Feminization of American Culture.* New York: Alfred A. Knopf, 1977.

Drake, St. Clair. *Churches and Voluntary Associations in the Chicago Negro Community.* Chicago: WPA, December 1940.

Dryer, Emma, Biographical File. Moody Bible Institute, Chicago.

Dubbert, Joe L. "Progressivism and the Masculinity Crisis." In Elizabeth

H. Pleck and Joseph H. Pleck, eds., *The American Man* (Englewood Cliffs, N.J.: Prentice Hall, Inc., 1980), 303–20.

Duis, Perry. *Public Drinking in Chicago and Boston, 1880–1920.* Chicago: University of Chicago Press, 1983.

———. "The Saloon in Changing Chicago." *Chicago History* 4 (Winter 1975–1976): 214–24.

Dunn, Roger F. "Formative Years of the Chicago YMCA—A Study in Urban History." *Journal of the Illinois State Historical Society* 37 (December 1944).

Dyer, Richard. *White.* New York: Routledge, 1997.

Edwards, Wendy J. Deishmann, and Carolyn DeSwarte Gifford, eds. *Gender and the Social Gospel.* Urbana: University of Illinois Press, 2003.

Ellis, William T. *Billy Sunday, The Man and His Message.* L. T. Meyers, 1914.

Epstein, Barbara Leslie. "Family, Sexual Morality, and Popular Movements in Turn-of-the-Century America." In Ann Snitow, Christine Stansell, and Sharon Thompson, eds., *Powers of Desire: The Politics of Sexuality* (New York: Monthly Review Press, 1983), 117–30.

———. *The Politics of Domesticity: Women, Evangelism, Temperance in Nineteenth Century America.* Middletown, Conn.: Wesleyan University Press, 1981.

Erenberg, Lewis A. *Steppin' Out: New York Nightlife and the Transformation of American Culture, 1890–1930.* Chicago: University of Chicago Press, 1981.

Evensen, Bruce J. *God's Man for the Gilded Age: D. L. Moody and the Rise of Modern Mass Evangelism.* New York: Oxford University Press, 2003.

Ewen, Elizabeth. "City Lights: Immigrant Women and the Rise of the Movies." *Signs* (Spring 1980 supplement): 45–65.

Farr, Finis. *Chicago: A Personal History of America's Most American City.* New Rochelle, N.Y.: Arlington House, 1973.

Feldman, Egal. "American Ecumenicism: Chicago's World's Parliament of Religions of 1893." *Journal of Church and State* 9 (Spring 1967): 180–99.

Filene, Peter. *Him/Her/Self: Sex Roles in Modern America.* Baltimore: Johns Hopkins University Press, 1986.

———. "In Time of War." In Elizabeth H. Pleck and Joseph H. Pleck, eds., *The American Man* (Englewood Cliffs, N.J.: Prentice Hall, 1980), 321–35.

Findlay, James. *Dwight L. Moody: American Evangelist 1837–1899.* Chicago: University of Chicago Press, 1969.

———. "Moody, Gapmen, and the Gospel: The Early Days of Moody Bible Institute." *Church History* 31 (September 1962): 322–35.

Fine, Lisa. "The Record Keepers of Property: The Making of a Female Clerical Labor Force in Chicago, 1870–1930." Ph.D. diss., University of Wisconsin–Madison, 1985.

Fishburn, Janet Forsythe. *The Fatherhood of God and the Victorian Family: The Social Gospel in America.* Philadelphia: Fortress Press, 1981.

Fogel, Robert William, *The Fourth Great Awakening and the Future of Egalitarianism.* Chicago: University of Chicago Press, 2000.

Forbes, Geraldine H. "In Search of the 'Pure Heathen': Missionary Women in Nineteenth Century India." *Economic and Political Weekly* (Review of Women's Studies) 21, no. 17 (April 26, 1986): WS2-WS8.

Foy, Jessica H., and Thomas J. Schlereth. *American Home Life, 1880–1930: A Social History of Spaces and Services.* Knoxville: University of Tennessee Press, 1992.

Frankenburg, Ruth, ed. *Displacing Whiteness Essays in Social and Cultural Criticism.* Durham: Duke University Press, 1997.

———. *The Social Construction of Whiteness.* Minneapolis: University of Minnesota Press, 1993.

Friedberg, Anne. *Window-Shopping: Cinema and the Postmodern.* Berkeley: University of California Press, 1993.

Frueh, Erne R., and Florence Frueh. "The Stained Glass Windows at the Second Presbyterian Church." *Chicago History* 6 (Winter 1977–1978): 210–17.

Gallagher, Sally K. *Evangelical Identity and Gendered Family Life.* New Brunswick, N.J.: Rutgers University Press, 2003.

Galloway, Thomas Walton. "The Responsibilites of Religious Leaders in Sex Education." Pamphlet, American Social Hygiene Association Papers, 1921.

Garber, Rebecca Perryman. "The Social Gospel and Its View of Women and the Women's Movement, 1880–1918." Master's thesis, Trinity Divinity School, Deerfield, Ill., 1978.

Giddings, Paula. *When and Where I Enter: The Impact of Black Women on Race and Sex in America.* New York: Quill William Morrow, 1984.

Gifford, Carolyn DeSwarte, ed. *The Ideal of the "New Woman" According to the*

Women's Christian Temperance Union. New York: Garland Publishing, Inc., 1987.

————. *Writing Out My Heart: Selections from the Journal of Frances E. Willard 1855–96.* Urbana: University of Illinois Press, 1995.

Gilbert, Frank. *Centennial History of the City of Chicago: Its Men and Institutions.* Chicago: Inter-Ocean, 1905.

Gilmore, Glenda Elizabeth. *Gender and Jim Crow: Women and the Politics of White Supremacy in North Carolina, 1896–1920.* Chapel Hill: University of North Carolina Press, 1996.

Ginzberg, Lori D. *Women and the Work of Benevolence: Morality, Politics, and Class in the 19th Century United States.* New Haven, Conn.: Yale University Press, 1990.

"Girls and Khaki." Pamphlet, American Social Hygiene Association Papers, 1918.

Goodspeed, Rev. E. J. *A Full History of the Wonderful Career of Moody and Sankey in Great Britain and America.* New York: Henry S. Goodspeed and Co., 1876.

Gordon, Linda. *Woman's Body, Woman's Right: A Social History of Birth Control in America.* New York: Penguin Books, 1974.

Gordon, Michael, ed. *The American Family in Social-Historical Perspective.* New York: St. Martin's Press, 1973.

Green, Paul M., and Melvin H. Holli, eds. *The Chicago Political Tradition.* Carbondale: Southern Illinois University Press, 1987.

Greene, T. P. *America's Heroes, The Changing Models of Success in American Magazines.* New York: Oxford University Press, 1970.

Greer, J. H. *The Social Evil and the Remedy.* Chicago: Charles Kerr and Co., n.d.

Gripe, Elizabeth Howell. "Women, Restructuring, and Unrest in the 1920s." *Journal of Presbyterian History* 52 (Summer 1974): 188–98.

Groetzinger, Leona Prall. *The City's Perils.* N.p., n.d.

Grossman, James R. *Land of Hope: Chicago, Black Southerners, and the Great Migration.* Chicago: University of Chicago Press, 1989.

Grossman, James R., Ann Durkin Keating, and Janice L. Reiff, eds. *The Encyclopedia of Chicago.* Chicago: University of Chicago Press, 2004.

Gundry, Stanley N. *Love Them In: The Proclamation Theology of D. L. Moody.* Chicago: Moody Press, 1976.

Halpern, Rick. *Down on the Killing Floor: Black and White Workers in Chicago's Packinghouses, 1904–1954.* Urbana: University of Illinois Press, 1997.

Hamm, Richard F. *Shaping the Eighteenth Amendment: Temperance Reform, Legal Culture, and the Polity, 1880–1920.* Chapel Hill: University of North Carolina Press, 1995.

Hammond, John. *The Politics of Benevolence, Revival, Religion and American Voting Behavior.* Norwood, N.J.: Ablex Publishing House, 1979.

Handbook of the YWCA. Chicago: Metropolitan Publicity Dept., 1944.

Handy, Robert T. *A Christian America: Protestant Hopes and Historical Realities.* New York: Oxford University Press, 1971.

Hanson, J. W., ed. *The World's Congress of Religions; the Addresses and Papers Delivered before the Parliament and an Abstract of the Congresses Held in the Art Institute of Chicago, Illinois, U.S.A. August 25 to October 15, 1893 under the Auspices of the World's Columbian Exposition.* Chicago: W. B. Conkey and Union Publishing, 1894.

Harrison, Dr. A. W. "Work of the Chicago Vice Commission." *City Club Bulletin,* vol. 4 (January 1911–December 1911): City Club of Chicago, January 1911–December 1911.

Hartzler, Rev. H. B. *Moody in Chicago or the World's Fair Gospel Campaign.* New York: Fleming H. Revell, Co., 1894.

Harvey, Turlington W., File. Moody Bible Institute, Chicago.

Hassey, Janette. *No Time for Silence: Evangelical Women in Public Ministry around the Turn of the Century.* Grand Rapids, Mich.: Zondervan Publishing House, 1986.

Hatch, Nathan O. *The Democratization of American Christianity.* New Haven, Conn.: Yale University Press, 1989.

Heidebrecht, Paul H. "Chicago Presbyterians and the Businessman's Religion." *American Presbyterians* 64 (Spring 1986): 39–48.

Hendricks, Wanda A. *Gender, Race, and Politics in the Midwest: Black Club Women in Illinois.* Bloomington: Indiana University Press, 1998.

Hewitt, Nancy. *Women's Activism and Social Change, Rochester, New York, 1822–1872.* Ithaca, N.Y.: Cornell University Press, 1984.

Higham, John. *Strangers in the Land: Patterns of American Nativism, 1860–1925.* New York: Atheneum, 1963.

Hill, Patricia R. *The World Their Household: The American Woman's Foreign Mission Movement and Cultural Transformation 1870–1920.* Ann Arbor: University of Michigan Press, 1985.

Higginbotham, Evelyn Brooks. *Righteous Discontent: The Women's Movement in the Black Baptist Church 1880–1920.* Cambridge, Mass.: Harvard University Press, 1993.

Historical Sketch of the Young Men's Christian Association of Chicago. Chicago: YMCA Publishing, 1898.

Hogeland, Ronald W. "Charles Hodge, The Association of Gentlemen, and Ornamental Womanhood: 1825–1855." *Journal of Presbyterian History* 53 (Fall 1975): 239–55.

Holli, Melvin, and Peter d'A. Jones, eds. *Ethnic Chicago: A Multicultural Portrait.* Grand Rapids, Mich.: William B. Eerdmans Publishing Co., 1995.

Howe, Daniel Walker. "The Evangelical Movement and Political Culture in the North during the Second Party System." *Journal of American History* 77 (March 1991): 1216–39.

———. ed. *Victorian America.* Philadelphia: University of Pennsylvania Press, 1976.

Hoyt, Homer. *One Hundred Years of Land Values in Chicago, 1830–1930.* Chicago: University of Chicago Press, 1933.

Humphrey, Mrs. S. J. *Two Decades of the Women's Board of Missions of the Interior.* Chicago: James Guilbert, Printer, 1889.

Hunter, James Davison. *Culture Wars: The Struggle to Define America.* New York: Basic Books, a Division of HarperCollins Publishers, 1991.

Hunter, Jane. *The Gospel of Gentility, American Women Missionaries in Turn-of-the-Century China.* New Haven, Conn.: Yale University Press, 1984.

Illinois Vigilance Association. Pamphlet, 1927.

Institute Tie. Publication of the Moody Bible Institute, 1900–1910.

Interior. 1900.

Jackson, Kenneth T., and Stanley K. Schulz, eds. *Cities in American History.* New York: Alfred A, Knopf, 1972.

Jaher, Frederic Cople. *The Urban Establishment: Upper Strata in Boston, New York, Charleston, Chicago, and Los Angeles.* Urbana: University of Illinois Press, 1982.

James, Janet Wilson, ed. *Women in American Religion.* Phildadelphia: University of Pennsylvania Press, 1980.

Jensen, Richard. *The Winning of the Midwest: Social and Political Conflict, 1888–1896.* Chicago: University of Chicago Press, 1971.

Jordan, Philip D. "The Evangelical Alliance and American Presbyterians, 1867–1873." *Journal of Presbyterian History* 51, no. 3 (Fall 1973): 309–26.

Juster, Susan. "In a Different Voice": Male and Female Narratives of Religious Conversion in Post-Revolutionary America." *American Quarterly* 41 (March 1989): 34–62.

————. *Disorderly Women: Sexual Politics and Evangelicalism in Revolutionary New England.* Ithaca, N.Y.: Cornell University Press, 1994.

————, and Lisa MacFarlane, eds. *A Mighty Baptism: Race, Gender, and Creation of American Protestantism.* Ithaca, N.Y.: Cornell University Press, 1996.

Kantowicz, Edward. *Polish American Politics in Chicago 1888–1940.* Chicago: University of Chicago Press, 1975.

Kasson, John F. *Houdini, Tarzan and the Perfect Man: The White Male Body and the Challenge of Modernity.* New York: Hill and Wang, 2001.

Keller, Rosemary Skinner. "Lay Women in the Protestant Tradition." In Rosemary Radford Reuther and Rosemary Skinner Keller, eds., *Women and Religion in America. The Nineteenth Century* (San Francisco: Harper and Row Publishers, 1980), vol. 1, 242–93.

Kessler-Harris, Alice. *Out to Work: A History of Wage-Earning Women in the United States.* New York: Oxford University Press, 1982.

Kleppner, Paul. *The Third Electoral System, 1853–1892: Parties, Voters, and Political Cultures.* Chapel Hill: University of North Carolina Press, 1979.

Knupfer, Anne Meis. *Toward a Tenderer Humanity and a Nobler Womanhood: African American Women's Clubs in Turn-of-the-Century Chicago.* New York: New York University Press, 1996.

Kraditor, Aileen. *The Ideas of the Woman's Suffrage Movement, 1890–1920.* New York: Columbia University Press, 1965.

Lambert, Frank. "'Pedlar in Divinity': George Whitfield and the Great Awakening, 1737–1745." *Journal of American History* 77 (December 1990): 812–37.

Lane, Kelsey, ed. *Reaching toward Tomorrow: The Moody Church.* Chicago: Randolph Street Press, 2000.

Larson, Erik. *The Devil in the White City: Murder, Magic, and Madness at the Fair That Changed America.* New York: Crown Publishers, 2003.

Lears, T. J. Jackson. *No Place for Grace: Antimodernism and the Transformation of American Culture, 1880–1920.* Chicago: University of Chicago Press, 1981.

Lerner, Gerda. *Black Women in White America: A Documentary History.* New York: Pantheon, 1972.

Lewis, Lloyd, and Henry Justin Smith. *Chicago: The History of Its Reputation.* New York: Harcourt, Brace and Co., 1929.

Lipsitz, George. *Time Passages: Collective Memory and American Popular Culture.* Minneapolis: University of Minnesota Press, 1990.

Long, Kathryn Teresa. *The Revival of 1857–58: Interpreting an American Religious Awakening.* New York: Oxford University Press, 1998.

Longstreet, Stephen. *Chicago, 1860–1919.* New York: David McKay Company, Inc., 1973.

Lukonic, Joseph Lee. "Evangelicals in the City: Evangelical Protestant Social Concerns in Early Chicago, 1837–1860." Ph.D. diss., University of Wisconsin–Madison, 1979.

Magnuson, Norris. *Salvation in the Slums: Evangelical Social Work, 1865–1920.* Metuchen, N.J.: Scarecrow Press, 1977.

Mallalieu, Willard F. "Mr. Moody's Ministry to Men." In Rev. Henry Davenport Northrop, ed., *Memorial Volume—The Life and Labors of Dwight L. Moody The Great Evangelist* (Pittsburgh: Methodist Board of Publication, 1899), 124–34.

Marks, Donald David. "Polishing the Gem of the Prairie: The Evolution of Civic Reform Consciousness in Chicago, 1874–1900." Ph.D. diss., University of Wisconsin–Madison, 1974.

Marsden, George M. *Fundamentalism and American Culture: The Shaping of Twentieth-Century Evangelicalism, 1870–1925.* Oxford: Oxford University Press, 1980.

Marsh, Margaret. "Suburban Men and Masculine Domesticity, 1870–1915." *American Quarterly* 40 (March 1988): 165–86.

Martin, Robert F. *Hero of the Heartland: Billy Sunday and the Transformation of American Society, 1862–1935.* Bloomington: Indiana University Press, 2002.

Martin, Roger. *R. A. Torrey: Apostle of Certainty.* Murfreesboro, Tenn.: Sword of the Lord Publishers, 1976.

Marty, Martin E. *The Irony of It All.* Vol. 1, *Modern American Religion.* Chicago: University of Chicago Press, 1986.

———. *Pilgrims in Their Own Land.* Boston: Little, Brown and Co., 1984.

May, Elaine Tyler. *Great Expectations: Marriage and Divorce in Post-Victorian America.* Chicago: University of Chicago Press, 1980.

May, Henry. *Protestant Churches and Industrial America.* New York: Octagon Books, 1963.

Mayer, Harold M., and Richard C. Wade. *Chicago: Growth of a Metropolis.* Chicago: University of Chicago Press, 1969.

Mayer, John Albert. "Private Charities in Chicago from 1871 to 1915." Ph.D. diss., University of Minnesota, 1978.

McCarthy, Kathleen. *Noblesse Oblige: Charity and Cultural Philanthropy in Chicago, 1849–1929.* Chicago: University of Chicago Press, 1982.

McCarthy, Michael P. "Prelude to Armageddon, Charles E. Merriam and the Chicago Mayoral Election of 1911." *Journal of Illinois State Historical Society* 67 (November 1974): 505–18.

McClure, Rev. James G. K. "The History of the Fourth Presbyterian Church." May 12, 1914.

McCormick, Nettie Fowler, Papers. McCormick Family Collection. Wisconsin State Historical Society, Madison.

McDannell, Colleen. *The Christian Home in Victorian America, 1840–1900.* Bloomington: Indiana University Press, 1986.

———, and Berhard Lang. *Heaven: A History.* New Haven, Conn.: Yale University Press, 1988.

McGovern, James R. "The American Woman's Pre–World War I Freedom in Manners and Morals." *Journal of American History* 55 (September 1968): 315–33.

McKibben, Bill. "The Christian Paradox—How a Faithful Nation Gets Jesus Wrong." *Harper's Magazine,* August 2005, 31–37.

McLoughlin, William. *The American Evangelicals 1800–1900.* New York: Harper and Row, 1968.

———. *Billy Sunday Was His Real Name.* Chicago: University of Chicago Press, 1955.

———. *Modern Revivalism: Charles Grandison Finney to Billy Graham.* New York: Ronald Press, 1959.

———. "Pietism and the American Character." *American Quarterly* 17 (Summer 1965): 163–86.

———. *Revivals, Awakenings, and Reform: An Essay on Religion and Social Change in America, 1607–1977.* Chicago: University of Chicago Press, 1978.

Merriam, Charles Edward. *Chicago: A More Intimate View of Urban Politics.* New York: Arno Press, 1970. Reprt., New York: Macmillan Co., 1929.

Meyer, D. H. "American Intellectuals and the Victorian Crisis of Faith." In Daniel Walker Howe, ed., *Victorian America* (Philadelphia: University of Pennsylvania Press, 1976), 59–77.

————. *The Instructed Conscience: The Shaping of the American National Ethic.* Philadelphia: University of Pennsylvania Press, 1972.

Meyerowitz, Joanne J. *Women Adrift: Independent Wage Earners in Chicago, 1880–1930.* Chicago: University of Chicago Press, 1988.

"Milestones in the March against Commercialized Prostitution, 1886–1949." Pamphlet, American Social Hygiene Association Papers, 1949.

Miller, Donald L. *City of the Century: The Epic of Chicago and the Making of America.* New York: Simon and Schuster, 1996.

Miller, Mark Crispin. "None Dare Call It Stolen: Ohio, the Election, and America's Servile Press." *Harper's Magazine,* August 2005.

Minutes, State President's Address and Reports of the Women's Christian Temperance Union of the State of Illinois. 1893, 1910, 1918.

Miscellaneous Pamphlets, First Presbyterian Church. Chicago Historical Society.

Moody Church Paper. 1888.

Moody Church Records. Billy Graham Center Archives, Wheaton, Ill.

Moody, Dwight L. *Sowing and Reaping.* Chicago: Fleming H. Revell, 1896.

————. *Weighed and Wanting.* Chicago: Moody Press, n.d.

Moody, William R. *The Life of Dwight L. Moody.* Chicago: Fleming H. Revell, Co., 1900.

Morgan, David T. "The Revivalist as Patriot: Billy Sunday and World War I." *Journal of Presbyterian History* 51 (1973): 199–215.

Morone, James A. *Hellfire Nation: The Politics of Sin in American History.* New Haven, Conn.: Yale University Press, 2003.

Noll, Mark A., ed. *Religion and American Politics from the Colonial Period to the 1980s.* New York: Oxford University Pres, 1990.

————. *The Scandal of the Evangelical Mind.* Grand Rapids, Mich.: William B. Eerdmans Publishing Company, 1994.

Northrop, Rev. Henry Davenport. *Memorial Volume: Life and Labors of Dwight L. Moody, the Great Evangelist.* Pittsburgh: Methodist Protestant Board of Publication, 1899.

Northwestern Christian Advocate. 1910, 1914, 1918.

Oberdeck, Kathyrn. *The Evangelist and the Impresario: Religion, Entertainment, and Cultural Politics in America, 1884–1914.* Baltimore: Johns Hopkins University Press, 1999.

Odegard, Peter. *Pressure Politics: The Story of the Anti-Saloon League.* New York: Octagon Books, 1966.

Official Report of the Strike Committee, Chicago Garment Workers' Strike 29 October–18 February, 1910. Chicago: Women's Trade Union League, 1910.

Omi, Michael, and Howard Winant. *Racial Formation in the United States from the 1960s to the 1990s.* New York: Routledge, 1994.

O'Neill, William L. *Divorce in the Progressive Era.* New Haven, Conn.: Yale University Press, 1967.

Pegram, Thomas R. *Battling Demon Rum: The Struggle for a Dry America, 1800–1933.* Chicago: Ivan R. Dee, American Way Series, 1998.

Phillips, George S. *Chicago and Her Churches.* Chicago: E. B. Meyers and Chandler, 1868.

Philpott, Thomas Lee. *The Slum and the Ghetto: Immigrants, Blacks, and Reformers in Chicago 1880–1930.* Belmont, Calif.: Wadsworth Publishing Company, 1998.

Pierce, Bessie. *A History of Chicago.* Vol. 3. New York: Alfred A. Knopf, 1937–1957.

Pivar, David J. "Cleansing the Nation: The War on Prostitution 1917–21." *Prologue* 12, no. 1 (Spring 1980): 29–40.

———. *Purity Crusade: Sexual Morality and Social Control, 1868–1900.* Westport, Conn.: Greenwood Press, 1973.

Protect Your Home, Property Values Injured by Immoral Neighbors. Illinois Vigilance Association leaflet. N.p., n.d.

Proudfoot, Wayne. *Religious Experience.* Berkeley: University of California Press, 1985.

Putney, Clifford. *Muscular Christianity: Manhood and Sports in Protestant America, 1880–1920.* Cambridge, Mass.: Harvard University Press, 2001.

Rabinovitz, Lauren. *For the Love of Pleasure: Women, Movies, and Culture in Turn-of-the-Century Chicago.* New Brunswick, N.J.: Rutgers University Press, 1998.

Reckless, Walter. *Vice in Chicago.* Montclair, N.J.: Patterson Smith Publishing, 1969. Reprt., 1933.

Record of Christian Work. New York: Fleming H. Revell Publishing, 1888–1895.

Records of the Chicago Presbytery, 1890–96, 1904–1910, 1910–1916. McCormick Theological Seminary, Chicago.

Report of the WCTU of the State of Illinois. President's Address. Chicago: Rogers and Co., 1909.

Reynolds, David S. "The Feminization Controversy: Sexual Stereotypes and the Paradoxes of Piety in Nineteenth-Century America." *New England Quarterly* 53, no. 1 (March 1980): 96–106.

Robertson, Darrell M. "The Chicago Revival, 1876: A Case Study in the Social Function of a Nineteenth Century Revival." Ph.D. diss., University of Iowa, 1982.

Robinson, Rev. F. A., ed. *Mother Whittemore's Records of Modern Miracles.* Toronto: Missions of Biblical Education, 1931.

Roe, Clifford G. *Panderers and Their White Slaves.* Chicago: Fleming H. Revell, 1910.

Rosen, Ruth. *The Lost Sisterhood: Prostitution in America, 1900–1918.* Baltimore: Johns Hopkins University Press, 1982.

———, ed. *The Maimie Papers.* New York: Feminist Press and Indiana University Press, 1977.

Rosenberg, Charles. "Sexuality, Class, and Role in Nineteenth-Century America." *American Quarterly* 25 (1973): 131–53.

Rothman, Sheila. *Woman's Proper Place: A History of Changing Ideals and Practices, 1870 to the Present.* New York: Basic Books, Inc., 1978.

Rotundo, E. Anthony. "Body and Soul: Changing Ideals of American Middle-Class Manhood." *Journal of Social History* 16 (Summer 1983): 23–38.

———. "Learning about Manhood: Gender Ideals and Middle-Class Family in Nineteenth-Century America." In J. A. Mangan and James Walvin, eds., *Manliness and Morality, Middle-Class Masculinity in Britain and America, 1800–1940* (New York: St. Martin's Press, 1987), 35–51.

Ryan, Mary. *Cradle of the Middle Class: The Family in Oneida County, New York, 1790–1865.* Cambridge: Cambridge University Press, 1981.

Sanders, Lena S. *The Council Torchbearer: A Tribute to Mrs. Virginia Asher.* Roanoke, Va.: Virginia Asher Business Woman's Bible Council, 1936.

Sandeen, Ernest R. *Roots of Fundamentalism, British and American Millennialism, 1800–1930.* Chicago: University of Chicago Press, 1970.

Scanzoni, Letha Dawson, and Susan Setta. "Women in Evangelical, Holiness, and Pentecostal Traditions." In Rosemary Radford Reuther and Rosemary Skinner Keller, eds., *Women and Religion in America, 1900–1968,* vol. 3 (San Francisco: Harper and Row, 1986), 223–35.

Scharff, Paulus. *History of Evangelism.* Grand Rapids, Mich.: William B. Eerdmans, 1966.

Schultz, Rima, and Adele Hast, eds. *Women Building Chicago: A Biographical Dictionary.* Bloomington: Indiana University Press, 2001.

Sennett, Richard. *Families against the City: Middle-Class Homes of Industrial Chicago, 1872–1890.* Cambridge, Mass.: Harvard University Press, 1970.

Session Records. Second Presbyterian Church, Chicago.

Sharlet, Jeff. "Inside America's Most Powerful Megachurch." *Harper's Magazine,* May 2005, 41–54.

Sinclair, Andrew. *Prohibition, the Era of Excess.* Boston: Little, Brown and Company, 1962.

Sizer, Sandra. *Gospel Hymns and Social Religion.* Philadelphia: Temple University Press, 1978.

Sklar, Kathryn Kish. *Catharine Beecher: A Study in American Domesticity.* New York: W. W. Norton, 1976.

———. "Protestant Women and Social Justice Activism, 1890–1920." Conference Keynote Essay. Women and Twentieth-Century Protestantism Conference, Chicago, April 23–23, 1998.

Slocum, Stephen Elmer, Jr. "The American Tract Society: 1825–1975. An Evangelical Effort to Influence the Religious and Moral Life of the United States." Ph.D. diss., New York University, 1975.

Smith, Alson J. *Chicago's Left Bank.* Chicago: Henry Regenry, Co., 1953.

Smith, Carl. *Urban Disorder and the Shape of Belief: The Great Chicago Fire, the Haymarket Bomb, and the Model Town of Pullman.* Chicago: University of Chicago Press, 1995.

Smith, Daniel Scott. "The Dating of the American Sexual Revolution: Evidence and Interpretation." In Michael Gordon, ed., *The American Family in Social-Historical Perspective* (New York: St. Martin's Press, 1973), 426–38.

———. "Family Limitation, Sexual Control, and Domestic Feminism in Victorian America." In Nancy F. Cott and Elizabeth H. Pleck, eds., *A Heritage of Her Own: Toward a New Social History of American Women* (New York: Simon and Schuster, 1979), 222–45.

Smith, Nellie. *The Mother's Reply, A Pamphlet for Mothers.* Educational Pamphlet no. 7. New York: Society of Sanitary and Moral Prophylaxis, 1914.

Smith, Timothy L. *Revivalism and Social Reform.* New York: Harper and Row, 1957.

Smith-Rosenberg, Carroll. *Disorderly Women, Visions of Gender in Victorian America.* New York: Oxford University Press, 1985.

————. *Religion and the Rise of the American City, the New York City Mission Movement, 1812–1870.* Ithaca, N.Y.: Cornell University Press, 1971.

————. "Sex As Symbol in Victorian Purity: An Ethnohistorical Analysis of Jacksonian America." In John Demos and Saranne Spence Boocockk, eds., *Turning Points: Historical and Sociological Essays on the Family* (Chicago: University of Chicago Press, 1978), 212–47.

Snitow, Ann, Christine Stansell, and Sharon Thompson, eds. *Powers of Desire: The Politics of Sexuality.* New York: Monthly Review Press, 1983.

Spears, Alan H. *Black Chicago: The Making of a Negro Ghetto, 1890–1920.* Chicago: University of Chicago Press, 1967.

Spinney, Robert G. *City of Big Shoulders: A History of Chicago.* DeKalb: Northern Illinois University Press, 2000.

Stead, William T. *If Christ Came to Chicago.* Chicago: Laird and Lee, 1894.

Stearns, Peter N. *Be a Man! Males in Modern Society.* New York: Holmes and Meier Publishers, 1979.

Stevenson, Andrew. *Chicago, Pre-Eminently a Presbyterian City.* Chicago: Winona Publishing Co., 1907.

Stout, Harry S., and D. G. Hart, eds. *New Directions in American Religious History.* New York: Oxford University Press, 1997.

Strong, Josiah. *The Challenge of the City.* New York: Young People's Missionary Movement, 1907.

Sunday, William Ashley, and Helen Amelia Sunday, Papers. Billy Graham Center Archive, Wheaton, Ill.

Swanson, Stephen, ed. *Chicago Days: 150 Defining Moments in the Life of a Great City.* Wheaton, Ill.: Cantigny First Division Foundation, 1997.

Szasz, Ferenc Morton. *The Divided Mind of Protestant America, 1880–1930.* Tuscaloosa: University of Alabama Press, 1982.

Szucs, Loretto Dennis. *Chicago and Cook County Sources: A Genealogical and Historical Guide.* Salt Lake City, Utah: Ancestry Publishing, 1986.

Taves, Ann. "Mothers and Children and the Legacy of Mid-Nineteenth Century American Christianity." *Journal of Religion* 67, no. 2 (April 1987).

Tax, Meredith. *The Rising of the Women: Feminist Solidarity and Class Conflict, 1880–1917.* New York: Monthly Review Press, 1980.

Timberlake, James H. *Prohibition and the Progressive Movement, 1900–1920.* Cambridge, Mass.: Harvard University Press, 1963.

To Girls in War Time. Pamphlet. American Social Hygiene Association Papers, n.d.

Torrey, R. A., File. Moody Bible Institute, Chicago.

Trachtenberg, Alan. *The Incorporation of America: Culture and Society in the Gilded Age.* New York: Hill and Wang, 1995.

Trotter, Joe William, Jr., ed. *The Great Migration in Historical Perspective: New Dimensions of Race, Class, and Gender.* Bloomington: Indiana University Press, 1991.

Turner, Victor W. *The Ritual Process: Structure and Anti-Structure.* Chicago: Aldine, 1966.

Turner-Zimmerman, Jean. *Chicago's Great Soul Market: An Article on the Great White Slave Question.* Pamphlet, 1908.

Tuttle, William M., Jr. *Race Riot: Chicago in the Red Summer of 1919.* Urbana: University of Illinois Press, 1996.

Tweed, Thomas, ed. *Retelling U.S. Religious History.* Berkeley: University of California Press, 1997.

Union Signal. 1890, 1893.

Vandermeer, Philip R., and Robert P. Swierenga. *Belief and Behavior: Essays in the New Religious History.* New Brunswick, N.J.: Rutgers University Press, 1991.

Vice Commission of City of Chicago. *The Social Evil in Chicago: A Study of Existing Conditions.* Chicago: Gunthrop-Warren Printing, 1911.

Vigilance 20, no. 11 (November 1912). New York: American Vigilance Association.

Vitrano, Steven P. *An Hour of Good News: The Chicago Sunday Evening Club, A Unique Preaching Ministry.* Chicago: Chicago Evening Club, 1974.

Wagenknecht, Edward. *Ambassadors for Christ: Seven American Preachers.* New York: Oxford University Press, 1972.

Waite, Caroline, File. Moody Bible Institute, Chicago.

Watt, David Harrington. *A Transforming Faith: Explorations of Twentieth-Century American Evangelicalism.* New Brunswick, N.J.: Rutgers University Press, 1991.

Weber, Timothy P. *Living in the Shadow of the Second Coming: American Premillennialism.* Chicago: University of Chicago Press, 1987.

Weekly Calendar. Fourth Presbyterian Church, Chicago.

Weiler, Sue. "Walkout: The Chicago Men's Garment Workers' Strike, 1910–1911." *Chicago History* (Winter 1979–1980): 238–49.

Weiman, Jeanne Madeline. *The Fair Women: The Story of the Woman's Building—World's Columbian Exposition, Chicago, 1893.* Chicago: Academy Chicago, 1981.

Weisberger, Bernard A. *They Gathered at the River: The Story of the Great Revivalists and Their Impact upon Religion in America.* Boston: Little, Brown and Co., 1958.

Wells-Barnett, Ida B. *Selected Works of Ida B. Wells-Barnett.* Compiled by Trudier Harris. New York: Oxford University Press, 1991.

Welter, Barbara. "The Cult of True Womanhood, 1802–1860." *American Quarterly* 18 (Summer 1966): 151–74.

———. *Dimity Convictions, The American Women in the Nineteenth Century.* Athens: Ohio University Press, 1976.

Wendt, Lloyd, and Herman Kogan. *Lord of the Levee, the Story of Bathhouse John and Hinky Dink.* Indianapolis: Bobbs, Merrill, Co., 1943.

Wertheimer, Barbara. *We Were There: The Story of Working Women in America.* New York: Pantheon Books, 1977.

Wharton, H. M. *A Month with Moody, His Work and Workers.* Baltimore: Wharton and Barron Publishing Co., 1893.

Willard, Mary. *The Story of A Great Conviction, or Why the W.C.T.U. of Illinois Seeks the Ballot.* Chicago: Union Signal Print, 1884.

Williams, A. W. *Life and Work of Dwight L. Moody: The Great Evangelist of the Nineteenth Century.* Chicago: P. W. Zeigler, 1900.

Williams, Fannie Barrier. "A Northern Negro's Autobiography." *The Independent* 57, no. 2902 (July 14, 1904).

Williams, Joan C. "Domesticity as the Dangerous Supplement of Liberalism." *Journal of Women's History* 2, no. 3 (Winter 1991): 69–88.

Wilson, Elizabeth. *The Sphinx in the City: Urban Life, the Control of Disorder, and Women.* Berkeley: University of California Press, 1991.

Wilson, Samuel Paynter. *Chicago by Gas Light.* Chicago: Wilson, 1909.

Winslow, Charles S. *Historical Events of Chicago.* Vol. 3. Chicago: Soderlund Printing Service, 1937.

Winston, Diane. *Red-Hot and Righteous: The Urban Religion of the Salvation Army.* Cambridge, Mass.: Harvard University Press, 1999.

Women's Christian Temperance Union of State of Illinois. Minutes, State President's Address and Reports of WCTU of State of Illinois, 1893. Illinois WCTU headquarters, Springfield, Ill.

Woman's Department of the Bible Institute. Pamphlet, 1895.

Woodcock-Tentler, Leslie. *Wage-Earning Women, Industrial Work and Family Life in the U.S. 1900–1903.* New York: Oxford University Press, 1979.

Yalom, Marilyn. *A History of the Wife.* New York: Perennial Harper-Collins, 2002.

Young Men's Christian Association of Chicago. Records, Chicago Historical Society, Chicago.

Young Women's Christian Association of Chicago. Records, University of Illinois at Chicago Manuscript Collections, Chicago.

Index

theory, 2, 6, 7; as profession, 133–34; waning influence of, 223–25
Rodeheaver, Homer, 203
Rosenwald, Julius, 130
Rounds, Mrs. T. C., 119

Saddleback Church, 233
Saloons: as political institutions, 31; as "evil," 67; and evangelicals, 73; and shutdown referendum, 130, 162; and Billy Sunday, 180, 185–86; and Prohibition, 183–86
Salvation Army: established in Chicago, 36–37; and vice, 72; and reform activity, 113; and Simultaneous Campaign, 144
Sankey, Ira, 53
Saxe, Grace, 119, 120, 202, 203
Scopes Trial, 225
Second Awakening, 1, 5, 8, 69
Segregation, 96–97, 115, 125, 170. *See also* Suburbs
Sherman Anti-Trust Act, 111
Smith, Adam, 3
Smith, Gypsy, 121, 130–32
Smith, Henry Justin, 38
Social Gospel, 14, 35, 36
Social Hygiene (movement), 163, 168, 211–13. *See also* Social Purity
Social Purity (movement): and reform societies, 10; at World's Fair, 69–72, 74, 75, 95; and prostitution, 124, 127; and Committee of Fifteen, 129; and female employment, 157–58; and hygiene focus, 163–64, 168; and Prohibition, 211–13; and World War I, 211–13; accomplishments, 227
Socialism, 18, 27, 30, 46, 179
Somerset, Lady Henry, 70
Spies, August, 49
Starr, Ellen Gates, 155
Stead, William T., 68, 112, 113, 129
Stevenson, Andrew, 34

Strong, Emily S., 119
Strong, Josiah, 33, 112
Suburbs: middle-class movement to, 27–28, 32; growth of, 115, 170, 172, 184; and current status, 233
Sunday, Billy: at Simultaneous Campaign, 159; and sports career, 186, 195–96; became evangelist, 187; influence of wife, 187, 204–6, 214; image, 193; later years, 225
Sunday, Helen Thompson: and Billy Sunday, 187; as administrator and celebrity, 202, 204–7; as writer, 210–11; on motherhood, 216
Sweitzer, Robert M., 178
Swift, Harold H., 130
Swing, David, 34

Taft, William Howard, 227
Third Awakening, x–xi; as social reform, 13–14; and gender roles, 15–17, 61–62; and cities, 18; and D. L. Moody, 40; and Emma Dryer, 44; and domesticity, 117; and women's influence, 119–20, 139; theology, 121; revival decline, 223–26; accomplishments, 227; and effect on current politics, 231–32
Thomas, Hiram, 34
Thompson, William Hale "Big Bill," 177–78, 183, 184, 199
Torrey, R. A., 13, 117, 119; and Simultaneous Campaign, 120, 134, 203
Traditional Values Coalition, 240
Trotter, Melvin, 159
Turner, Victor, 16, 99
Turner-Zimerman, Jean, 128

Unions. *See* Labor unions
Unitarians, 10
United Garment Workers, 154
University of Chicago Divinity School, 121